STUDIES IN
LATE ANTIQUITY AND EARLY ISLAM
10

THE *CONTINUATIO* OF THE SAMARITAN CHRONICLE OF ABŪ L-FATḤ AL-SĀMIRĪ AL-DANAFĪ

STUDIES IN
LATE ANTIQUITY AND EARLY ISLAM
10

THE *CONTINUATIO* OF THE SAMARITAN CHRONICLE OF ABŪ L-FATḤ AL-SĀMIRĪ AL-DANAFĪ

TEXT, TRANSLATED AND ANNOTATED
BY

MILKA LEVY-RUBIN

THE DARWIN PRESS, INC.
PRINCETON, NEW JERSEY
2002

Library of Congress Cataloging-in-Publication Data

Abu al-Fath ibn Abi al-Hasan, al-Samiri, fl. 1355
[Kitab al-tarikh mimma taqaddama 'an al-aba'. English & Arabic. Selections]
The continuatio of the Samaritan chronicle of Abu L-Fath Al-Samiri Al-Danafi
[edited and translated by Milka Levy-Rubin].
p. cm. -- (Studies in late antiquity and early Islam ; 10)
Includes bibliographical references and index.
ISBN 0-87850-136-3 (alk. paper)
1. Samaritans--History. 2. Dhimmis. 3. Islamic Empire--Ethnic relations. I. Levy-Rubin, Milka, 1955- II. Title. III. Series.

DS129 A213 2002
956.95'3004922--dc21

2002019996

The paper in this book is acid-free neutral pH stock and meets the guidelines for permanence and durability of the Committee on Production Guidelines for Book Longevity of the Council on Library Resources.

Printed in the United States of America

To my father,
scholar and mentor,
who imbued me with the love of history
and taught me the intricate ways of its texts.

CONTENTS

ABBREVIATIONS

ADAJ	*Annual of the Department of Antiquities of Jordan*
AJBA	*Australian Journal of Biblical Archeology*
BASOR	*Bulletin of the American Schools of Oriental Research*
BF	*Byzantinische Forschungen*
BJRL	*Bulletin of the John Rylands Library*
BSOAS	*Bulletin of the School of Oriental and African Studies*
CCSL	*Corpus Christianorum Series Latina*
CH	*Church History*
DOP	*Dumbarton Oaks Papers*
EI [1]	*Encyclopaedia of Islam*, ed. M.T. Houtsma *et al.* 4 vols. Leiden and London, 1913–34.
EI [2]	*Encyclopaedia of Islam*, New Edition, ed. H.A.R. Gibb *et al.* Leiden and London, 1960–proceeding.
IEJ	*Israel Exploration Journal*
IJMES	*International Journal of Middle Eastern Studies*
JEH	*Journal of Ecclesiastical History*
JESHO	*Journal of the Economic and Social History of the Orient*
LA	*Liber Annuus*
RB	*Revue biblique*
REJ	*Revue des études juives*
ROC	*Revue de l'orient chrétien*
RSO	*Revista degli studi orientali*
SI	*Studia Islamica*

PREFACE

THE TEXT PRESENTED HERE first came to my attention while working on my Ph.D. thesis, which concerned the Patriarchate of Jerusalem during the early Muslim period (638–1099). The paucity of material concerning the state, during this period, of the Christians in particular and the non-Muslim inhabitants of Palestine in general, obliged me to search for new and as yet unknown material on the subject. I discovered that a relevant part of the Samaritan chronicle of Abū l-Fatḥ was being cited by scholars from a Latin summary published by Edward Vilmar in 1865. A new edition of the *Chronicle* recently made by Father Paul Stenhouse only extended to the time of Muḥammad and did not include this later part, which he believed to be a continuation of the *Chronicle* rather than an integral part of the original work of Abū l-Fatḥ.

My curiosity was aroused. I ordered a copy of the manuscript from the Bibliothèque Nationale, and discovered a document rich in information concerning not only the situation of the Samaritans in Palestine during the early Muslim period, but in fact much more than that: an interesting and unusually colourful and detailed portrait of Palestine and its environs in early Islamic times until the reign of the 'Abbāsid caliph al-Rāḍī (d. 322/934). The text was especially interesting because it described events as seen by the local population living in Palestine at the time. I therefore made extensive use of the manuscript for a chapter describing the state of the *dhimmīs* in Palestine during the said period.

After completing my Ph.D. thesis, I contemplated the idea of publishing the text. Examination of all the manuscripts of the chronicle that I suspected might contain this continuation revealed that it is unique to the Paris manuscript. This, coupled with the fact that the language of the text is very irregular even as Middle Arabic texts go, thus making it difficult to understand in certain places, and in many others difficult to translate, was cause for hesitation. I was encouraged to carry on, first and foremost, by my friend and colleague Dr. Amikam Elad of the Institute of Asian and African Studies at the Hebrew University of Jerusalem. I am especially indebted to him for his dedicated support and aid in all stages of the preparation of this book, investing in it not only his special knowledge, but also much of his time. I owe many thanks to my *SLAEI* editor, Lawrence I. Conrad, for the great effort he invested in the preparation of the manuscript for publication, as well as for the helpful and creative suggestions he offered throughout the text. Prof. B.Z. Kedar of the Dept. of History, who recognized the importance of the text, also constantly encouraged me to have it published. I should also like to thank Prof. Joshua Blau for his help in reading some the most difficult passages, Prof. Y. Naveh for his aid in reading the passages in Samaritan Arabic, and Prof. Z. Ben-Hayyim for his advice on some Samaritan matters. I owe thanks to many scholars in the Oriental Reading Room of the National and University Library in Jerusalem for their ideas and suggestions, among whom are Prof. Etan Kohlberg, Prof. Yohanan Friedmann, and Prof. Michael Lecker. The errors remain, of course, mine alone.

Most of all, I am grateful to my husband, Buni, who gave me constant support and encouragement throughout my work on this text, continuously urging me on to the finish.

Milka Levy-Rubin
Jerusalem, 3 March 1999

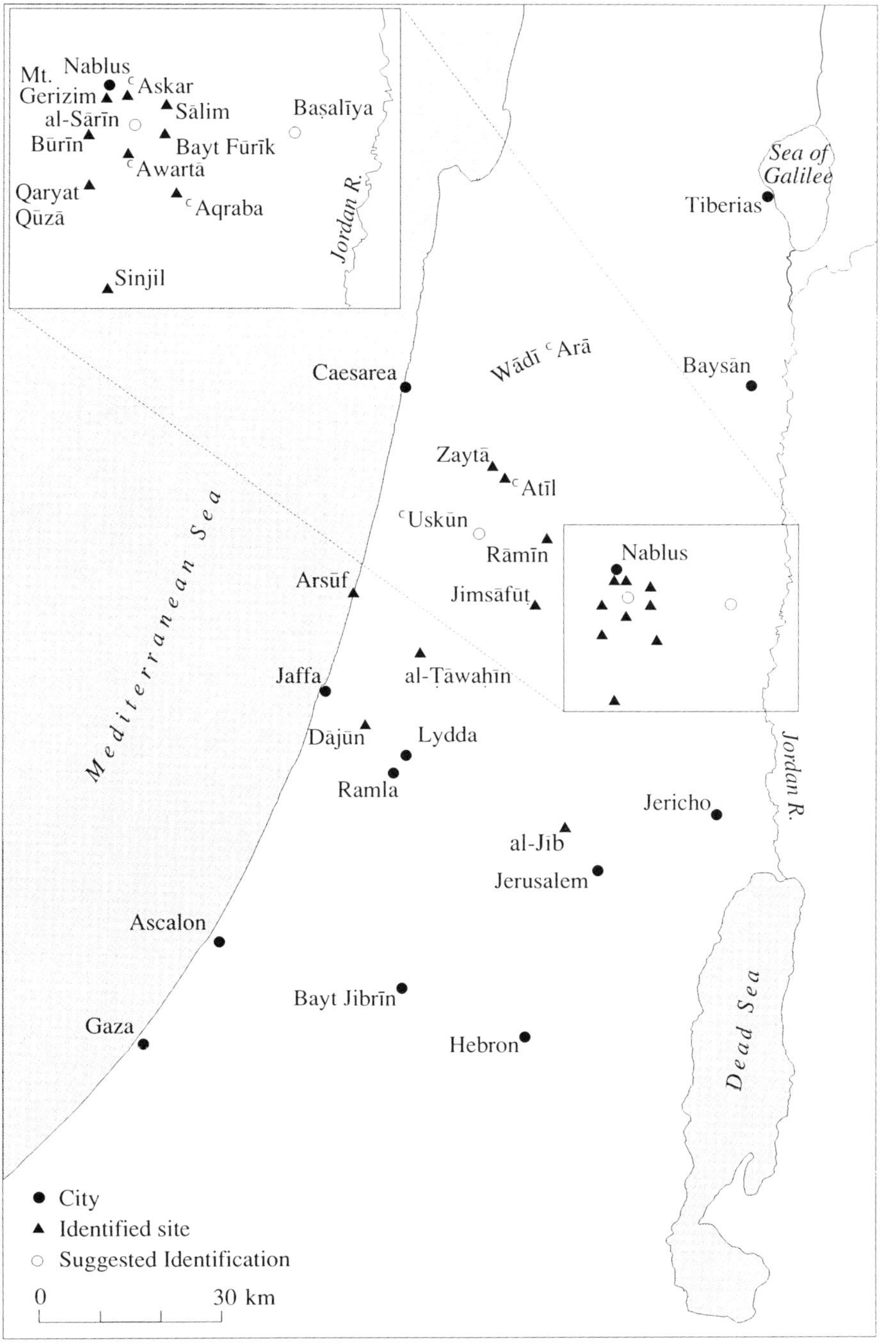

Sites Mentioned in the *Continuatio*

INTRODUCTION

THE PURPOSE OF THIS BOOK is to make available an important but hitherto neglected text that sheds light on the history of Palestine and its neighbouring countries, Syria and Egypt, during the early Muslim period, from the time of the Arab conquest to the fourth decade of the tenth century. This text, which will be called the *Continuatio* (for reasons that will be clarified below), appears at the end of the Samaritan chronicle *Kitāb al-ta'rīkh*, written in Arabic and compiled from earlier sources by Abū l-Fatḥ ibn Abī l-Ḥasan al-Sāmirī al-Danafī in CE 1355.

The text, the main part of which appears solely as part of one of the oldest and most trustworthy Mss. of the chronicle,[1] the Bibliothèque Nationale Ms. Samaritain no. 10,[2] describes the history of the Samaritans in Palestine during the early Muslim period up to and including the first third of the tenth century. It contains considerable information not only about the history of the Samaritan people, but also about political events of the period in Palestine, Syria and Egypt. What makes the information in this text especially valuable is the fact that it is of a completely different character from that conveyed in the Muslim chronicles pertaining to the same period. While the latter focus upon events, changes and intrigues that influenced the Muslim world in general, and the ruling class in its political centres in particular, our text presents the history of the period from two

[1]The first part of the text presented in this book, covering the period from Muḥammad to Hārūn al-Rashīd, exists in a number of Mss. and has appeared already as part of Vilmar's edition of the Arabic text. For more detailed discussion of this part, see below, pp. 4, 43.

[2]See below, pp. 5–10, for a detailed discussion of the Ms., its history and relation to the other Mss.

other points of view. The first is the point of view of the *dhimmīs*, the "protected non-Muslim population" living under Muslim rule, whose conditions of life were essentially different from that of any Muslim of any class or status; a description of the life of the *dhimmīs* thus provides us with many new facts concerning how they lived, as well as a completely different outlook upon the events themselves. The second differentiating characteristic lies in the fact that Muslim chronicles were usually written in important Muslim centres of government such as Iraq (Baghdad) or Egypt (Fusṭāṭ/Cairo), Palestine being just a marginal and neglected province serving mainly as a throughway or, at most, as a post given to an aspiring general. The Samaritan text, on the other hand, is a local chronicle that naturally considers Palestine as the centre and views other countries and provinces as peripheral and marginal to its concerns. It provides the reader, therefore, with a special viewpoint of Palestine under Muslim rule, revealing many new facts concerning local events. These include the imposition of various restrictions upon the non-Muslim population, local rebellions, relations between the local rulers and the population, the attitude of the local population towards Muslim rule, processes such as Islamization and Arabization, and much more.

While chronicles of a similar nature were written mainly by members of different Christian groups in Egypt and in Mesopotamia (e.g. the Coptic Arabic chronicles of Eutychius and ps.-Severus ibn Muqaffaʿ in Egypt, and the Jacobite Syriac history of Michael the Syrian and the Melkite Arabic chronicle of Agapius, both in north Syria), no such chronicle describing the history of Palestine during the early Muslim period exists. As Palestine is pushed to the margins in Muslim historiography, and since no other local history for this region is known, this chronicle seems to bear special importance. It is the purpose of this book to make this text available to scholars with an English translation and notes, in the hope that it will contribute to research on this period, not only for those interested in Samaritan history, but also, more broadly, for historians interested in various developments in Palestine and its neighbouring areas during the first three centuries of Islamic history.

Previous Research on the *Kitāb al-ta'rīkh* of Abū l-Fatḥ

Scholars in the West have been familiar with the Samaritan chronicle of Abū l-Fatḥ since 1653, when the chronicle was first brought to the attention of European scholarship by Abraham Ecchellensis. Different sections of the chronicle were then referred to and translated by various scholars, amongst them Edward Bernard (1691), Christian Friedrich Schnürrer (1790), and the famous orientalist Silvestre de Sacy (1806).[3] The first full critical edition of the text, based upon five manuscripts, was published by Vilmar in 1865.[4] Eighteen years ago, a new and more comprehensive critical edition based on additional manuscripts was made by Paul Stenhouse.[5] The latter also presented readers with a full English translation of the text for the first time.[6] Since its discovery, this chronicle, which is in fact the only extended description of the history of the Samaritan people, has been a major source for the study of Samaritan history.[7] This subject, it should be noted, has lately attracted considerable interest, and great progress has been made in the field in the past two decades.[8]

In spite of the considerable interest taken in Samaritan history in general, and in *Kitāb al-ta'rīkh* in particular, our text, which appears as part of the Paris Ms. Samaritain no. 10 of the *Kitāb*, has been neglected. The question, of course, is why this part of the Paris manuscript was overlooked in both the Vilmar and Stenhouse editions of the *Kitāb al-ta'rīkh*.

The answer to this question lies in two different considerations. The first, applied by Vilmar, is technical. Vilmar based his edition of the *Kitāb* upon five manuscripts:

[3]For a complete and thorough survey of the history of research on this chronicle, see Stenhouse, *Kitāb*, Introduction (below, n. 5), Vol. I, Part I, introduction, Chap. 1, pp. 1–6.

[4]E. Vilmar, ed. *Abulfathi Annales Samaritani* (Gothae, 1865), to be referred to subsequently as "Vilmar."

[5]P. Stenhouse, ed., *The Kitāb 'l-Ta'rīkh of Abū 'l-Fatḥ—A New Edition with Notes*, Ph.D. thesis (Sydney, 1980), to be referred to subsequently as "Stenhouse, *Kitāb*" (available in microfiche form from the Mandelbaum Trust, University of Sydney, Sydney, Australia).

[6]*The Kitāb 'l-Ta'rīkh of Abū 'l-Fatḥ—Translated and Annotated by P. Stenhouse* (University of Sydney: Mandelbaum Trust, 1985; *Studies in Judaica* 1), to be referred to subsequently as "Stenhouse, trans."

[7]As has already been pointed out by Stenhouse, scholars have in the past accused Abū l-Fatḥ of distorting facts intentionally, of (unintentional) confusion, and of "plagiarizing" other sources; see, e.g., J.W. Nutt, *Fragments of a Samaritan Targum* (London, 1874), p. 126; J.A. Montgomery, *The Samaritans* (Philadelphia, 1907), p. 69 n. 49. But the value of the chronicle as a document reflecting a Samaritan view of their history has since then been recognized. Sec Stenhouse, *Kitāb*, Chap. 5, pp. 3–4.

[8]See A.D. Crown, ed., *The Samaritans* (Tübingen, 1986), an updated volume summing up research on the subject. See also recently A.D. Crown and L. Davey, eds., *Essays in Honour of G.D. Sixdenier—New Samaritan Studies of the Société d'Études Samaritaines III & IV* (Sydney, 1995).

Ms. A = Berlin, Staatsbibliothek Stiftung Preussischer Kulturbesitz, Or. Ms. 4° no. 471 (copied 1859);
Ms. B = Berlin, Staatsbibliothek, Petermann I 8 (copied 1813);
Ms. C = Paris, Bibliothèque Nationale, Ms. Samaritain no. 10 (copied 1523);
Ms. D = Oxford, Bodleian Library, Ms. Huntington no. 350 (copied 1596);
Ms. F = Berlin, Staatsbibliothek, Petermann I 5 (copied 16th c.?).

Three of these Mss., Vilmar's B, D and F, carried the chronicle up to the time of Muḥammad, including the story of his recognition by the three astrologers—the Jew, the Christian and the Samaritan. The two other Mss., A and C, continued beyond this point. Vilmar published this additional section, continuing up to the point where Ms. A stopped, i.e. the reign of the caliph Hārūn al-Rashīd (r. 170–93/786–809). From that point onwards, he was left with only Ms. C, which continued up to the time of the caliph al-Rāḍī (r. 322–29/934–40). The Arabic in this section, according to Vilmar's report, was corrupt to such a degree that he declared that he could not copy it and was therefore unable to publish it; neither did he want to take the risk of emending the text.[9] This situation may nowadays be rectified to some degree. First, it is possible to provide a facsimile copy of the manuscript, thus avoiding the need to "correct" the text in difficult places; in addition, dialects of Middle Arabic (= *MA*) are now recognized as such, with their special style and grammar, and do not need to be "corrected" to adhere to the conventions of Classical Arabic (*CA*). Moreover, due to the great advances made in the study of the dialects of *MA* (see below), many stylistic difficulties may now be solved. Yet, in spite of all this, Vilmar was indeed justified in noting that the text is difficult and problematic in many places, as will be discussed below.

Although Vilmar decided not to publish the text, he considered it to be of great importance[10] and therefore gave a short summary of this part in Latin (no impediment for Orientalists in those days!) on pp. lxxx–lxxxiv of his introduction. It was therefore only technical limitations that prevented Vilmar from publishing the unique *Continuatio* found in the Paris manuscript.

---

[9] Vilmar, intro., lxxix: "Quae praeter primum horum additamentarum caput... in codice C, reperiuntur tam corruptis litteris scripta sunt, ut verba Arabica typis exscribi et in lucem edi nequeant. Neque enim ausus sum librum, qui gravissimis scripturae vitiis laboraret et difficilimus esset intellectu, pro meo arbitrio emendare emendatumque edere."

[10] *Ibid.*

The considerations guiding Stenhouse were methodological rather than technical. His task was to present a new critical edition of the *Kitāb*, based on all the new additional manuscripts known to him. This *per se* should not, of course, have excluded the *Continuatio* found in the Paris manuscript. Rather, it was Stenhouse's decision that only the original chronicle compiled by Abū l-Fatḥ himself would be included in his edition. Stenhouse accepted Vilmar's conclusion that Abū l-Fatḥ's chronicle extended as far as Muḥammad's career and did not continue beyond it;[11] he therefore limited his edition and translation of the *Kitāb* to that part considered to be original, and left out all those parts that continued beyond Muḥammad's time in the manuscripts before him, considering them to comprise a different composition.[12]

The Relationship between the *Continuatio* and the *Kitāb*

In the prologue to *Kitāb al-ta'rīkh*, Abū l-Fatḥ explains the circumstances that led him to write the chronicle and presents the scope of his work, its sources and his methodology. He states[13] that it was a meeting with the high priest Pinḥas in AH 753 (= CE 1352–53) that had encouraged him to take upon himself the task of compiling this chronicle. Abū l-Fatḥ had complained that there was no knowledge of the history of the Samaritans; the people themselves were scattered, he says, and their chronicles were in a state of disarray. Pinḥas had then imposed upon him the task of compiling a chronicle based on the existing sources, a work that would record all the events "from the Creation of Adam until recent times." It was only three years later, in the year 756/1355, that Abū l-Fatḥ actually sat down to write the chronicle.

On the face of things it would thus seem very plausible that the latter part of the text, following the time of Muḥammad, is an integral part of Abū l-Fatḥ's chronicle, and was intended to carry the history of the Samaritan people up to his own time. Nevertheless, Vilmar advances several convincing arguments in support of the claim that the original chronicle written by Abū l-Fatḥ went only up to the time of Muḥammad.[14] The first is that two of his manuscripts ended with Muḥammad's emergence, while the scribe of the third (C, the Paris Ms., which included the longest additional part) created

[11] Cf. the discussion in the next section below.

[12] Stenhouse, *Kitāb*, Chap. 6, p. 19.

[13] For the description of these circumstances see Vilmar, pp. 4–5; Stenhouse, trans., pp. 2–3.

[14] See Vilmar, intro., lxxv–lxxvii.

a clear division between the first (original) part, and the second (additional) part, inserting his colophon at the end of the first part, and once again at the end of the composition. The fourth Ms. (A, Berlin no. 471) was the only one that continued straight on, with no interruption, and it was the latest among the manuscripts. Ms. F was only partial, and could not therefore provide useful testimony on this point. The second substantial argument is that at the point of Muḥammad's emergence, the author chooses to cite the full list of Samaritan high priests, after which he concludes with the date of the writing of this chronicle, giving both the *hijra* date and the computation from the time of the Creation.

In addition, Vilmar suggests that it is logical that the chronicle should stop at the time of Muḥammad, since the rise of Islam is considered by the Samaritans as a crucial turning point in history. The period of God's "turning away"—the Age of Disfavour, *fanūta* in Aramaic—is to last 3000 years. In the year 2950 the *tāhib*, the Samaritan "Messiah," will arrive, and the Age of Grace, *raḥūta* or *riḍwān*, will return.[15] According to these eschatological computations, the *hijra* occurred in the year 2000 of the *fanūta*, and ushered in, therefore, the last third of the *fanūta*, a time of expectation. These last 1000 years were also the sixth millennium from the time of the Creation, the last millennium before the return of the *raḥūta*, which will occupy the seventh millennium—the Jubilee.[16] According to this concept, the days of Islamic rule could be considered as part of this last period, the main import of which is expectation, the waiting for the end of the *fanūta* and the arrival of the *tāhib*.

This last argument can be turned around, since if the *hijra* is indeed such a crucial turning point in Samaritan history, it might justify this specific structure of the chronicle as it appears in Ms. C (Paris), which chooses to distinguish sharply between the period before Muḥammad and that following his arrival. This counter-argument is weakened, however, by two other arguments advanced by Vilmar. One refers to the system of dating: in the second part a new method of calculation, according to the Sabbatical Year, appears beside the former ones, which include the calculation according to the years of Creation, the *hijra*, and according to the priesthood. The second argument refers to the style of the chronicle. The additional material

[15]On Samaritan eschatology, see F. Dexinger, "Samaritan Eschatology," in Crown, *Samaritans*, pp. 266–92.
[16]*Ibid.*, p. 280.

after the *hijra* is written in a very careless and loose style, which is obviously different from the concise and clear style of Abū l-Fatḥ in the first part, although both are written in Middle Arabic. If Abū l-Fatḥ had incorporated this part into his chronicle, he would no doubt have improved its style.

It should be noted, however, that although the difference in style is clear it cannot be said that the style of the first part is completely uniform. Stenhouse states that "Abū l-Fatḥ does not present a uniformly unconventional style—but rather an irregularity of style that can be explained, at least in part, by the variety of sources from which he is quoting verbatim."[17] It is thus possible to argue that having a fluent Arabic source in front of him, Abū l-Fatḥ did not make the effort to go over it, edit it, and improve its style.

This said, Vilmar's arguments as a whole still appear to be convincing. It still seems very likely that this additional part was not, in fact, part of the original composition of Abū l-Fatḥ.

It is important to add that the fact that the *Continuatio* does not seem to be part of the original compilation of Abū l-Fatḥ does not diminish its significance. The Paris manuscript was copied 170 years after the original *Kitāb* was compiled, while Abū l-Fatḥ himself wrote his composition hundreds of years after the events actually took place. What is significant in our case, therefore, is not so much the identity of the compiler as the credibility of his sources. This question will be dealt with separately below.

The Paris Ms. and its Relation to the Other Mss.

As already mentioned above, two of Vilmar's five manuscripts included the *Continuatio*: A (Ms. Berlin no. 471) stopped at Hārūn al-Rashīd's time, while C (Ms. Paris) alone continued on until the days of al-Rāḍī. Since Vilmar, numerous other manuscripts have come to light. It should be noted that many of these are copies made by the Samaritans in the second half of the nineteenth and in the first half of the twentieth century in response to the brisk demand of Western scholars for such texts. Many of these were thus actually copied around the time in which Vilmar produced his edition and afterwards. Moreover, there is a large group of late amplified versions of Abū l-Fatḥ,[18] written freely, which include many later additions and interpretations for the convenience of the modern reader. Some of these additional

[17] Stenhouse, *Kitāb*, Chap. 4, p. 5.

[18] *Ibid.*, Chap. 2, p. 2 and n. 13. These include: Berlin, Staatsbibliothek, Ms. 4° no. 963; London, British Library, Or. Ms. no. 7927; Cambridge, Girton College, Ms. no. 18; New York, Jewish Theological Seminary, Sulzberger Ms. no. 3473; Vatican City, Bibliotheca

manuscripts include the first part of the *Continuatio*, after the model of Vilmar's Ms. A, and were considered during the work done here on the first part of the *Continuatio*.[19]

It should be stressed, however, that none of these manuscripts include the section from Hārūn al-Rashīd's time until the reign of al-Rāḍī (i.e. the period from CE 809 until about 940); this is so in spite of the fact that some of them pretend to give a full and complete history up to the time the manuscript was copied. They in fact pick up again later, in the tenth century, with Kāfūr's reign (called "al-Malik al-Sarīs from Kūsh or Sūdān") at the end of the tenth century, or with the reign of al-Ḥākim, called here al-Ḥākim ibn al-Mu'īz (*sic.*), at the beginning of the eleventh century—all of them skip completely the intervening period covered by our text. In so far as the extant textual tradition allows us to judge, then, among all the manuscripts of the *Kitāb* the Paris manuscript with its augmented *Continuatio* seems to stand alone.

Thanks to the comprehensive and thorough work done by Stenhouse on the manuscripts of Abū l-Fatḥ while working on his critical edition,[20] we have comprehensive and well-established information concerning the Paris manuscript and its relationship to the other manuscripts.[21] According to its colophons, the Paris Ms. (Vilmar's Ms. C) was copied during the years 1523–24: the first part was completed on 18 Jumādā I 930/24 March 1524,[22] while the second part, covering the period from Muḥammad to al-Rāḍī, was completed on 20 Ramaḍān 930/22 July 1524.[23] The copyist was Musallam ibn Yūsuf ibn Ibrāhīm ibn Hiba ibn Qabāṣ the Samaritan, of the clan of Yūsuf, the Israelite. It is the oldest, or perhaps second oldest, extant manuscript of the *Kitāb*; the Sassoon Samaritan Ms. no. 36 may be older, since, although it bears no copying date, another composition copied by the same scribe was completed in 1502.[24] The Paris Ms. remained in the copyist's family at least until 4 March 1560 (see colophon at Ms. p. 257 and note thereto). Other

Apostolica Vaticana, Sbath Ms. no. 742; Manchester, John Rylands Library, Sam. Ms. no. 234. Another manuscript mentioned by Stenhouse is Boston, Barton College, Mugar Library, Sam. Ms. no. 7; this Ms. could not, however, be identified by the librarians of the Mugar Library.

[19]See below, pp. 43–44.

[20]See Stenhouse, *Kitāb*, Chap. 2.

[21]*Ibid.*, Chap. 3.

[22]Ms. p. 201.

[23]*Ibid.*, p. 264.

[24]See Stenhouse, *Kitāb*, Chap. 2, pp. 5–7.

names of members of the Qabās family are scribbled in notes at the end of the Ms.[25]

The history of the Paris manuscript, which was somewhat obscure,[26] was finally clarified by Stenhouse.[27] The manuscript arrived in Europe not long afterwards. Already at the end of the sixteenth century or the beginning of the seventeenth it formed part of the collection of Nicholas Claude Fabri de Peirsac (1580–1637). From there it passed into the hands of the Cardinal Mazarin (1602–61), receiving the signature Ms. no. 2008; after his death, it came into the possession of the Bibliothèque du Roi (no. 839 of the Catalogue de Clément); in 1739 it was recatalogued as Ms. no. 5 of the Bibliothèque du Roi, and at the end of the nineteenth century it finally received its present signature.

Stenhouse's research into the manuscripts also shows that the Paris manuscript occupies a unique place in the stemma of the extant manuscripts. It is the sole manuscript to derive in an independent line from the archetype, in that no other known manuscripts are related to it.[28] This is clearly reflected by the fact that the manuscripts that belong to Stenhouse's Family A all seem to derive from a no-longer-extant copy made in 1492.[29] This is attested by the fact that the earliest surviving member of Family A, the Huntington manuscript (Vilmar's D), states the date of completion of the manuscript by Abū l-Fatḥ on the last page as AH 898 (= CE 1492),[30] instead of the correct original date on which Abū l-Fatḥ finished compiling the *Kitāb* (756/1355). The year 1492 was obviously the date when the direct source used by the copyist of the Huntington Ms. was completed. It should be noted that there is no doubt as to the date of compilation by Abū l-Fatḥ, since he takes care to mention it already at the beginning of the *Kitāb*.[31] In fact, it is only the Paris manuscript that preserves the original date (rather than 1492) of Abū l-Fatḥ's completion at the end of the text as well.

That the Paris manuscript has no later relations is explained by the fact that it left the possession of the Samaritans and was transferred to Europe

[25] I would like to thank my editor, Lawrence I. Conrad, for drawing my attention to this fact.

[26] See Vilmar, intro., xvii; Stenhouse, *Kitāb*, Chap. 2, p. 3.

[27] Stenhouse, *Kitāb*, Chap. 2, p. 38.

[28] *Ibid.*, Chap. 3, pp. 19, 25.

[29] *Ibid.*, Chap. 2, pp. 9–11.

[30] Vilmar, p. 178.

[31] *Ibid.*, pp. 4–5.

very early in its history, and thus could not have been used as a model for later copyists in the Near East. In addition, it seems that no earlier or contemporary relatives of the Paris manuscripts remained in the hands of the Samaritan community in Nablus after the removal of the Paris Ms., otherwise they would have been copied. The Paris manuscript therefore seems to stand completely alone among the manuscripts of the *Kitāb*.

The special status of the Paris manuscript accounts well for the fact that it is the sole manuscript among all of them to carry the *Continuatio* about 140 years beyond the other manuscripts, to the time of al-Rāḍī. It is also alone in preserving a very important and intriguing section in the first part of the *Continuatio*.[32] This part, which preserves an ancient and quite detailed local Samaritan description of the Muslim conquest of Caesarea, is not to be found in any of the other manuscripts that contain the *Continuatio* up to the time of Hārūn al-Rashīd.

Unless the unexpected happens and another manuscript belonging to this same branch of the stemma turns up, we shall have to make do with this one unique manuscript that preserves the *Continuatio* all the way to the tenth century.

The *Continuatio* as a Historical Source

The *Continuatio* exhibits close proximity, both in time and in place, to the events described in the text. It is clearly familiar not only with events that take place in the local arena, but is also acquainted with the main events in the Muslim world at large.

The Local Character of the Chronicle

When Vilmar reviewed the *Continuatio* (*Additamenta* in his terms) of Abū l-Fatḥ, he expressed his opinion that the sources employed seem to have been contemporary to the events described. This, he notes, is made evident by the fact that they often write in the first person plural.[33]

The use of the first person plural in the description of events indeed stands out prominently. Thus, for example, at the end of the hardships

[32] See Vilmar, pp. 178–80; Ms. pp. 205–207.

[33] Vilmar, intro., lxxvii: "E sermonis pravitate negligentique scriptionis genere equidem conjecerim, a librariis has narrationes exeuntibus libris adjectas esse. Sed libri, e quibus depromatae sunt, a scriptoribus rerum narratarum aequalibus compositi esse videntur. Nam rerum auctores, quippe qui rebus a se narratis ipsi interfuerint, persaepe prima persona loquuntur. Horum igitur additamentorum antiquissimi sunt fontes."

encountered by the Samaritans during the days of Hārūn al-Rashīd the text reads: "All these hardships [came upon us] when we defied our God".[34] In the time of Muḥammad al-Amīn's rule, the Samaritans suffered: "And we were terrified by night and by day," then "we returned to our homes".[35] During al-Ma'mūn's reign (r. 198–218/813–33), "we were scattered amongst the people and fled in fear of the sword".[36] When describing the annulment of the system of the *ḥakākima* the text reads: "We were forced to call upon judges without wisdom".[37] It is of course possible that the use of the first person plural is just a manner of speech denoting the identification of the author with the "Samaritan people" rather than a reference to his own times. Yet this is not the case in the original chronicle of Abū l-Fatḥ, where the usual expression is "the Samaritans" or just "they" (*passim*). Abū l-Fatḥ says distinctly that he is basing his history upon written sources.[38] I would therefore tend to believe that this style of writing attests to the fact that the author or authors (see below on sources) not only lived at the time of the events, but actually experienced them as well.

This conclusion is further supported by the fact that the author reports minute details exhibiting an intimate knowledge of the time and circumstances in which the events took place. Thus, the location of the grave of the *ra'īs* Nethan'el is described as "opposite the tomb of Zeno, close by the road that leads to al-Sārīn...,"[39] revealing the author's first-hand acquaintance with the local burial grounds and traditions concerning them. When describing the arrival of the rebel Abū Ḥarb in the vicinity of Nablus during the 840s, he informs the reader that "fighting broke out on Thursday".[40] The author also reveals precise knowledge of natural phenomena—earthquakes, shooting stars, droughts, etc.—and often specifies such details as the exact time, place and the intensity in which they occurred, e.g.: "On Thursday, which fell upon the fourth day of Tishrīn, stars were seen falling at night from the east towards the west, and towards the south—a momentous event....After four

[34] See below, p. 67.

[35] See below, p. 70.

[36] See below, p. 71.

[37] See below, p. 83.

[38] This is said both at the beginning of the chronicle (Vilmar, pp. 4–6; Stenhouse, trans., pp. 2–5), and, e.g., Vilmar, p. 145 (= Stenhouse, trans., p. 201), where he refers to disagreement vs. agreement among the sources.

[39] See below, pp. 81–82.

[40] See below, p. 86.

days there came a great sandstorm....";[41] or: "For ten days in the month of Tishrīn stars were seen falling from the sky; in their descent they coughed up fires, like immense lightning, and they continued from the middle of the night until after sunrise, falling one after the other";[42] or the following description of a great drought:

> After that the heavens held back the rain for three years, and the sky became like copper and the earth like iron in the winter [for a long] time. The springs dwindled, the trees and the vegetation dried up, the trees dropped their blossoms, and there was a rise in prices so great that it led to fatalities.[43]

There are many such detailed descriptions of earthquakes,[44] droughts,[45] locust attacks,[46] and plagues.[47]

On another occasion the author reveals to the reader that his sources are first-hand witnesses of the events: "The Samaritans of Kafr Tiya [who] related the story suffered with those who fled, but those who reached the coast were not harmed".[48] It seems that the information was written down soon after the events themselves, and the impression is that the author himself heard the moving account from injured refugees.

It seems, in fact, that the chronicle was written so close to the time of the events that at times they were recorded in a confused and hurried fashion, like a reporter writing a first draft in the field. This is directly supported in one place where the author expressly apologizes for not having had time to record the events:

> We did not write down their recollection [of events] during this period, nor that of the kings of the land, because we were preoccupied with our own affairs; there was no one left who had the zeal, or was interested in taking it upon himself, except a few people from amongst all the groups of the Muslims.[49]

[41] See below, pp. 94–95.
[42] See below, p. 115.
[43] See below, pp. 100–101.
[44] See below, pp. 56, 94, 111.
[45] See below, pp. 100–101, 112.
[46] See below, pp. 62, 71, 72, 113.
[47] See below, pp. 64–65, 87, 105.
[48] See below, pp. 96–97.
[49] See below, p. 90.

This crude style of writing sometimes makes it difficult to understand the exact meaning of the text. Thus, in some cases a certain situation is described, and then, without any warning, the events leading up to it are reported. This can be seen, for example, in the story concerning ʿAbd Allāh ibn Ṭāhir, the commander who "had mercy upon the people, and lightened their affliction except for the [damage] done by the rebels, to which there was no limit." Without warning the text then goes on to describe that former situation: "All the people had left their places vacant, run away and strayed from their beliefs. . . ."[50] Only after this sentence does it become evident that this is in fact a description of the situation that was corrected by Ibn Ṭāhir.

This proximity in time and place to the events, in addition to the distinctly Samaritano-centric character of the *Continuatio*, accounts also for the strong local colour that the text bears. Thus, although the author always starts with a general picture of events and describes the political background of the situation, he invariably zooms in and focuses upon occurrences in Palestine, and more specifically in Samaria, and it is quite obvious that he was a resident of Nablus or one of its neighbouring villages.

Thus, for example, the "War of the Watermelon," which took place between the Qays and Yaman factions in Palestine in the last decade of the eighth century, is first described by the author in general; he then moves on to describe in detail the effects of this war—the famine and plague that followed it—upon the residents of the area in general and the Samaritans in particular.[51] After describing the general background and events concerning the revolt of Abū Ḥarb, the author continues and describes in minute detail his attacks on the villages of Samaria and their consequences: he describes how the rebels wreaked havoc in the vicinity of Nablus, and how, after several attempts by the authorities in Ramla to suppress them failed, they continued to rob, loot and terrorise the local population, which fled in fear. The description culminates in the murder of the *ra'īs*, the high priest of the Samaritans.[52] Another example is the restrictions imposed by the caliph al-Mutawakkil (r. 232–47/847–61) upon the *dhimmīs*. The *Continuatio* first provides a detailed description of the restrictions imposed in Palestine;[53] then the author goes on to describe in particular how the Samaritan community in

[50]See below, p. 76.

[51]See below, pp. 62–67; Vilmar, pp. 184–86.

[52]See below, pp. 84–89.

[53]For this there is no other evidence; see below, p. 16.

Palestine contended with them.[54] The order that every *dhimmī* should affix an idol to his doorpost was considered especially offensive by the Samaritans in Palestine, and they managed to alleviate this indignity by receiving permission to choose their own image—a candelabrum. It should be noted that although many of these cases are specific incidents concerning the Samaritans, they provide us with an insight into the daily life of the local population, vividly illustrating the specific local effects that large-scale political, military and social events and decisions had upon the inhabitants of the country.

Familiarity with Events in the Muslim Empire

In spite of this strong local flavour, the author of the chronicle is far from being narrow-minded and provincial and is surprisingly knowledgeable about general events occurring in the Muslim world. Thus, he reports about the ʿAbbāsid revolution, its course and its consequences.[55] He also displays impressive knowledge about the contract drawn by Hārūn al-Rashīd concerning the division of the empire among his heirs;[56] like some of the Muslim sources, he reports not only that Muḥammad al-Amīn was neglectful of his kingdom, but also that he "adorned himself, cleaving to the boys, dressing them as women, adorning them with women's ornaments, sleeping with them and clinging to them".[57] He reports in detail the movements of Khālid ibn Yazīd and ʿAbd Allāh ibn Ṭāhir, the two generals sent by al-Ma'mūn to quell the revolts against him. He knows of Khālid's journey to Egypt, his initial success and later his defeat and departure; he is also familiar with ʿAbd Allāh's success in defeating the rebel Nāṣr ibn Shabath in Ḥimṣ, and with his victory over the rebels in Egypt and his conquest of North Africa.[58] He knows about al-Mutawakkil's unsuccessful short-term attempt to move his capital to Damascus, mentions the deposition of the caliph al-Mustaʿīn and his epithet *al-makhlūʿ min banī Hāshim*, and is aware of the complicated relationship between the caliph al-Muʿtamid (r. 256–79/870–92) and his brother Abū Aḥmad.[59] Despite the fact that it is clearly a local Samaritan chronicle, it is very well tied in, therefore, with the political and social developments and events that occurred in the Muslim empire, describing the events, however,

[54] See below, pp. 92–94.
[55] See below, pp. 56–57; Vilmar, p. 181.
[56] See below, pp. 67–68.
[57] See below, pp. 68–69 and nn. 175–79.
[58] See below, pp. 74–76.
[59] See below, pp. 96–99.

from a very unusual angle—not that of a Muslim intellectual in Baghdad, Cairo or Damascus, who would usually view circumstances through the eyes of the ruling elite, but rather that of a *dhimmī* in Palestine.[60]

The argument for the proximity of the *Continuatio* to the events is strengthened even further by the fact that in certain cases names belonging to the history of the period, which were preserved in the *Continuatio*, were no longer known to the copyist, who had difficulty in identifying them and copying them correctly. Thus, the name Qays is erroneously written as Qabs;[61] Judhām is spelt Ḥudām;[62] the word Kināniyīn, which appears twice, is written on both occasions without diacritical points (كاىس) implying that the copyist was not familiar with this name.[63] Khumārawayh's name is copied consistently as Jumāz instead of Khumār;[64] Aḥmad ibn Ṭūlūn's name is twice copied as Ibn Tūbūn before it is correctly spelt a few pages later;[65] and the name Ibn Ṭughj appears several times as Ibn Ṭufḥ.[66]

Thus, although no specific date can be determined, the use of the first person plural, in addition to the presence of many details pertaining to local and general matters, including numerous names, events and dates (some of which could no longer be identified by the copyist), all point to the proximity of the *Continuatio*'s sources to the events in time and place.

The Credibility of the Chronicle

Since the *Continuatio* supplies us with plentiful new information, it is of special importance to establish its credibility, especially when it comes to information that is not directly or exclusively connected with the area of Samaria. This can of course be done by comparing facts that appear in the chronicle with those known from other sources, in this case mainly Muslim sources. Several of these cases, which are well corroborated with the Muslim sources, have already been presented above. There are many others beside these, including: a) the well-known earthquake in Palestine in 749 (in the days of Marwān ibn Muḥammad, the last of the Umayyad caliphs),

[60]The importance of this sort of perspective has recently been stressed in R.W. Bulliet, *Islam: the View from the Edge* (New York, 1994), pp. 1–12.

[61]See below, p. 70.

[62]See below, p. 69.

[63]See below, p. 70.

[64]See below, pp. 106–108.

[65]See below, p. 99.

[66]See below, pp. 114–16.

known from Jewish and Muslim sources;[67] b) the depiction of the extortionate ruler of Palestine during the days of al-Manṣūr (r. 136–58/754–75), ʿAbd al-Wahhāb, which is corroborated by Ibn ʿAsākir—a reliable source containing much information concerning Palestine and Syria in this period that is not to be found elsewhere;[68] c) the building of a fortress by al-Mutawakkil in Damascus, also corroborated solely by Ibn ʿAsākir;[69] d) al-Maʾmūn's successful military attack against Byzantium in the year before his death,[70] and al-Muʿtaṣim's famous expedition in 838, which culminated with the destruction of Amorium,[71] mentioned here in passing; e) the famous rebellion of Abū Ḥarb, described in detail by our chronicle and well corroborated by Muslim sources,[72] as is its final suppression by Rajāʾ ibn Ayyūb al-Ḥiḍārī;[73] f) the list of restrictions applied by al-Mutawakkil, as presented in the *Continuatio*, is almost identical to the list in al-Ṭabarī, proving the author's close acquaintance with the issue and contributing much to our knowledge concerning this matter.[74] Additional corroborations may be found in the mention of al-Mutawakkil's murder by his son, the future caliph al-Muntaṣir (r. 247–48/861–62);[75] the rebellion of a man named al-Qiṭāmī, which was quelled by a general named Muzāḥim ibn Khāqān;[76] the report about the caliph al-Muʿtamid and his relations with his brother al-Muwaffaq, called Abū Aḥmad, who actually detained the caliph in his palace at Jawsaq;[77] the reports concerning the growth of Aḥmad ibn Ṭūlūn's dominion, the course of his expanding hegemony over Syria, Palestine, and Egypt,[78] and the fortress he built in Jaffa;[79] and his surprisingly intricate knowledge about the heirs of Ibn Ṭūlūn and about wars waged by his generals against al-Muwaffaq's commanders both in Shayzar and in Nahr al-Ṭawāḥīn.[80]

---

[67]For references, see below, p. 56 n. 77.
[68]See below, pp. 58–59 and n. 92.
[69]See below, p. 96 and n. 438.
[70]See below, p. 79.
[71]See below, p. 84 n. 309.
[72]See below, pp. 84–89.
[73]See below, pp. 88–89 and notes.
[74]See below, pp. 91–93 and notes.
[75]See below, pp. 97–98 and n. 454.
[76]See below, pp. 96–97 and notes.
[77]See below, pp. 98–99 and nn. 462–63.
[78]See below, pp. 99–100, 102–105, and notes.
[79]See below, p. 104 and n. 518.
[80]See below, pp. 106–108 and notes.

There are, however, several cases of imprecision and confusion. These fall into the following categories:

1. Most of the dates given in the *Continuatio* are indeed correct. But in one case, that of al-Ma'mūn's attack upon Byzantium, the date given is April 833,[81] while the successful expedition referred to actually took place in 832.[82] Al-Ma'mūn left on his second expedition, from which he never returned, on 9 August 833. There seems to have been some confusion here between the two expeditions. The other cases of imprecision in dating pertain to the list of the reigns of the caliphs: the reign of Yazīd ibn Mu'āwiya is omitted; Marwān ibn al-Ḥakam reigned for nine or ten months, not four; 'Abd Allāh ibn al-Zubayr ruled, according to tradition, for nine years and one month, and not eight years and five months; 'Abd al-Malik ibn Marwān ruled for 21 years and one month, not for thirteen years and six months. In a few other places there are slight inaccuracies: 'Umar ibn 'Abd al-'Azīz reigned for two years and five months, while our source cites two years and six months; Yazīd ibn 'Abd al-Malik ibn Marwān ruled for four years and a month, not for four years. Some of these are no doubt just mistakes, the clearest being 'Abd al-Malik ibn Marwān; still others, the less clear-cut ones, might reflect the different Muslim traditions that were "in the air," as attested by al-Ṭabarī himself, who chooses to cite other available traditions beside the widely accepted one that he presents.[83] There are also a few errors and inaccuracies concerning the ruling period of some 'Abbāsid caliphs. Thus, al-Musta'īn reigned for four years, not for two and a half,[84] and al-Mu'tamid reigned for 22 and not 24 years.[85]

2. Cases of imprecision and error concerning events are few in number. They include a reference to Aḥmad ibn Ṭūlūn's "conquest" of Barqa and Alexandria, which according to Muslim sources were handed over to his jurisdiction by Yārjūj, the Egyptian apanagist, not taken by force;[86] a gross error where Ibrāhīm ibn al-Mahdī, al-Ma'mūn's uncle,

[81] See below, p. 79 and n. 273.
[82] *Ibid.*
[83] See, e.g., below, pp. 54–56, nn. 60, 65, 70–71, 74.
[84] See below, p. 98 and n. 458.
[85] *Ibid.*
[86] See below, p. 100 and n. 478.

who acted as caliph for a short term and then abdicated, is confused with Abū Isḥāq ibn Hārūn al-Mu'taṣim, who first served as governor of Syria and was proclaimed caliph after al-Ma'mūn's death;[87] and a mistaken reference to Khumārawayh's two generals as "his sons," a mistake that seems to correct itself in the next sentence.[88]

3. There are several instances of imprecision in names. Al-Mu'tamid's brother, al-Muwaffaq, who bore the *kunya* Abū Aḥmad, is called Abū Muḥammad in the text;[89] the leader of the rebels in Damascus during the days of al-Wāthiq, Ibn Bayhas, is called here Ibn 'Abbās;[90] Khumārawayh's general, Sa'd al-Aysar, is called here Sa'īd,[91] and the Umayyad caliph Hishām ibn 'Abd al-Malik is called Hāshim.[92] Names are sometimes spelt wrongly or awkwardly: the caliph Abū Bakr's name, 'Atīq ibn Abī l-Quḥāfa, is spelt 'Atīk,[93] and Shayzar is spelt Shayjar. In at least some cases these imprecisions seem to point to the use of oral sources. Thus Ibn Bayhas could easily be turned by an unaccustomed ear into Ibn 'Abbās; and Abū Aḥmad could easily be memorized as Abū Muḥammad. This seems much less feasible when using a written source. The cases of 'Atīq being spelt 'Atīk, and Shayzar as Shayjar, also serve as an indication of the use of an oral source, since they obviously could not be copyist's errors.

The number of errors, however, is on the whole quite small. Thus it seems that although the author had access most of the time to accurate information concerning the periods of the reigns of the caliphs, he was sometimes misguided by his sources, or alternatively was not sufficiently alert to the potential for error in this matter.

It can therefore be concluded that the *Continuatio* is, most of the time, a reliable source. It bears detailed and trustworthy information concerning activities and events in Palestine and its surroundings, and is normally reliable in conveying information about general events in the Muslim world. It should be noted, however, that naturally the latter sort of information

[87] See below, pp. 76–77, 78, 80, 84, and nn. 246, 261, 264, 278, 308.
[88] See below, p. 106 n. 537.
[89] See below, pp. 98–99 and nn. 462–63.
[90] See below, p. 88 and n. 352.
[91] See below, p. 106 and n. 538.
[92] See below, p. 55 and n. 69.
[93] See below, p. 53 and n. 50.

is sometimes partial and incomplete. This is exemplified well by the problematic cases of the time-spans of the reigns of the caliphs, by an awkward mistake such as putting Ibrāhīm in place of Abū Isḥāq, or of calling al-Muwaffaq Abū Muḥammad instead of Abū Aḥmad. Also awkward is the use of the first names of the caliphs instead of their titles, a practice unheard of among Muslim historians. In this case, a Samaritan historian living in a far-off province can in no way be compared to Muslim historians, who had the advantage of a profound knowledge of Muslim culture and were usually close to the centre of events and thus had easy access to reliable information.

Language, Style and Terminology

The *Continuatio* is written in Samaritan Arabic (= *SA*), a dialect of what is called Middle Arabic (= *MA*), which also comprehends Christian Arabic (= *ChA*) and Judeo-Arabic (= *JA*). *MA* serves as the link bridging between Classical Arabic and the modern Arabic dialects; it represents, so it seems, the vernacular Arabic that developed in the East after the Arab conquest, but was not represented by Muslim writers of Arabic due to their strict concept of *ʿarabīya*.[94] *MA* is therefore often best documented by non-Muslim groups who adopted the Arabic language. The different dialects of Middle Arabic have been intensively researched in the past few decades, Joshua Blau being responsible for the main breakthrough in this field through his investigations of *CA* and *JA*.[95] Lately, Paul Stenhouse has paid special attention to Samaritan Arabic in his new edition of Abū l-Fatḥ.[96] Important progress in the field of *SA* is also being made by Haseeb Shehadeh, whose first volume of the Arabic version of the Samaritan Pentateuch, including Genesis and Exodus, was published in 1989.[97]

[94] J. Blau, "The Importance of Middle Arabic Dialects for the History of Arabic," *Scripta Hierosolymitana* 9 (1961), pp. 206–28; *idem*, *A Grammar of Christian Arabic Based Mainly on South-Palestinian Texts from the First Millennium*, I (Louvain, 1966), pp. i–ii, 19–20.

[95] For *ChA* see his monumental *Grammar*; for *JA* see *idem*, *The Emergence and Linguistic Background of Judaeo-Arabic* (Oxford, 1965). See also B. Knutsson, *Studies in the Text and Language of Three Syriac–Arabic Versions of the Book of Iudicum with Special Reference to the Middle Arabic Elements* (Leiden, 1974).

[96] P. Stenhouse, "Samaritan Arabic," in Crown, *Samaritans*, pp. 585–623.

[97] H. Shehadeh, ed., *The Arabic Translation of the Samaritan Pentateuch* (Jerusalem, 1989). See also *idem*, "When did Arabic Replace Samaritan Aramaic?," in M. Bar-Asher, A. Dotan *et al.*, eds., *Hebrew Language Studies Presented to Professor Zeev Ben Hayyim* (Jerusalem, 1983), pp. 515–28 (in Hebrew); *idem*, "The Arabic of the Samaritans," in

Since the general rules of the grammar and syntax of *MA* are to be found in Blau's *Grammar*, and specific guidelines for *SA* have been laid out by Stenhouse, there is no need to delve further into this matter, and I will refer here briefly to the special orthography, language and style of the *Continuatio*.

The Paris manuscript bears some special orthographic characteristics. In addition to the well-known practice according to which letters of identical skeletal forms bear additional differentiating marks (thus ط, س and ر are usually marked by a small hacek above the letter in order to confirm that ظ, ش or ز are not meant), letters are marked by a small form of the letter above or beneath them in order to denote the difference; thus, ع and ح have the same letter written above themselves in a smaller form to confirm that غ and ج or خ are not meant. The letter و often carries, arbitrarily it seems, a *sukūn* above it, while the conjunction و often carries a *ḍamma* above it, perhaps denoting its pronunciation. In addition, ص, ح and the combination لا all bear a *shadda* quite consistently. Other signs that resemble *fatḥa* and *kasra* seem to be mostly ornamental rather than functional, and fill up the spaces between the lines. Line endings are sometimes marked by one of two signs that seem to have no difference between them apart from the fact that one fills up more space than the other; in cases where the last word reaches the end of the line, there are no such signs at all.

As for language and style, Vilmar already observed that the language of the *Continuatio* is unmistakably different from the "first section" of Abū l-Fatḥ, which extends to the time of Muḥammad.[98] While the first section is written in a clear and concise manner and strives to imitate "Classical Arabic" in style, the *Continuatio* is composed much more carelessly; its style is quite common, and the vernacular language is dominant, making it a much more difficult text for the reader.

The linguistic imprecision of the author is also expressed in the inconsistency of the terminology used. The author does not seem to be very familiar with the administrative or military hierarchy of the Muslim authorities. The term *muqaddam* often bears the meaning of an officer or commander (of various ranks, so it seems) representing the Muslim authorities, yet it is also used sometimes in reference to leaders of the Samaritan community.[99] The

---

Crown and Davey, eds., *Essays in Honour of G.D. Sixdenier*, pp. 551–75.

[98]Vilmar, intro., lxxvi, xcvii; see also Stenhouse, "Samaritan Arabic," p. 587.

[99]See below, pp. 86, 102. The term *muqaddam* with reference to the leaders of the

exact meaning of the term *za'īm* is also unclear. It appears at times as a local authority[100] and at others as a higher authority.[101] The Samaritan high priest is called interchangeably *ra'īs* and *imām*; this may imply, however, the use of multiple sources by the author, each deploying different terminology.

It should be noted that the *Continuatio*, like other compositions written in *SA*, bears some special usages in Arabic. Thus the Hebrew word נטמא ("to become impure") is transferred into Arabic as *taṭamma'a*; the word *dājin* is equivalent to the Hebrew דגן ("cereals");[102] the very unusual use of *shām* for "north,"[103] the use of *būq* to denote the *shōfar* (a horn used for liturgical purposes)[104] and others. Also characteristic is the adoption of typical Muslim terminology, such as *qibla* to denote "south" (obviously the Muslim direction of prayer),[105] *muftī* for a Samaritan expounder of law,[106] or *imām* to denote the Samaritan high priest. This phenomenon testifies to the extent of the process of Arabization among the Samaritans at an early date. Our text might therefore cast doubt on the accuracy of the claim presented in the *Tōlīdah* that Samaritans started writing in Arabic only in the twelfth century; or perhaps this claim may refer to the use of Arabic script, which replaced the Samaritan script in use by Samaritans formerly when writing in the Arabic language.[107]

Another characteristic of the Paris manuscript is its occasional use of Samaritan script.[108] Throughout the text the names of the Samaritan high

---

community was also in use by the Arabic-speaking Jewish community. See S.D. Goitein, *A Mediterranean Society*, II (Berkeley, 1971), pp. 33, 35, *passim.*

[100]See below, pp. 80, 82.

[101]See below, p. 85.

[102]For *taṭamma'a*, see Ms. p. 218:5, = trans. p. 67 n. 164; Ms. p. 249:10, = trans. p. 101 n. 492. For *dājin*, see Ms. p. 216:5, = trans. p. 65 n. 154. This usage also appears in the Hebrew–Aramaic–Arabic dictionary of biblical words, written around the eleventh century and published by Z. Ben Hayyim, *The Literary and Oral Tradition of Hebrew and Aramaic amongst the Samaritans* (Jerusalem, 1961), II, 446 (in Hebrew).

[103]Ms. p. 206:7, = trans. p. 52. Cf. Ben Hayyim, II, 576.

[104]Ms. p. 243:8, = trans. p. 94. Cf. Ben Hayyim, II, 598.

[105]See below, Ms. p. 236:2, = trans. p. 87 n. 341; also Stenhouse, trans., nn. 3, 210, 221.

[106]See below, Ms. p. 238:3, = trans. p. 89.

[107]See B.Z. Kedar, "The Frankish Period," in Crown, *Samaritans*, p. 89, referring to the *Tōlīdah*; M.A. Neubauer, *Chronique Samaritaine* (Paris, 1873), pp. 26, 65 (trans.); E.N. Adler and M. Seligsohn, "Une nouvelle chronique samaritaine," *REJ* 45 (1902), pp. 95–96; J. Bowman, *Transcript of the Original Text of the Samaritan Chronicle Tolidah* (Leeds, 1957), p. 23a–b.

[108]In the present translation, words written in Samaritan script are in sans serif type.

priests, as well as other important figures (such as Ṣarmaṣa) or places (Mt. Gerizim) are often written in Samaritan script, as is the name Muḥammad (not only the Prophet). The special treatment of the latter name seems to denote its special status in the eyes of the Samaritans; this fits in well with the positive image of the Prophet exhibited in the *Continuatio*.[109] In other cases words quoted in Hebrew or in Samaritan Aramaic appear in the text in Samaritan characters, e.g. המכתב ("the letter," Ms. p. 205:1), הישמעאלים ("the Ishmaelites," *ibid.*), הנערים ("the boys," Ms. p. 219:6), הגוים ("the Gentiles," Ms. p. 227:4). This is not especially surprising in light of the fact mentioned already, that Arabic was first written by the Samaritans in Samaritan characters before they adopted the Arabic script, and Samaritan characters were still being used by the Samaritans for liturgical purposes (as they still are today). This may well explain some of the errors in personal and place names mentioned above.

There are, however, several cases in which the use of Samaritan script is not so easily explained. In these cases, whole sentences of Arabic are suddenly written in Samaritan characters for no apparent reason. Such is the case on Ms. p. 242, where several of al-Mutawakkil's restrictions on the *dhimmīs* are suddenly written in Samaritan script, the change actually beginning and ending in the middle of the sentence. It might be claimed that fear of the Muslims may have been the cause of this, were it not for the fact that the bulk of the restrictions is enumerated on the preceding page in Arabic characters. An identical case appears on the following page (Ms. p. 243), where the text relates a prohibition against the Samaritans' going up to Mt. Gerizim and raising their voices in prayer. The fact that several days later they went up to the mountain and raised their voices without disturbance is, however, related in Arabic characters. On Ms. p. 250, the characters again switch from Arabic to Samaritan in the middle of a sentence when suspicion of murder falls upon the Samaritans and their leaders are arrested; the Samaritans are forced to pay an apparently enormous sum—15,000 *dīnār*s—in order to free them. On the following page (Ms. p. 255) some of the restrictions imposed by Aḥmad ibn Ṭūlūn appear in Samaritan characters, while others appear in Arabic script. It may be that special restrictions or punishments imposed especially on the Samaritans, as opposed to general restrictions that included all *dhimmīs*, were concealed in Samaritan script so that such "ideas" would

---

[109] See below, p. 53.

not reach the eyes of those who might be inspired to enforce them. It may also be that in certain cases the sources used by the author of the *Continuatio* were themselves written in Samaritan script, and thus may have sometimes confused the author as he copied from them.

Sources and Relationship to Other Samaritan Chronicles

When referring to the nature of the so-called *additamenta*, Vilmar emphasized that these additions must have their origin in very early sources.[110] Indeed, as already demonstrated above, the source or sources employed in the *Continuatio* were, no doubt, local materials produced in the area of Nablus itself by eyewitnesses to the events in some cases, and actual participants in others. This would lead us to the simple and obvious conclusion that the *Continuatio* is an unedited and uncontaminated, direct, first-hand account of the events described in the text.

Yet even if we accept Vilmar's claim, as indeed we do, that Abū l-Fatḥ's original text ended with the advent of Muḥammad, we are still left with a text describing a period of over 300 years, from Muḥammad until the time of al-Rāḍī. So long a period obviously cannot be attributed to a single author; we thus still have to contend with the question of the sources of the *Continuatio*. It follows that most probably the *Continuatio* was written by several authors who each wrote first-hand accounts of the events in his own day. Whether these accounts were then edited by one hand, or written one after the other and then strung together in the conventional style of a chronicle, is difficult to determine.

As to the first part of the text extending to the time of Hārūn al-Rashīd, for which there are several parallel Mss., there are a number of indications that may point to the conclusion that the first part of the *Continuatio* was based on a more authentic text, or alternatively, that it tended not to intervene or edit the text as much, and thus retained a more original text. The Paris manuscript distinguishes quite clearly, as has been mentioned above, between the first part, Abū l-Fatḥ's *Kitāb al-ta'rīkh*, and the second part, the *Continuatio*. At the end of Abū l-Fatḥ's chronicle the list of high priests is given, after which there is a colophon (Ms. p. 202). However, the *Continuatio*, which begins on p. 203 of the Paris Ms., opens with the story describing the recognition of Muḥammad by the three astrologers, a story already told at the end of Abū l-Fatḥ's text (Paris Ms., pp. 194–202, and parallel Mss.

---

[110] See above, p. 10 n. 33.

of Abū l-Fatḥ). Not only is there such a repetition in the same manuscript, but when the Abū l-Fatḥ version of the story is compared to the *Continuatio* (Ms. pp. 203–207), it becomes obvious that although they present the same text, there are essential differences between them. Although it is immediately evident that the language and style of the Abū l-Fatḥ version are closer to *CA* and superior to that of the *Continuatio*, which uses a much more vulgar and vernacular language, the *Continuatio* seems to bear the better and more reliable text. The most obvious example is the text on Ms. p. 204:3 of the *Continuatio*, which reads: انت تدين بدين وشريعه ("you will be the one to profess [the Muslim] faith and law"); this version appears solely on p. 204 of the Paris Ms., while all the other manuscripts of the Abū l-Fatḥ version, including the first version of this story appearing on pp. 197–202 of the Paris Ms.,[111] carry the corrupt and almost meaningless: انت تدين بدين وسيعه (trans. by Stenhouse as: "you have a magnanimous religion"[112]). The *Continuatio* also preserves a whole section describing the conquest of Caesarea, which is completely missing in the Abū l-Fatḥ version and appears to be an important and completely integral part of the text.[113] Another point that may indicate the superiority of the text used in the *Continuatio* is the fact that it states on Ms. p. 203 that the Christian astrologer, named in the Abū l-Fatḥ version and later on in the *Continuatio* as ʿAbd al-Salām, was called ʿAbd Allāh; this fits in very well if he is indeed to be identified with ʿAbd Allāh ibn Salām.[114] The *Continuatio* is also the only source to add that he was originally from Lydda.

If we were to assume that the Abū l-Fatḥ version and the *Continuatio* draw on the same source, then the former seems to have recast and refined the text (perhaps omitting and corrupting some material), while the latter seems to have been unedited, and preserves, in that sense, a better and more accurate text. It seems quite plausible that the *Continuatio* relied upon sources mentioned in the list of sources used by Abū l-Fatḥ and cited by him at the beginning of his composition.[115] The following materials are listed:

---

[111]See Vilmar, p. 173.

[112]Stenhouse, trans., p. 244.

[113]See Vilmar, pp. 179–80.

[114]See below, p. 46 nn. 1, 5.

[115]Vilmar, p. 5. For a comprehensive review of Samaritan chronicles and the state of research in the field, see P. Stenhouse, "Samaritan Chronicles," in Crown, *Samaritans*, pp. 218–65.

1. Two books concerning the *Allotment of Regions* (قطع البلدى, *sic*!), unknown compositions referring, no doubt, to the division of the land during the period of the Israelite settlement.[116]

2. *The Book of Joshua and Others* (سفر يهوشع وغيره), written in Arabic.

3. *The Catena* (السلسله المنقولة), the list of high priests, which was expanded into the *Tōlīdah* (*Genealogy*) in the middle of the twelfth century, and was continued further in the fourteenth century.[117]

4. "Three defective histories" (i.e. histories with some of their pages missing: ثلاث تواريخ مخرومة); and "quires" (كراس or كراسة).

Of these listed sources, we are familiar with the *Book of Joshua* (in Hebrew and in Arabic versions); and with the *Catena* and the *Tōlīdah*. Although this last source[118] contains some information concerning the early Muslim period, it is scant and faulty and could in no way have served as the source for the *Continuatio*. Another Samaritan chronicle (not included in Abū l-Fatḥ's list) that contains information relevant to the period under discussion is the so-called *New Chronicle* or *Chronicle Adler*.[119] It too is quite confused and poor in evidence. Moreover, Abū l-Fatḥ's *Kitāb al-ta'rīkh* seems to serve as one of his sources; it cannot, therefore, be considered as a source of the *Continuatio*.[120]

We are therefore left with two sources mentioned by Abū l-Fatḥ that may have served as the source of the *Continuatio*: the "three defective histories" and the "quires." The former were written in Hebrew script and language (perhaps meaning Samaritan Aramaic?), which he received according to his testimony from "the house of the headship" (*dār al-riyāsa*) in Damascus;[121]

[116] See Stenhouse, "Samaritan Chronicles," pp. 241–42.

[117] *Ibid.*, pp. 218–19.

[118] Neubauer, *Chronique Samaritaine*, pp. 23–24; Bowman, *Transcript*, pp. 20a–21b.

[119] See E. Adler and M. Seligsohn, "Une nouvelle chronique samaritaine", *REJ* 44 (1902), pp. 188–222; 45 (1902), pp. 70–98, 160, 223–54; 46 (1903), pp. 123–46; Stenhouse, "Samaritan Chronicles," p. 222.

[120] *Ibid.*, pp. 228–30.

[121] Vilmar, p. 5. This could hardly be "the seat of Government in Damascus," as translated by Stenhouse (trans., p. 4), and is much more likely to be the centre of the Samaritan community in Damascus, as he himself notes elsewhere (see "Samaritan Chronicles," p. 248 and n. 149).

nothing is known about the latter. However, it is plausible that these "histories and quires" included material recorded at different periods by the Samaritan community; it may well be that such histories were written in chronicle form: i.e. events were recorded in the order of their occurrence in proximity to the events, by members of the community who were appointed to the task.

This form of *chronographia* fits in well with the use of the first person plural already emphasized above. Certain references in the text itself also point in this direction: thus the author says: "We did not set down records of their (i.e. the Muslims') past, nor that of the kings of the land during this period, because we were preoccupied with our own affairs...."[122] This seems to imply that the chronicle was written at the time of the events, and its writing was therefore itself influenced by prevailing circumstances; if there had simply been no information concerning these matters in the sources, a later editor or copyist would have had no way of knowing that there was anything missing at this point or why it was missing. The author actually feels that he has to apologize for his lack of dedication to his task. He then goes on to say: "...and there was no one left who had the zeal, or was interested in taking it upon himself, except a few of the schools of all the Muslims." This discloses another interesting point: Samaritan chroniclers were familiar with some forms of Muslim historiography. This may well be, at least partially, the source of some of the information concerning Muslim history that was incorporated quite generously into the chronicle. Another source, no doubt, was news that travelled by word of mouth. This is made evident by the corruption of toponyms and personal names.[123]

In conclusion it seems, therefore, that the *Continuatio* was based upon information contained in the histories or quires mentioned by Abū l-Fatḥ. These were actually parts of a chronicle or chronicles written by Samaritans in Nablus or its surroundings close to the time in which the events occurred. Sometimes they themselves witnessed the events described, while at other times they received information from other Samaritans, or in certain cases probably from non-Samaritan informants who passed by and informed them of events in other places in Palestine and Syria. In addition, they had access to both oral and written information concerning events in the Muslim empire. The chronicle was thus made up of a series of descriptions and notes, each

---

[122]See below, p. 90.
[123]See above, p. 18.

pertaining to a certain time and situation. In contrast to Abū l-Fatḥ, these lists do not seem to have been edited at all, since there are repetitions and lacunae, as well as references that are sometimes obscure or ambiguous, as if the author was writing a "journal" rather than an organized historical tract.[124]

The Historical Contribution of the *Continuatio*

The absence of a chronicle or any other composition of historical character that centres specifically upon the history of Palestine during the early Muslim period makes the *Continuatio* an especially important document. It is undoubtedly Samaritano-centric, but nevertheless provides us with ample information about events and developments in Palestine during the period. In contrast to other sources of the same period, such as Christian hagiographical and theological compositions, which mention political and military events only in passing, the *Continuatio* places the historical events at centre stage. Here it may be worthwhile to survey at least some of the most prominent and outstanding contributions of the *Continuatio* to our knowledge of the period.

As I have already mentioned, the section describing the Arab conquest, culminating in the capture of Caesarea, is of special importance.[125] This description of the conquest clearly implies that although the Samaritans living along the coast felt threatened to such an extent that they decided to flee along with the Byzantines to Byzantium,[126] the Samaritan inhabitants of the inland areas did not feel as imperilled; not only did they remain in their places, but the Samaritan high priest also took it upon himself to guard all their belongings and possessions (which were enormous, according to the text) until the danger had passed and they could return ("and they have not returned to this day"). This description supplies us with an interesting view of events. It seems that it was the Byzantine *poleis* centred along the coast-

[124]On the subject of "layered chronicles," see L.I. Conrad, "Syriac Perspectives on Bilād al-Shām during the 'Abbāsid Period," in M.A. Bakhit, ed., *Bilād al-Shām During the 'Abbāsid Period—Proccedings of the Fifth International Conference on the History of Bilād al-Sham* (Amman, 1991), pp. 1–44, esp. pp. 18–26.

[125]See below, pp. 50–53.

[126]A remarkable fact in itself, since there was great tension and animosity between Samaritans and Byzantines in Palestine; this was a result of the Samaritan revolts of the 5th–6th centuries that caused great havoc in Palestine and resulted in the cruel humiliation of the Samaritans by the Byzantines and in extreme anti-Samaritan legislation. See A.D. Crown, "The Byzantine and Moslem Period", in Crown, *Samaritans*, pp. 68–77.

line,[127] and especially Caesarea the Metropolis, as our text clearly states, that offered resistance to the invaders and thus placed their inhabitants in danger, while the inhabitants of the inland area felt comparatively secure. This fits well with our growing realisation that the Muslim conquest of Palestine was essentially non-violent and that many of the cities surrendered in return for a guarantee of security for themselves and their possessions and a promise of religious freedom, all of which were included in the *amān* (a pledge of protection of life and property) written and granted to each city specifically.[128]

---

[127]The coastal cities were indeed abandoned by their inhabitants and resettled by the Muslims, who introduced a non-Arab mostly Persian population. See A. El'ad, "The Coastal Cities of Palestine during the Early Middle Ages," *The Jerusalem Cathedra* 2 (1982), pp. 146–67, esp. pp. 146–51.

[128]On the nature of the conquest, see F.M. Donner, *The Early Islamic Conquests* (Princeton, 1981), pp. 152–53. A detailed review of the *amāns* given to different cities is found in D.R. Hill, *The Termination of Hostilities in the Early Arab Conquests* (London, 1971); see also A. Noth's discussion in his book *The Early Arabic Historical Tradition: a Source-Critical Study* (Princeton, 1994), pp. 146–67, where he demonstrates that "the summons to Islam (*da'wa*)" included the option of *amān* before the final option of fighting; W. al-Qāḍī, "Madkhal ilā dirāsat 'uhūd al-ṣulḥ al-islāmīya zaman al-futūḥ," in M.'A. al-Bakhīt and I. 'Abbās, eds., *Proceedings of the Second Symposium on the History of Bilād al-Sham During the Early Islamic Period up to 40 A.H./640 A.D.* (Amman, 1987), II, 193–269; R. Schick, *The Christian Communities of Palestine from Byzantine to Islamic Rule* (Princeton, 1995), pp. 68–90, esp. pp. 77–84, 222–24. To these should be added the results of numerous archaeological excavations made in recent years. These investigations reveal no sign of any traumatic break or crisis in the seventh century. See, for example, the cases of Apollonia (Arsūf) in I. Roll and E. Ayalon. *Apollonia and Southern Sharon* (Tel-Aviv, 1989), pp. 67–81, esp. 78–81; Tiberias in Y. Hirschfeld and G. Foerster, "Tiberias," in E. Stern, ed., *The New Encyclopedia of Archeological Excavations in the Holy Land* (Jerusalem, 1993), IV, 1464–73; Beth-Shean in Y. Tsafrir and G. Foerster, "From Scythopolis to Baysān—Changing Concepts of Urbanism," in G.R.D. King and A. Cameron, eds., *The Byzantine and Early Islamic Near East*, II: *Land Use and Settlement Patterns* (Princeton, 1994), pp. 95–115, esp. pp. 111–15, also their article "Urbanism at Scythopolis–Bet Shean in the Fourth to Seventh Centuries," *DOP* 51 (1997), pp. 85–146; Jerusalem in R. Arav, L. Di Segni, and A. Kloner, "An Eighth-Century Monastery near Jerusalem," *LA* 40 (1990), pp. 313–20. The same applies to numerous sites excavated in Transjordan in the past decade; for a general survey see H.I. MacAdam, "Settlements and Settlement Patterns in Northern and Central Transjordania, *ca.* 550–750," in King and Cameron, eds., *Land Use and Settlement Patterns*, pp. 49–94, esp. pp. 91–92. See also M. Piccirillo, *Chiese e mosaici di Madaba* (Jerusalem, 1989); J.P. Humbert and A. Desreumaux, "Huit campagnes de fouilles au Khirbet es-Samra (1981–1989)," *RB* 97 (1990), pp. 252–69; M. Piccirillo, "Le iscrizioni di Um er-Rasas–Kastron Mefaa in Giordania I (1986–1987)," *ADAJ* 30 (1986), pp. 341–51; M. Piccirillo, "Le chiese di Quweismeh

The version given here concerning the manner in which Caesarea was captured is unfamiliar and especially interesting.[129] The author describes the discovery of a small unknown postern gate facing the sea (with which, he adds, the Muslims were not acquainted), the penetration of the city through this postern, and the massacre in the lower market, which lasted a full day before it spread into the upper market.[130] The author seems to have been familiar with the layout of the Byzantine city, and was well informed about the story of its conquest.

His positive evaluation concerning both conditions in Palestine during the Umayyad period and the positive attitude of these rulers towards the local population seems to fit well with the existing historical and archaeological evidence about Palestine under Umayyad rule.[131] The Umayyads, according to the *Continuatio*, "ruled according to what he (i.e. Muḥammad) had enjoined upon them; they did no more or less, and did not harm anyone".[132]

Of special interest, therefore, is the concept of a sharp and categorical change in the conditions of the *dhimmīs* and in the attitude towards them with the ascendency of the ʻAbbāsids to power. The writer states unequivo-

---

Amman," *LA* 34 (1984), pp. 329–40; *idem*, "Una chiesa nell'Wadi ʻAyoun Mousa ai piedi del Monte Nebo," *LA* 34 (1984), pp. 307–18. See also the following note about Caesarea.

[129]For a survey of the sources concerning the capture of Caesarea, see M. Gil, *History of Palestine, 634–1099* (Cambridge, 1992), pp. 59–60. See also *ibid.*, n. 61, which relates to Noth's observation, concerning the uniformity in the pattern of conquest of cities found in the Muslim sources. The description in our text is completely non-stereotypical! It should be emphasized that although all of the sources agree that the siege and the fighting over Caesarea were long and difficult, the city seems to have been left intact after the conquest, since recent excavations in the city have discovered no trace of any break or catastrophe such as destruction or fire; see K. Holum, "Archeological Evidence for the Fall of Caesarea," *BASOR* 286 (1992), pp. 73–85.

[130]Concerning the city plan reflected here, see below, pp. 52–53 n. 45.

[131]See Schick, *Christian Communities of Palestine*, pp. 68–90, esp. pp. 77–84; Donner, *Conquests*, esp. pp. 152–53; Hill, *Termination of Hostilities*, pp. 59–84; M. Sharon, "The Cities of the Holy Land under Islamic Rule," *Cathedra* 40 (1986), pp. 83–120 (in Hebrew).

On the Muslim taxation policy of the *ahl al-dhimma* see M.J. Kister, "The Social and Political Implications of Three Traditions in the *Kitāb al-Kharāj* of Yaḥyā b. Ādam," *JESHO* 3 (1960), pp. 326–34; *idem*, " *ʻAn Yadin* (Qur'ān IX/29)," *Arabica* 11 (1964), pp. 272–78. The Muslim sources preserve traditions relating that one of the main reasons for the dismissal of the famous commander Khālid ibn al-Walīd by ʻUmar ibn al-Khaṭṭāb was disagreement over the treatment of the local population. ʻUmar insisted that the liberty and property of the local inhabitants be guarded and preserved. See Ġil, *History of Palestine*, pp. 48–50.

[132]See below, p. 53.

cally that "the kingdom of Banū l-'Abbās was a strong and mighty kingdom. They doubled the tax upon the land (*kharāj*) and raised the poll tax (*jāliya*) and made its burden heavier; they levied *waṣriya*[133] from all the provinces and afflicted the people with it".[134] According to the description presented here, the change of government in Baghdad was felt immediately and strongly in the provinces.

This is well demonstrated by the following description of the miseries and injustices brought upon the *dhimmīs*, and the Samaritans in particular, by 'Abd al-Wahhāb ibn Ibrāhīm (who according to the text was called Abū Shindī), the governor of Palestine appointed by the caliph al-Manṣūr. This Abū Shindī did not hesitate to incite Samaritans and Christians against one another in order to impose heavy penalties that were, of course, collected by him. The detailed evidence concerning his rule is corroborated by a tradition preserved by the Muslim historian Ibn 'Asākir stating that 'Abd al-Wahhāb left Palestine looking like "a plucked pigeon."[135]

A succession of calamities that fell upon Palestine towards the end of the eighth century completes this dire image of the history of Palestine at this time. This period, which began with the horrendous earthquake of 748–49[136] and continued with the worsening conditions brought on by the rise of the 'Abbāsids to power, ended, according to our text, with a series of calamities, including a severe attack of locusts, the outbreak of a bitter *fitna* between the Qays and Yaman factions in Palestine (known as the "War of the Watermelon") that brought ruin upon large parts of the country, a drought followed by a terrible famine, and a devastating plague.[137] Only in our text is this succession of events, whose details are indeed corroborated separately by other sources, described in a full and comprehensive account, thus giving us a clear view of the comparatively rapid decline of Palestine during the second half of the eighth century.

The text goes on to present an interesting account of the strife and havoc wreaked in Palestine as a result of the dissension that broke out after Hārūn

---

[133]For this unclear term, see below, p. 57 n. 88.

[134]See below, pp. 57–58.

[135]Ibn 'Asākir, *Ta'rīkh madīnat Dimashq*, facsimile ed. (Amman, 1989), X, 592; = Ibn Manẓūr, *Mukhtaṣar ta'rīkh madīnat Dimashq*, ed. Rūḥīya al-Naḥḥās *et al.* (Damascus, 1404–1409/1984–89), XV, 272.

[136]See below, p. 56; see n. 77 for other sources and bibliography concerning this earthquake.

[137]See below, pp. 62–67 and notes.

al-Rashīd's death between the supporters of al-Amīn and al-Ma'mūn. It appears that the strife was not limited to the important centres, but spread throughout the empire to a distant and marginal province such as Palestine, bringing with it much killing and looting and awakening great internal tension and strife between the local tribal elements.[138] These local skirmishes among different Muslim elements for control and power were the cause of great calamities for the local non-Muslim population. Besides the immediate horrendous effects of looting, killing and captivity, the economy of the land was greatly damaged, prices rose and people suffered from famine, gradually lost their property, and lived in constant fear. The state of affairs was so fragile and unstable that although a good and supportive local governor brought relief, this was only temporary, and peace and security were immediately shattered when he was killed by local Muslims.[139] There was dissension and opposition to al-Ma'mūn in Palestine throughout his reign, and our text describes numerous cases of resistance and rebellions, which were periodically quelled by the caliph's forces only to be rekindled after their departure. Thus when Khālid ibn Yazīd passed through Palestine on his way to Egypt with a large army, all the rebels hid in great fear, only to emerge again after he was gone to harry and harm the local non-Muslim population and to bring devastation upon the people.[140] 'Abd Allāh ibn Ṭāhir, who was appointed by al-Ma'mūn to rule the western part of the empire, and another later governor (probably Abū Isḥāq ibn Hārūn al-Rashīd, the future caliph al-Mu'taṣim) seem to have succeeded in establishing some law and order, only for it to be disrupted immediately upon their departure when another rebel by the name of Ibn Firāsa rose and oppressed the local population without hindrance.[141] The struggle culminated when al-Ma'mūn himself, later joined by his brother al-Mu'taṣim, came to Palestine in order to face the rebels and fight them on his way to Egypt sometime around January 832.

The fact that al-Ma'mūn came to Palestine accompanied by his brother, the future caliph al-Mu'taṣim, and visited Jerusalem on this occasion, is only recorded one place else to the best of my knowledge; yet it is very well supported by the inscriptions appearing on the copper plates above the eastern and northern entrances of the Dome of the Rock. These bear al-Ma'mūn's name and the date Rabī' II 216 (May–June 831), just before

[138] See below, pp. 69–70.
[139] See below, pp. 71–72.
[140] See below, pp. 74–75.
[141] See below, p. 77.

al-Ma'mūn must have left for Egypt. This may very well also have been the occasion when he replaced 'Abd al-Malik's name with his own in the dating inscription in the mosaic in the Dome of the Rock.[142]

Also otherwise unknown is the fact that he faced strong resistance in Palestine; he seems to have succeeded finally in subduing the rebels and in destroying their strongholds, and appointed governors on his behalf. This success had its drawbacks, as these governors did not always treat the local population very favourably.[143] Another otherwise unattested matter mentioned in the text is al-Ma'mūn's building of "very strong forts" when he returned to Damascus from Egypt in the autumn of 832.[144]

The new order did not last long, since dissension broke out again with the rise of al-Mu'taṣim to power after the death of al-Ma'mūn (9 August 833). As before, the consequences of these outbreaks for the local population were ruinous and included looting and burning. We are informed that two commanders were sent by the caliph to quell this revolt.[145] All of this was once again followed by oppressive tyranny on the part of the local governors, who according to the text "oppressed the Muslims more than they oppressed the Samaritans," a remark indicating that the tyranny was not always motivated by religious zeal.[146]

Here the text supplies information concerning local Samaritan affairs, including disruption of the structure of leadership within the Samaritan community when the system of the *ḥakākima* established by the great Samaritan leader Baba Rabbah (second or third century CE) was annulled, leaving the community, in the author's opinion, without a competent judicial system. This revision was carried out by the *ra'īs* Pinḥas. The *ra'īs* who followed him, Dartā, rebuilt the synagogue in Nablus that had been burnt down, presumably during one of the rebel raids.[147]

The *Continuatio* next describes in detail the rebellion of Abū Ḥarb al-Mubarqa' al-Yamanī, which started at the end of al-Mu'taṣim's reign (r. 218–27/833–42) and continued in the days of al-Wāthiq (r. 227–32/842–47), lasting about nine years. This rebellion, which is widely described in the Muslim sources, is related here in detail from a completely different point

[142] See below, p. 77 n. 257.
[143] See below, pp. 77–80 and notes thereto.
[144] See below, p. 79.
[145] See below, pp. 80–81, 82.
[146] See below, p. 83.
[147] See below, p. 83.

of view. While the author of our text, unlike the Muslim sources, is not interested or indeed familiar with the reasons for this rebellion or with the factions that took part in it, he follows the moves of Abū Ḥarb closely, describing how at first the governor of Ramla tried to subdue his rebellion at a local level, "but could not master him." The Samaritans of Nablus take the governor's side, the commander appointed in Nablus by the governor flees back to Ramla, and Abū Ḥarb feels free to roam about Nablus and its villages, exacting money and plundering. When another attempt to crush him finally fails, the inhabitants of Nablus flee, leaving their possessions behind. As a result, Abū Ḥarb enters the city, looting, burning and plundering the city for seventeen days. The head of the Samaritan community (*ra'īs*), who had not left the city, was subsequently killed. According to the text, Abū Ḥarb roamed around the country for quite a long time, wreaking havoc and causing panic and destruction; the text mentions the whole area of Samaria up to Baysān (Beth Shean), and all the way to Ramla. We may presume that his influence spread much further than the area mentioned in our text, in which the Samaritan population was concentrated. Abū Ḥarb certainly does not seem to have been a messianic Sufyānī[148] in the eyes of the local non-Muslim population, though he seemed to play such a role at least in the eyes of some of the Muslim rebels who joined him.[149] All of these occurrences took place at a local level, before the arrival of Rajā' ibn Ayyūb al-Ḥiḍārī, who was finally sent with a great army to face him. The author knows that on his way to Palestine Rajā' subdued the leader of the rebels in Damascus, Ibn Bayhas, and describes in detail the battle that took place in the area of 'Atīl in which Abū Ḥarb was finally defeated. We thus gain here a close look at a rebellion that is otherwise described succinctly and briefly by Muslim historians located hundreds of miles away and kept informed only by messages and messengers from the governors and military commanders of the caliphate.[150]

After the suppression of Abū Ḥarb's rebellion another problem arose: the local rulers appointed by the caliph fell to extorting the local population, a habit to which the caliph al-Wāthiq finally put an end. Two other interesting reports relate to the days of this caliph. The first informs us that al-Wāthiq prohibited the Christians from striking the *nāqūs*, the wooden clapper used

---

[148]On this subject see W. Madelung, "The Sufyānī between Tradition and History," *SI* 63 (1984), pp. 5—58.

[149]See Gil, *History of Palestine*, pp. 295–96.

[150]See below, pp. 84–89.

for calling to prayer. This report, which to my knowledge has no parallels in other sources, indicates that such restrictions upon the *dhimmīs* were indeed not only issued, but also applied already in the first half of the ninth century, and in the provinces of the Muslim empire as well as at the centre. The other report cited here seems quite strange and says literally that "the Jews prevented the Muslims from worshipping, even from afar." It seems that this should definitely be turned around and read as: "the Muslims prevented the Jews from worshipping, even from afar," since the first statement is in no way possible.[151] This probably refers to the fact that Jews were no longer allowed to worship in the area of the Temple Mount, even from afar; we know that the Jews were accustomed to worshipping on and around the ruined Temple Mount already in the Byzantine period, and that the Byzantines applied restrictions in this matter and levied considerable sums from the Jews in return for permission to worship and lament in the area of the Temple Mount on the day of the Temple's destruction, the ninth of Āb.[152]

The report concerning restrictions imposed upon the *dhimmīs* during the days of the caliph al-Mutawakkil are very detailed and of considerable significance. Although the decrees issued by al-Mutawakkil are well known, and were reported in detail by the Muslim chroniclers, there is little evidence concerning their application in the major centres;[153] information regarding peripheral areas is practically non-existent. Our text confirms unequivocally that not only were *dhimmīs* in distant and marginal provinces like Palestine and Jordan familiar in detail with these decrees, but also that the restrictions were put into practice quite strictly. This is well demonstrated by practical consequences related in the text, such as the story of the image that the *dhimmīs* had to attach to their doorpost.[154] The Samaritans of Palestine went to considerable trouble in order to circumvent this decree,

---

[151]See below, p. 90 and n. 383.

[152]See *Itinerarium Burdigalense*, in P. Geyer and O. Cuntz, eds., *Itineraria Hierosolymitana*, in *CCSL* 175 (Turnhout, 1965), 591.4–6, p. 16; Hieronymus, *Commentarium in Sophoniam*, in *CCSL* 76 (Turnhout, 1969), 1.15, p. 673; *The History of Barsauma of Nisibis*, in F. Nau, "Résumé de monographies syriaques," *ROC* 9 (1914), p. 119. For evidence of Jewish worship in the area of the Western Wall during the early Muslim period, see Gil, *History of Palestine*, pp. 607–608.

[153]For Egypt see Saʿīd ibn Baṭrīq, *Ta'rīkh*, ed. L. Cheikho (Leipzig, 1906; *CSCO*, *Scr. arabici*, Ser. iii, IV.2), p. 63; Bar Hebraeus, *Chronography*, ed. and trans. E.A.W. Budge (Oxford, 1932), I, 141.

[154]See above, pp. 13–14.

which in their eyes was equivalent to idol worship; still, they had to settle for a compromise—use of an image of a candelabrum. The Samaritans of Jund al-Urdunn were granted not even this concession from their governor, and had to accept the decree in full. Another example of the strict execution of the decrees is the levelling of the grave of the Samaritan head Nethan'el because it resembled a Muslim grave. It may be presumed that these decrees were imposed in an equal measure of severity upon all the other *dhimmīs* in Palestine as well.[155]

Other important events mentioned during the days of al-Mutawakkil are an earthquake that took place during the Feast of Tabernacles, probably in 853,[156] another major quarrel with the Dositheans, ending in their excommunication by the *ra'īs*,[157] and finally a very interesting report about a great rise in prices that brought about a terrible famine and led to the conversion of many Samaritan families to Islam, since conversion exempted them from payment of the *jizya*, a heavy financial burden especially at such times. This report, as well as several other references to similar events concerning mass Islamization in Palestine during the early Muslim period, are, as far as I know, unique.[158] Although we know of individuals who left their religion and accepted Islam for personal reasons,[159] there is no other testimony that actually declares that families and groups accepted Islam *bloc* due to worsening economic conditions. The author of the text here laments openly: "How many left their faith as a result of the terrible rise in prices and because they were exhausted by the *jizya*! Many sons and families who left the faith were lost!"[160] Moreover, it is reported that al-Mutawakkil actually increased the *jizya*. The text also reports that al-Mutawakkil ordered a survey, the purpose of which was the reevaluation of property and resources. This may well be the survey carried out by al-Mutawakkil in 240/854–55, which is mentioned

[155]See below, pp. 91–94.

[156]See below, p. 94.

[157]See below, p. 94.

[158]See my article on the subject of conversion to Islam among Samaritans, "New Evidence Relating to the Process of Islamization in Palestine in the Early Muslim Period: the Case of Samaria," *JESHO* 43 (2000), 258–76.

[159]See M. Levy-Rubin, "Arabization versus Islamization in the Palestinian Melkite Community during the Early Muslim Period," in A. Kofsky and G. Stroumsa, eds., *Sharing the Sacred: Religious Contacts and Conflicts in the Holy Land, First to Fifteenth Century C.E.* (Jerusalem, 1998), pp. 149–62.

[160]See below, p. 95.

by al-Yaʿqūbī.[161] A similar case in which the worsening economic situation brought on the dwindling of the Samaritan community is also described.[162]

Although it seems that al-Mutawakkil managed to introduce some law and order into the land, this was short-lived. At the end of his reign, and during the days of his successor al-Muntaṣir, anarchy reigned again. A rebel named Qūmaṭī (probably to be identified with al-Qiṭāmī)[163] succeeded in killing the Muslim commander in Nablus, and proceeded to rob, loot and kill. He was followed by another bandit who also kidnapped people. Anarchy was again replaced by tyranny when a new ruler named Majmūra (or Amājūr according to other sources) extorted money from the local inhabitants. The information concerning the governor Amājūr and, most probably, the former governor of Palestine ʿĪsā ibn al-Shaykh,[164] seems to have been greatly disordered by one of the copyists, since it is interpolated into the text quite awkwardly and confusedly; the incoherent text that results from this has to be corrected and rearranged in order to be understood.

During the days of Amājūr, before Ibn Ṭūlūn gained control of Palestine, the text informs us of the involvement of the authorities in an internal Samaritan affair. The head of the Samaritan community, Yōshaʿ, died, and a dispute developed between two individuals who claimed a right to the title: the brother of Yōshaʿ, Yūsuf, who was apparently accepted as the new *ra'īs* by the community, and his uncle Madī, who contested his right. Madī had apparently been quick and cunning and had bought the diploma of appointment of the Samaritan community (*kitāb ru'asā' al-sāmira*), thus gaining the support of the authorities. The community apparently rebelled against this coerced appointment, and was consequently punished and heavily fined by the authorities.[165] Such an official diploma of appointment issued by the authorities was indeed required from each of the religious groups among the *dhimmīs*.[166]

---

[161]See below, p. 96 and n. 443.

[162]See below, p. 102.

[163]See below, pp. 96–97 nn. 444, 448.

[164]See below, p. 99 n. 467.

[165]See below, pp. 101–102.

[166]See, for example, L.I. Conrad, "A Nestorian Diploma of Investiture from the *Tadhkira* of Ibn Ḥamdūn: the Text and its Significance," in Wadād al-Qāḍī, ed., *Studia Arabica et Islamica: Festschrift for Iḥsān ʿAbbās* (Beirut, 1981), pp. 83–104; S.D. Goitein, "New Sources on the Palestinian Gaonate," in S. Lieberman, ed., *Salo Whitmeyer Baron Jubilee Volume on the Occasion of his Eightieth Birthday* (Jerusalem, 1974), pp. 503–37. An updated version of this latter study exists in Hebrew; see S.D. Goitein, "Government In-

There is ample and interesting information concerning the reign of Aḥmad ibn Ṭūlūn (r. 254–70/868–84). The reports about his gradual takeover of Egypt and North Africa are basically true, though somewhat naive and exaggerated and apparently based on popular hearsay. Thus the author reports about the new palace built by Ibn Ṭūlūn north of al-Fusṭāṭ. He adds that the money for building it came from a treasure trove uncovered by Ibn Ṭūlūn while digging in a fireplace: it was with this money that Ibn Ṭūlūn allegedly bought Sudan and other countries; this is in fact corroborated in Ibn Ṭūlūn's *Sīra.*[167] Uncorroborated and somewhat suspicious information concerning Ibn Ṭūlūn includes the claim that he conquered Barqa (i.e. Cyrenaica), and that the people of Alexandria submitted to him. In fact, the whole of Egypt and the frontier districts were submitted to his jurisdiction by the apanagist Yārjūj. Another interesting fact, uncorroborated but not contested elsewhere, is the claim that the island of Crete submitted to his rule.[168]

The new information on Ibn Ṭūlūn's rule in Palestine and Syria, about which little has been known until now, seems to be accurate and based upon the personal experience of the author or upon the reports of other eyewitnesses. The author describes Ibn Ṭūlūn's arrival in Palestine in June 878, mourning the "ruin that the black soldiers brought upon the people," and describing the looting and rape that took place in the villages along the road.[169] He goes on to describe the consequences of his siege of Antioch, which ended in mass murder, adding sympathetically that "a great sorrow came upon the Muslims".[170]

It should be especially emphasized that it has been supposed that, as in Egypt, Ibn Ṭūlūn's rule was favourable both towards the *dhimmī* population and towards the farmers, and greatly improved the condition of these populations.[171] This supposition has to be rejected in light of our text. In complete contradiction to Ibn Ṭūlūn's positive image as a ruler who was generous, considerate and benevolent towards both Muslims and *dhimmī*s in Egypt, he is depicted in the text as "a bad man" who exploited and abused the inhab-

stallation of Gaons and Jewish Judges," *Palestinian Jewry in Early Islamic and Crusader Times in the Light of the Geniza Documents* (Jerusalem, 1980), pp. 70–81.

[167] See below, p. 100 n. 477.

[168] See below, p. 100 n. 479.

[169] See below, pp. 102–103.

[170] See below, p. 103.

[171] Gil, *History of Palestine*, p. 307.

itants of Palestine and made their lives unbearable. According to the text, Ibn Ṭūlūn returned with his army from Syria to Egypt through Palestine, and ordered the local inhabitants to provide for him and his forces. The text mentions several times that he confiscated the draught animals, the farmers' most precious possessions, and actually seized people from their villages and sent them to Egypt in ships, perhaps to take part in the intensive rehabilitation of Egypt, which was carried out under his rule, as mentioned on the next page. In addition, the governor appointed by him imposed a series of restrictions upon the *dhimmīs* similar to those imposed by al-Mutawakkil, including distinguishing signs, images upon the doors, restrictions upon prayer in public, and submissive behaviour towards Muslims; he also prohibited the drinking of wine. Further, he seems to have threatened the churches and synagogues, arousing in the *dhimmīs* fear that their places of worship might be confiscated for his needs. It appears that this repressive and humiliating attitude employed by the authorities had its effect upon the local Muslim inhabitants, who "behaved insolently towards the *dhimmīs*" and plundered anything they could.

Of special interest is the corroboration of the report about a fortress built in Jaffa by Ibn Ṭūlūn.[172] It seems that a major part of the affliction and abuse brought about by Ibn Ṭūlūn was actually a result of his massive building projects, both in Palestine and in Egypt, which required provisions, a large work force, and draught animals—all of which he seized and confiscated without mercy.[173]

The text sheds new light on the events leading up to the battle of al-Ṭawāḥīn in which Ibn Ṭūlūn's son, Khumārawayh, fought against the caliph's nephew, Abū l-ʿAbbās ibn al-Muwaffaq, the future caliph al-Muʿtaḍid, on 5 April 885.[174] The news of the death of Ibn Ṭūlūn caused the governor of Palestine, ʿAbd Allāh ibn al-Fatḥ, otherwise unknown to us, to spread his wings; feeling free to do as he liked, he started oppressing the local population and extorting money from them. The news that Khumārawayh was sending his commanders northwards was enough to send him flying. Khumārawayh's generals, who were on their way to protect the Ṭūlūnid territories in Syria, once again threatened by the ʿAbbāsids, appointed a new governor by the name of Iṣbaʿ, who turned out to be as bad as his

[172]See below, p. 104 n. 518.
[173]See below, pp. 102–106.
[174]On this battle, see Gil, *History of Palestine*, pp. 308–309.

predecessor, if not worse. When things took a turn for the worse and the 'Abbāsids began to gain the upper hand in Syria, one of these generals, by the name of Aḥmad ibn Muḥammad al-Wāsiṭī (or Abū 'Abd Allāh), decided to change sides. Thus, upon arriving in Palestine, he arrested Iṣba', the loyal Ṭūlūnid governor, and apparently started levying taxes on the order of the 'Abbāsid ruler. Upon hearing of his betrayal, the other general, Sa'd al-Aysar, arrived immediately, fought him and defeated him, killing 130 of his officers and many of his soldiers. Abū 'Abd Allāh fled to Damascus, where, upon being informed of Khumārawayh's unstable state, he tried to lure Sa'd to rebel against Khumārawayh as well. It was this threat that brought Khumārawayh and his army to al-Ṭawāḥīn. We thus find here a much more detailed account, given from a local point of view, of the events that brought about the battle of al-Ṭawāḥīn (identified in the text as Ra's al-'Ayn). According to the text, it was the discord between these two generals over the question of loyalty to the Ṭūlūnid ruler—a break that occurred in Palestine—that drove Abū 'Abd Allāh to Damascus and finally led to the confrontation at al-Ṭawāḥīn. When the battle of al-Ṭawāḥīn ended with Khumārawayh's victory, Iṣba' was again appointed governor, only to continue oppressing the inhabitants.[175]

Following this we are informed of a seemingly important yet obscure reform in Samaritan liturgy, pursued throughout the reigns of two of the Samaritan high priests. Since the text here has been deleted and corrected by the copyist, it is difficult to be certain what this reform involved. It seems, however, to have been applied to a certain manner of reading the Pentateuch. The operative term seems to be *ramī*, in which case this would probably mean that the Aramaic version in use for the reading of the Pentateuch was supplanted by an Arabic version,[176] a shift quite common among other groups in Palestine at the end of the tenth century,[177] by which time the most common language spoken among the Samaritans was Arabic. It is

[175]See below, pp. 106–109.

[176]See below, pp. 110–11 n. 578.

[177]On this subject see S.H. Griffith, "Anthony David of Baghdad, Scribe and Monk of Mar Sabas: Arabic in the Monasteries of Palestine," *CH* 58 (1989), pp. 7–19; *idem*, "Greek into Arabic: Life and Letters in the Monasteries of Palestine in the Ninth Century—the Example of the *Summa Theologiae Arabica*," *Byzantion* 56 (1986), pp. 117–38; *idem*, "Stephan of Ramlah's and the Christian Kerygma in Arabic in 9th-Century Palestine," *JEH* 36 (1985), pp. 23–45; *idem*, "The Arabic Account of 'Abd al-Masīḥ an-Naǧrānī al-Ghassānī," *Le Muséon* 98 (1985), pp. 331–74. See also M. Levy-Rubin, "Arabization versus Islamization," above, p. 35 n. 106.

also possible to read this word as *rūmī*, in which case it would be the Greek language that was supplanted by Arabic. This, however, seems very unlikely; we do know, in fact, that Greek was used by Samaritans during the Byzantine period, and Abū l-Fatḥ himself notes that he chose to omit many Greek expressions included in his sources in order to make the text more legible and comprehensible.[178] It is known that Greek expressions were preserved in Samaritan marriage contracts,[179] and there is also an argument concerning the existence of an independent Greek version of the Torah.[180] Nevertheless, it seems most unlikely that during the tenth century the Pentateuch was being read in Greek. It seems very probable, on the other hand, that it was the Samaritans' traditional language, Aramaic, that was gradually being replaced, a process also familiar among the Aramaic-speaking Christians in Palestine.

The *ra'īs* mentioned here in connection with this reform, Dartā, may be related in some manner to the well-known poet and author of the composition known as *The Rules of Ibn Dartā Regarding the Reading*, Ṭabiya ibn Dartā, who flourished in the tenth century.[181]

As for the date mentioned at the beginning of the paragraph, the year AH 369 (= CE 979–80), this seems quite out of place here since the preceding event mentioned—the swarm of locusts—occurred in 297/909–10, while the following events refer to the end of the third decade and the fourth decade of the tenth century. It may be that this section is a mislocated interpolation, although it seems much more likely that the date was copied wrongly. If indeed this reform took place in the first third of the tenth century, then it would also agree well with the dates of Ṭabiya ibn Dartā, who may have been continuing his father's project, which aimed at defining the rules for reading the Pentateuch.

New information is added concerning the rule of the Ikhshīd (r. 323–34/935–46) in Palestine. A series of events leads to the rule of Muḥammad ibn Ṭughj al-Ikhshīd in Palestine. After the death of an unknown governor of Palestine named al-Rā'irī, a governor named Abū 'Abd Allāh, who is to be identified with al-Rāshidī, was appointed. According to the text, al-Rāshidī adopted a favourable attitude towards the local population.[182] He was ousted

---

178 Vilmar, p. 5.
179 R. Pummer, "Samaritan Rituals and Customs", in Crown, *Samaritans*, p. 662.
180 See S. Noja, "The Samareitikon," in *ibid.*, pp. 408–12.
181 See A. Tal, "Samaritan Literature," in *ibid.*, pp. 416–19.
182 See below, pp. 111 and n. 583, 113 and n. 592.

and sent to Damascus by Muḥammad ibn Ṭughj al-Ikhshīd, whose governorship of Palestine, which lasted seven months, is described as distressing and harmful.[183] These remarks demonstrate once again the precariousness of the conditions endured by the *dhimmīs* in Palestine, whose fate was decided to a large degree by the policy adopted by the local ruler towards the local non-Muslim inhabitants. Another event mirroring this reliance upon the good will and positive attitude of the ruler is the story about the miraculous recovery of the governor of Egypt's son, al-Takīn—a recovery brought about by Samaritan priests. Their success in healing him was generously rewarded, and they were given special privileges for a period of a year and two months. These gifts and privileges improved the conditions of the whole Samaritan community, as is emphasized in the text.[184]

The Ikhshīd's return to Palestine following his victory over Muḥammad ibn 'Alī al-Mādharā'ī in 935 was again bad news for the local non-Muslim inhabitants. Not only was anarchy and crime rampant everywhere, but Ibn Ṭughj adopted a policy of outright extortion and oppression of the Samaritans, such as is rarely mentioned previously in the text, giving the reader again the special Palestinian angle on the rule of Muḥammad ibn Ṭughj.

To conclude, it may be said that excluding a certain period between the reign of the Ṭūlūnids and al-Takīn (*ca.* 886–910), the *Continuatio* supplies us with a generally continuous and quite detailed description of events in Palestine during the early Muslim period, up to the days of Muḥammad ibn Ṭughj. Its continuity and the local angle on events that it provides are of great advantage, since Muslim chronicles are devoid of either of these elements when dealing with Palestine. Nevertheless, it should be remarked that the *Continuatio* cannot be treated as a full and comprehensive history of Palestine during the said period; this is due to the nature of the chronicle, which tends to concentrate on the area of Samaria and neglect other areas of Palestine. In other cases, as is attested, conditions did not allow the luxury of recording the events. We thus may appreciate the ample information given us about the behaviour of local governors, the movements and actions of rulers in Palestine, rebellions and battles, the attitude towards the *dhimmīs*, the economic situation and the physical conditions at different periods, and so on; yet we should bear in mind that there were other developments that are not mentioned in the text. Thus we do not hear, for example, of al-Manṣūr's

[183] See below, p. 113 and n. 595.
[184] See below, pp. 111–12.

visit to Jerusalem, or in fact about any other events that took place there. Naturally other religious communities are very rarely mentioned, and then only in passing. It should therefore be borne in mind that although much can be learned from this text about Palestine in the early Muslim period, the material is presented from a specific local angle, and therefore nothing can be learnt or deduced *ex silentio*. This said, it should once again be emphasized that information about Palestine for this period is very meagre, and that the contribution of this text to our knowledge of the period is indeed a substantial and meaningful one.

About this Translation

This translation was meant, at first, to include only that section of the Paris manuscript that was not printed by Vilmar and does not appear in any of the other manuscripts. However, it soon became apparent that the present work should begin with the appearance of Muḥammad on the scene. Vilmar did indeed print the part from Muḥammad to Hārūn al-Rashīd, but this remained without translation or notes. It thus seemed that the present work would be more complete if it started both where Stenhouse's translation left off and where a new era in Palestine's history began.

The Paris manuscript includes a version of this section that is quite unlike what appears in the other manuscripts, and seems to be more accurate.[185] This version, which appears after the more common version (located at the end of the first part of the manuscript up to p. 202, before the colophon), is not represented by Vilmar's apparatus. This repetition, which appears in the beginning of the new section following the colophon, makes it evident that the *Continuatio* begins, in fact, at this point. This claim, which is supported by technical and morphological proofs, is also in line with the Samaritan eschatological scheme, which sees in Muḥammad the herald of the last period of the *fanūta*, the "Age of Disfavour," after which the Samaritan Messiah, the *tāhib*, will arrive. This and the list of Samaritan High Priests appearing at the end of the first section was in fact the basis for Vilmar's initial claim that Abū l-Fatḥ's original composition extended only to the time of Muḥammad.[186]

---

[185]See above, pp. 7–10.

[186]See above, pp. 5–7.

For all these reasons, it became clear that a complete text of the *Continuatio* should start after the first colophon, with the second version of the advent of Muḥammad, covering pp. 203–64 of the Paris manuscript.

Unlike the part from Hārūn al-Rashīd onwards, the first section of the text, from Muḥammad to Hārūn al-Rashīd, finds parallels in some other manuscripts, to which it therefore had to be compared. Some of these Mss. were already included in Vilmar's edition; these are Berlin, Or. Ms. 4° no. 471 (Vilmar's A); Berlin, Petermann I 8 (Vilmar's B); Paris, Ms. Sam. no. 10 (Vilmar's C) = the first version, fol. 197–202; and Oxford, Bodleian Library, Ms. Huntington 350 (Vilmar's D). Of these four, only Vilmar's A and C continue beyond the legend of Muḥammad's identification as a prophet by the three astrologers and cover the period from the rise of the Umayyads until Hārūn al-Rashīd.

Additional manuscripts have been discovered since Vilmar's time; all of these were listed and thoroughly collated in Stenhouse's critical edition and translation, which includes the text up to and including the time of Muḥammad. Several of these manuscripts continued beyond the legend of Muḥammad and the three astrologers until the time of Hārūn al-Rashīd.

In establishing the text I have proceeded as follows. For the first part—the legend of Muḥammad's identification as a prophet—Stenhouse's work includes a full critical edition. I concentrated, therefore, on comparing the second version of this legend, appearing on pp. 203–207 of the text, with the version that appears at the end of the first part of the manuscript (pp. 197–202) and its parallels, which are accounted for in Stenhouse's translation and in Vilmar's text. Since there were no meaningful differences between Vilmar's and Stenhouse's editions, I chose to refer to the former; this was done for practical reasons only, since Stenhouse's edition exists only in a limited microfiche edition and is not as yet readily available.

As for the part covering the period from the Umayyads to Hārūn al-Rashīd, I chose to present only the meaningful differences, rather than to publish a full critical edition. This is justified by the fact that in effect, there were not many variants that did not appear already in Vilmar's edition. In fact, the additional manuscripts covering this period seem to adhere loyally to the version presented by Vilmar's edition, which is based on his Ms. A, i.e. Berlin, Or. Ms. 4° no. 471, while most of the variants are actually found in the Paris manuscript.

For comparing the parallel versions of the part covering the period from the Umayyads to Hārūn, I chose several of the manuscripts, basing my choice on the stemma of the manuscripts constructed by Stenhouse. I thus examined the following manuscripts:

1. London, British Library, Ms. Or. no. 1447 (Stenhouse's B/BA), copied in 1865. This manuscript was the source of BL, Ms. Or. no. 10,875 (Stenhouse's G), which in turn was the source of Yale University, Beinecke Rare Book and Manuscript Library, Landberg Ms. no. 663 (Stenhouse's Y), copied in 1868.

2. London, British Library, Ms. Or. no. 2080, copied in 1859 (Stenhouse's E).

3. Vatican City, Bibliotheca Apostolica Vaticana, Sbath Ms. no. 744 (end of 19th/beginning of 20th c. = Stenhouse's Va). This Ms. and no. 2 above, in addition to Berlin, Or. Ms. 4° no. 471, copied in 1859 (Stenhouse's F), all depend on the same source, probably the archetype of family B.

4. Jerusalem, Jewish National and University Library, Sam. Ms. 8° no. 5, copied in 1908 (Stenhouse's J). This manuscript and Leningrad Ms. Sam. VI 19, copied in 1863 (Stenhouse's M), were both copied from the same source.

I also made use of the later amplified Mss. mentioned above, that were copied rather loosely and included many later extensions, finding no meaningful variants there. Altogether, it may be said quite confidently that the section covering the period from the Umayyads to Hārūn al-Rashīd was in all the manuscripts based on the same archetype. Meaningful differences are to be found mainly in the Paris text following the colophon, which renders another version of the story of the identification of Muḥammad as a prophet and seems to carry an earlier and more accurate version, including some difficult passages, terms and names omitted in the other manuscripts.

I have chosen to present the Arabic text in facsimile for two reasons. First, the main body of the *Continuatio* (pp. 218–64) has no parallels at all, while its first part (pp. 203–18) is notably different from the other versions. Second, the language of the text is very colloquial and grammatically quite unsystematic; on the other hand, the writing is quite legible and clear. I thus saw a great advantage in presenting it in its original form, allowing the reader to examine for himself all the problematic words and expressions—both those that cannot be readily understood and those that can be read in several ways.[187]

The task of translating the text proved to be quite problematic in some places. The colloquial style in which the text was written at times uses expressions that are unclear and undocumented in other texts, and are therefore sometimes difficult to understand. Hypothetical readings may at times be offered, but these cannot always be convincingly supported. A second obstacle lies in the fact that there seem to have been copying mistakes: in some of these cases the copyist himself did not comprehend completely what he was copying, while in others he may inadvertently have skipped words or lines. The copyist in fact admits to this when he begs the reader's forgiveness, as this is the first book that he has ever copied (Ms. p. 202), and mentions elsewhere (p. 264) that he is an amateur. Since the manuscript is unique, there is no certain way of knowing what the mistake is and what the correct text looked like. In such cases one can hardly do more than suggest what appears to be the most plausible reading. Alternative readings, or points where doubts remain, appear in the notes. These considerations should be taken into account when using the translation. Readings that were suggested by my *SLAEI* editor, Lawrence I. Conrad, are marked "L.C."

For ease of cross-reference the page numbers of the Paris manuscript have been indicated in bold type in the translation. It is this pagination that is used when reference is made to the manuscript in this book.

[187]I would like to thank the Bibliothèque Nationale for kindly granting me permission to publish photographs of the Paris manuscript.

TRANSLATION

[203] AT THAT TIME[1] there were three men, astrologers, who used to foretell coming events:[2] the first, Ṣarmaṣa, a Samaritan from ʿAskar;[3] the second, Kaʿb al-Aḥbār, a Jew; and the third,[4] ʿAbd Allāh, a Christian from Lydda (Ludd).[5] These three were aware of each other's skill, and they saw in their

---

[1]The following story presents another version of the famous story of Baḥīra, the Christian monk who met Muḥammad in his youth and identified him as the future prophet by finding on him the stigmata of prophecy in the form of a mole between his shoulders. See al-Ṭabarī, *Taʾrīkh al-rusul wa-l-mulūk*, ed. M.J. de Goeje *et al.* (Leiden, 1879–1901), I, 1123ff.; *EI* [2], *s.v.* "Baḥīra". The name Baḥīra, though, is not mentioned here; instead, two figures beside the Samaritan Ṣarmaṣa take his place. The first, it seems, is to be identified with ʿAbd Allāh ibn Salām, who appears in the Paris Ms. once as ʿAbd Allāh and later as ʿAbd al-Salām, while in all the other Mss. he appears only as ʿAbd al-Salām (see Vilmar, p. 173:3), who is presented here as the Christian monk. The second is Kaʿb al-Aḥbār, the renowned Jew who accompanied ʿUmar ibn al-Khaṭṭab (see *EI* [2], *s.v.*). ʿAbd Allāh ibn Salām, Kaʿb al-Aḥbār and Baḥīra appear together in Muslim tradition along with several other figures from the *ahl al-kitāb* who joined Islam, bringing with them certain written traditions into the faith. See Ibn al-Nadīm, *Kitāb al-fihrist*, ed. G. Flügel (Leipzig, 1871–72), I, 22. ʿAbd Allāh ibn Salām was in fact a converted Jew (*EI* [2], *s.v.* "ʿAbd Allāh ibn Salām"). On the legend of Baḥīra and the traditions of Jews who embraced Islam, according to different Muslim, Jewish and Christian traditions, see M. Gil, "The Story of Baḥīra and its Jewish Versions", *Hebrew and Arabic Studies in Honour of Joshua Blau* (Jerusalem, 1993), pp. 193–210 (in Hebrew); see also the article by J. McDonald, who cites a Hebrew version of this same story and compares it to the story of the magi and Jesus in *AJBA* 1 (1969), pp. 3–12.

[2]Cf. Vilmar, p. 173:1: ماهرين في صناعتهم, "proficient in their trade".

[3]See Geographical Appendix.

[4]The word ثالث is somewhat unclear in the text.

[5]Cf. Vilmar, p. 173:2–3: نصراني راهب واسمه عبد السلام, "a Christian monk by the name of ʿAbd al-Salām".

dreams[6] that the rule of Byzantium had ended, that the rule of Ismāʿīl[7] was beginning, and that a leader (*qā'im*) was arising for them[8] from amongst the descendents of Hāshim. His sign would be found on his back [in the form of] a yellow mole the size of a palm, and the first thing to occur would be that he would emerge from a city called "the city of the messenger".[9] The three met together and said: "Let us go and see whether it is he or not; if it is he, we shall contemplate what we should do,[10] [so that] we will not be hurt [by him like we were] by those who preceded [him]."[11] The three departed and arrived at his city, where he was staying. When they approached him and saw him they said: "Who could overcome him?"[12] They decided that Kaʿb al-Aḥbār should approach him. So [Kaʿb] approached him and greeted him, and Muḥammad asked him: "Who are you?" He answered: "I am one of the Jewish dignitaries, and I found in my Torah that [one] of the descendents of Ismāʿīl will arise, **[204]** who will rule and conquer the world,[13] and no one will stand in his way." [Then] ʿAbd Allāh said likewise: "I found the same in the Gospel", and they did not recognize any authority but his.[14] When

---

[6]Ms. نظروا في حلومتهم. See R. Dozy, *Supplément aux dictionnaires arabes* (Leiden, 1881), I, 318: "certaines mots barbares que l'on prononce avant s'endormir, et qui amènent une vision par laquelle on apprend ce qu'on désire savoir". They saw in their dreams, therefore, as a result of these incantations.

[7]Muslim rule is often called Ismāʿīlīya by the Samaritans. Cf. below, p. 50 n. 30.

[8]Ms. وان قايم لهم قايم من اولاد هاشم. The term *qā'im*, literally "riser", is a loaded term that in Shīʿī and Sunnī circles usually denotes the *mahdī*, and often appears as *al-qā'im bi-amr Allāh*, the one who shall rise by the order of God, or *al-Qā'im al-Mahdī*. It should be noted that it is only this version of the story of Muḥammad's appearance that uses this term, while the first version appearing in the first part of the Paris manuscript, as well as all the other manuscripts, choose to use the much more neutral word *rajul*, "man". See Vilmar, p. 173:4–5: على يد رجل من اولاد اسماعيل من بنى هاشم. On the *qā'im*, see *EI*^{2}, *s.v.* "Ḳā'im āl Muḥammad"; M. Sharon, *Black Banners from the East* (Jerusalem and Leiden, 1983), p. 142 and n. 160; al-Balādhurī, *Ansāb al-ashrāf*, III, ed. ʿA.ʿA. al-Dūrī (Wiesbaden, 1978), p. 178.

[9]Ms. مدينه الرسول: this phrase is missing in Vilmar's version.

[10]Ms. دبرنا ما نفعله.

[11]Ms. ولا سيلحقنا من هولاي الذي تقدمو. Vilmar, p. 173:8–9, is more complete: لئلا يلحقنا منه ما لحقنا من الذين تقدموا.

[12]This is an unusual usage of the verb قدر. See E.W. Lane, *Arabic–English Lexicon* (London, 1863–93), I.6, 2495: ما لي عليك مقدرة, "I have not power over thee".

[13]Vilmar, p. 173:13, has: ان يقوم ملك من نسل اسماعيل ويملك الدنيا.

[14]Presumably this refers to the fact that they submitted themselves to Muḥammad

Ṣarmaṣa, the Samaritan, approached him he said to him: "You will be the one to profess [the Muslim] faith and law; with it you will subdue the necks of the infidels and you will rule the world through it. We were told that there is a sign between your shoulders." [Muḥammad] stood up and revealed his back,[15] and they saw the mole on his back. When Ka'b al-Aḥbār heard Ṣarmaṣa's words he became a hypocrite in his religion;[16] 'Abd al-Salām[17] too became a hypocrite. The man[18] was pleased with them, and also with the words he heard from Ṣarmaṣa. He said: "Why are you not doing the same as these [two] did?" [Ṣarmaṣa] had already gained from him[19] concessions with respect to taxation and protection[20] before he proclaimed the message of Islam to him, so that he would not force him to do what he did not want to do; and Ṣarmaṣa, the Samaritan, said to him: "My need is satisfied by that which I have"[21]—that is, the law and the faith[22]—and [Muḥammad]

---

totally and accepted the Muslim faith, as is indeed noted later on. Vilmar's version (p. 173:14–15) is different: ولم يعرفوا شيئًا الا من صناعتهم, i.e. "they did not know anything except for matters of their craft", alluding to the fact that they did not in fact find it in the Scriptures, but through their craft, i.e. through astrological observations.

[15]Ms. ضهره; read ظهره. For the merging between ض and ظ in MA, see Blau, *Grammar*, I, 114.

[16]Ms. انفق, here in the sense of نافق في الدين; see J.G. Hava, *Al-Farā'id: Arabic–English Dictionary* (Beirut, 1970), p. 789; A. de Biberstein Kazimirski, *Dictionnaire arabe–français* (Paris, 1860), II, 1315. This word, which in Islam is considered a derogatory term denoting someone who has left the Muslim faith, serves here to denote someone who has left his own religion in order to become a Muslim. For the connotation of this term in Islam, see *EI*², *s.v.* "Munāfiḳūn".

[17]Earlier he is called 'Abd Allāh.

[18]Referring to Muḥammad.

[19]Ms. اخذ عليه is an elliptical form of اخذ عليه عهدا. See Dozy, *Supplément*, I, 12.

[20]Ms. وكان قد اخذ عليه الاحد والميثاق, with الاحد to be corrected to الاجل. For this sense of اجل see Lane, *Lexicon*, I.1, 25. Vilmar's text (p. 175:7) reads: جئتك لاجل عهد وميثاق, "I came to you for the sake of a pact and a treaty". This may be a *lectio facilior* of the Paris Ms.

[21]Ms. عندي من هذا حاجتي. Cf. Vilmar, p. 175:4–7, who has the same sentence in a different context. According to the present text, Ṣarmaṣa deliberately asked Muḥammad for the treaty before he let him know that he would not adopt his religion, while the other Mss. claim that Ṣarmaṣa revealed his intentions to Muḥammad, who was offended by his rejection, and only then asked Muḥammad for the treaty. This latter order of events would have obviously demanded from Muḥammad a much greater measure of generosity.

[22]One of the late and amplified versions, and therefore not a direct parallel of the text (see above, Introduction, p. 7 n. 18), found in John Rylands Library Ms. no. 234 (1161),

said to him in answer to this:[23] "What do you want, O Samaritan?,"[24] and so on to the end of the discussion.[25] This was [the work] of Ka'b al-Aḥbār,[26]

---

fol. 156r, adduces here a somewhat different version, including a paragraph in Samaritan Aramaic. According to this version Muḥammad invited the three to share his meal with him. 'Abd al-Salām and Ka'b al-Aḥbār accepted his offer, while Ṣarmaṣa refused, claiming that his religion did not allow him to do so. This is what made Muḥammad angry, and he then exclaimed: "Well then, what do you want from me, O Samaritan?" See also McDonald's version above, p. 46 n. 1.

[23]See Vilmar, p. 174:6, which adds: وانجرح محمد منه, "and Muḥammad was offended by him" (i.e. by his rejection).

[24]Vilmar, p. 174:6, reads: فقال له ما خطبك.

[25]It seems that the formula of the treaty that Ṣarmaṣa allegedly received from Muḥammad was so well known that the author of the present text chose to omit it. This seems to contradict somewhat the previous statement claiming that Ṣarmaṣa had received some form of agreement from Muḥammad previously; this may be explained, however, as some form of a general commitment, which was later followed by a formal and detailed treaty. The text omitted here is given by the other Mss., cited by Vilmar, pp. 174–75, and translated by Stenhouse, pp. 245–46. The following is Stenhouse's translation of the omitted part: "Ṣarmaṣa said to him: 'O my master, I have come to you to get a covenant and a treaty that we can rely upon, I and the people of my faith and my religion: a covenant of peace and security: as a protection for persons and families and property and religious endowments, and for freedom to erect houses of worship.' Muḥammad instructed a scribe to draw up a covenant for them, of peace and security according to what he had requested. The scribe entered his presence [and wrote]: 'I, Muḥammad ibn 'Abd Allāh ibn Muṭṭalib, have commanded that a treaty of peace and security be written down for the Samaritans concerning themselves and their families and their property and houses of worship and religious endowments throughout all my realm and in all their territories. And that this be effective for them and as a covenant of peace among the people of Palestine; and as a safe conduct.' Then Ṣarmaṣa took it and left his presence. But 'Āmir ibn Rabī'a and 'Abd Allāh ibn Jaḥsh advised him to get the covenant endorsed by 'Alī ibn Abī Ṭālib. So he went back to Muḥammad and stood before him and said: 'O my master, I have come to you from an extensive, vast and distant land and from a religious group which is weak and which the polytheists have persecuted and which the idol worshippers have overcome. We look for deliverance to God, by means of you. I have been advised to obtain the endorsement of 'Alī ibn Abī Ṭālib for this covenant.' So he instructed 'Alī to sign the document, and he wrote for them from him [as follows]: 'I append to this covenant of peace for the Samaritans, a guarantee for themselves, their families, their belongings, their houses of worship and their religious endowments throughout all my lands in every place and throughout all my possessions—that it be for them a safe conduct.' This was written on a piece of leather, and he ('Alī) gave it to him. Ṣarmaṣa kissed the ground from a respectful distance and said farewell. Muḥammad said: 'O Samaritan, depart! In your lifetime you can indeed say, "Let no one touch me". You have a pledge. Do not violate it. Look to your God whom you are still loyally following.'"

[26]This sentence refers to an event that apparently stood at the end of the section that

since [Ṣarmaṣa] had not done as he did—every affliction that comes upon us is due to the Jews, may God punish them. Ṣarmaṣa left, and Ka'b al-Aḥbār and 'Abd al-Salām stayed; Ka'b al-Aḥbār became his secretary,[27] [**205**] and he was the one who administered everything and directed all the correspondence[28] and the rest.[29]

From the creation of Adam until the rule of Yishmā'el[30] there are 5047 years.[31] After this the Ishmaelites, Muḥammad and all his army, went forth to wage war against the Byzantines; they conquered the land and defeated

---

the scribe of our text chose to omit, obviously believing that it was common knowledge. Surprisingly, the event is not recounted in its entirety even in the other Mss., which did choose to tell the story of the *amān* given to the Samaritans. In the latter, there appears only one sentence, which itself seems to be out of context: لنحرقه ثم لننسفه في اليم نسفا (Vilmar, p. 175:7–8), "Let us burn it, and then let us tear it up and throw [the pieces] into the sea" (Stenhouse, *trans.*, p. 246). The following sentence, appearing only in our text and in the first version of the story in the Paris manuscript (Vilmar, p. 175:13–14; see above, Introduction, pp. 22–23), attributes this act to Ka'b al-Aḥbār, who seems to have done this in order to punish Ṣarmaṣa for not having accepted Islam, as he himself had done. Having lost this crucial piece of evidence, the Samaritans were not protected as they could have been in the first place, and were afflicted by many misfortunes. It is thus logical to conclude that while our text chose to omit the detailed version of the *amān*, and returned only to remark that subsequent problems were all Ka'b al-Aḥbār's fault, the other manuscripts were missing a vital point at the end of the story.

[27]See Vilmar, p. 175:11–12: وصار كعب الاحبار عنده يكتب له ويرتب ما يرتب ويعرفه كل قضية, "and Ka'b al-Aḥbār became his secretary, organized [affairs for him] and advised him on all issues" (Stenhouse, *trans.*, p. 246).

[28]Ms. המכתב, Hebrew for "the letter", or perhaps Arabic, مكتب, "office".

[29]The amplified John Rylands Ms. mentioned above (p. 8 n. 18), fols. 156v–157r, adds here another paragraph in Samaritan Aramaic reporting the bad advice and false wisdom that these two gave to Muḥammad, including many things that they inserted into the Qur'ān.

[30]Ms. يشمعال, sic! In genealogical schemes formulated by both Muslims and non-Muslims in the medieval Near East, the Arabs are the descendents of Ishmael. See *EI* [2], *s.v.* "Ismā'īl"; R. Hoyland, *Seeing Islam as Others Saw It: a Survey and Evaluation of Christian, Jewish and Zoroastrian Writings on Early Islam* (Princeton, 1997), pp. 131–32, 266, 280 n. 68, 336, 509–10.

[31]This is according to the computation of Abū l-Fatḥ, which is, however, not universally agreed upon by the Samaritans. See S. Powels, "The Samaritan Calendar and the Roots of Samaritan Chronology", in Crown, *Samaritans*, pp. 691–742. In fact, Berlin Ms. Or. 4° 471, gives an additional computation according to which from Adam to Muḥammad there are 4869 years. See Vilmar, p. 173.

the Byzantines and killed them as they fled before them.[32]

The *imām* in those days was ʿAqbūn ben Elʿazar, who lived in Bayt Ṣāma.[33] When the Muslims attacked and the Byzantines fled, all of the Samaritans who lived along the coast fled with the Byzantines from the advancing Muslims, [thinking][34] that they would return. When the Samaritans began to leave with the Byzantines for Byzantium (Rūmīya), they came to the *ra'īs* ʿAqbūn ben Elʿazar, to Bayt Ṣāma, because he lived there, and said to him: "You are a trustworthy man, so we will deposit our possessions with you until we return," thinking[35] that they would be returning soon. They collected their possessions and deposited them with him, and there accumulated in his charge an amount of wealth greater than anything either encountered or known. The people who deposited [their wealth] were the people of Caesarea (Qaysārīya), Arsūf,[36] Maioumas (Mīmās),[37] Jaffa (Yāffa), Lydda, Ascalon (ʿAsqalān), Gaza (Ghazza), and all of the interior villages[38] and those **[206]** along the coast. After this they left for Byzantium[39] and remained there and have not returned to this day.

---

[32]According to the Islamic tradition, which consistently regards almost all of the campaigns of the Syrian conquest as having occurred after the death of Muḥammad, this information must be wrong. But in non-Islamic sources it is often stated that Muḥammad personally led campaigns into Syria; see Theophanes Confessor, *Chronographia*, ed. K. de Boor (Leipzig, 1883–85), I, 333–34; Agapius, *Kitāb al-ʿunwān*, ed. L. Cheikho (Paris, 1912), II, 334–35; Constantine VII Porphyrogenitus, *De administrando imperio*, ed. Gy. Moravcsik, trans. R.J.H. Jenkins (Washington, D.C., 1967), XIV:1–36, XVII:1–10 (text), 77–79, 81 (trans.); Michael the Syrian, *Chronique de Michel le Syrien*, ed. and trans. J.-B. Chabot (Paris, 1899–1924), II, 403–405; *Chronicon ad annum Christi 1234 pertinens*, ed. J.-B. Chabot (Paris, 1916–20), I, 227–30. This bears on the question of the sources of the *Continuatio*. Before the adoption of Arabic the main language used by the Samaritans was Samaritan Aramaic, so access to Syriac would have been a simple matter for any educated Samaritan who could read Syriac script.

[33]See Geographical Appendix.

[34]The scribe seems to have dropped the word يظنوا by mistake. See Ms. p. 205:10–11: وكانوا يظنوا انهم عايدين عن قرب.

[35]The verb here should be يظنوا, as commented in the preceding note.

[36]Ms. وارشوف; read وارسوف. Arsūf, called also Apollonia, was a town on the coast between Jaffa and Caesarea (presently near Herzliya). See Geographical Appendix.

[37]Maioumas, on the coast near Gaza. The text reads ميماس.

[38]In this text the word ضياع consistently denotes "villages" rather than "estates".

[39]Ms. شرقميه, but this should most probably be شرق رومية (L.C.). See Ms. p. 205:8, where شرقميه is clearly given; and cf. Vilmar, p. 179:10, who reads شرقية.

The Muslims rose and entered the land of Canaan, and took control of it; they seized all the cities and inhabited them, and ruled over all the places until there was no place left which they had not taken over but Caesarea, which rebelled and did not submit to them because it was called the mother of cities[40] and took precedence over them. [The Muslims] set camp against it and besieged it for six years before they conquered it.[41] [Now] the Byzantines were making use[42] of the sea before the Muslims were acquainted with it. In the fortress of Caesarea, at its north (*min al-Shām*), in the northwest corner, there was a small[43] gate which was hidden from view.[44] The Byzantines used to come and go through it without the Muslims knowing. [The Byzantines] forgot and left it open, and a dog came out of it. When [the Muslims] saw it, they followed it to the gate without raising the alarm.[45] They rode in,

---

[40]Caesarea was the metropolis of Provincia Palaestina Prima.

[41]Caesarea was under siege already in Jumādā I AH 13/July 634, according to al-Balādhurī, *Futūḥ al-buldān*, ed. M.J. de Goeje (Leiden, 1866), p. 140. He reports that Caesarea was besieged on and off between this date and its capture in Shawwāl 19/September–October 640. He adds that altogether it was besieged about seven years before it was captured. Al-Ṭabarī, I, 2579, also mentions another tradition according to which this event took place in 20/641. On the conquest of Caesarea, see Gil, *History of Palestine*, pp. 59–60. Noth lists Caesarea among the cities whose capture fits well into an accepted *topos*. See A. Noth, *The Early Arabic Historical Tradition*, second ed. in collaboration with L.I. Conrad, trans. M. Bonner (Princeton, 1994), pp. 167–68. The account appearing here, however, does not fit into this *topos*.

[42]Ms. يستخدموا. This use of the root خدم with reference to an inanimate noun is quite irregular. It appears once more in the the Ms. on p. 251pu.

[43]For this sense of لطيف see Dozy, *Supplément*, II, 532.

[44]Ms. يخمن; see Lane, *Lexicon*, I.2, 813.

[45]Ms. ما علم بهم. The following sentences seem to include authentic details about the city of Caesarea. Especially interesting is the reference to the upper and lower market, which seem to have been located so far apart that the massacre which took place throughout the day in the lower market was not felt in the upper market. Although extensive excavations have taken place in Caesarea in recent years, it is not possible to identify these sites with confidence. It would be hard to imagine that these names refer to features of topography, since Caesarea is flat; they may, however, refer to their relative locations in the city. It is known that Byzantine Caesarea was a large city in the shape of a large semi-circle 2500 meters in diameter, and that it flourished as never before, with a population estimated at around 100,000. For a description of Caesarea during the Byzantine period, see K. Holum and R.L. Hohfelder, eds., *King Herod's Dream: Caesarea on the Sea* (New York and London, 1988), pp. 155–99, esp. pp. 173–76. Two markets have been identified in Caesarea: one was the original *agora*, and the other was called the *pedion* or the *Campus Martius* (*ibid.*, p. 176); however, according to the map (*ibid.*, p. 163), these must have

and there was[46] killing in the city. They continued killing for a whole day in the lower market before it was known in the upper [market], because it was built in the form of one city above another. Whoever was able to flee fled by sea, whoever opposed them they killed, and whoever submitted to them was unharmed. The city was captured, and they inhabited it. After they captured it, every place else stood in awe of them.

[207] The Banū Ismāʿīl gained control of all the places, and the *jizya* was set at four *dirhams*[47] and a sack of barley, in addition to the tax upon the land (*kharāj*). The prophet of Islam did not cause anyone distress throughout his life. He would present his belief before the people, accepting anyone who came to him, [yet] not compelling one who did not. He remained in power for ten years, and all the world obeyed him. From him, his rule was transferred to his relatives, the Banū Umayya,[48] [and they ruled] according to what he had enjoined upon them; they did no more or less, and did not harm anyone. From them descended nineteen rulers, descendents of Muḥammad. Muḥammad lived for 63 years; for 43 years he did not reveal anything to anyone; for ten years [he was occupied in] wars, and for ten years [he was] a prophet.[49] He ruled and died, and after him rose ʿAtīq ibn Abī Quḥāfa,[50] known as Abū Bakr al-Ṣiddīq. He ruled for two years and three months.[51] After him rose ʿUmar ibn al-Khaṭṭāb, who ruled for ten years and seven

been quite close to each other, if we are to accept the evidence in the *Vita* of Anastasius; concerning this, see W.E. Kaegi, "Some Seventh Century Sources on Caesarea," *IEJ* 28 (1978), pp. 178–79.

[46]For the use of بقى in the sense of "to be", see Blau, *Grammar*, II, 440–41.

[47]On this coin see *EI* [2], *s.v.* "Dirham", "Jizya". The terms *jizya* and *kharāj* were not clearly defined at first, and the use of these terms here seems to be somewhat anachronistic. This specific amount does not seem to be mentioned elsewhere. For taxes in Palestine after the conquest, see Gil, *History of Palestine*, pp. 143–46.

[48]As will soon become clear, the Rāshidūn are included among Banū Umayya. On the nature of the conquest and conditions in Palestine under the Umayyads, see Introduction, pp. 27–28 and nn. 128, 131 above.

[49]Ms. נבי = نبي.

[50]In the Samaritan script here the personal name ʿAtīq is misspelt عتيك, instead of the correct form عتيق.

[51]According to the accepted tradition Abū Bakr ruled from 12 Rabīʿ I 11 (7 June 632) until 22 Jumādā II 13 (23 August 634).

months;[52] in the seventh year [of his reign][53] Caesarea was captured. He was killed by a man named Abū Lu'lu'a,[54] who was the slave of a great (?) man.[55] After him rose ʿUthmān ibn ʿAffān; he ruled for twelve years[56] and was killed. After that dissent broke out among the Muslims,[57] and they remained in dissent for four years and nine months.[58] After that Muʿāwiya **[208]** ibn Abī Sufyān rose to power and ruled for twenty years and eight months.[59] After Muʿāwiya rose his son, who ruled four months and died.[60] After him rose Marwān ibn al-Ḥakam, who ruled four months and died.[61] After him rose ʿAbd Allāh ibn al-Zubayr,[62] who ruled eight years and five

---

[52] I.e. from 634 until 644. There are indeed a further seven months in addition to the ten years from 22 Jumādā II (23 August 634) to 26 Dhū l-Ḥijja 23 (4 November 644).

[53] This is the accepted version of the date according to the *futūḥ* traditions; see above, p. 29 n. 129.

[54] This is Abū Lu'lu'a Fayrūz al-Nihāwandī, who was taken prisoner by the Byzantines during the war with Persia and later captured by the Muslims. See al-Ṭabarī, I, 2632. He was the slave of al-Mughīra ibn Shuʿba and assassinated ʿUmar because the caliph refused his request for a reduction of his tax. See al-Ṭabarī, I, 2722; also *EI* ², *s.v.* "Abū Lu'lu'a", "al-Mughīra ibn Shuʿba".

[55] Ms. عبد لرجل قيسارالي. This last word appears in all the other Mss. simply as قيساري, which cannot mean "from Caesarea" since there is no evidence connecting al-Mughīra to this city; perhaps the correct sense of the word is "Caesar-like", i.e. "eminent" or "great".

[56] 23 Dhū l-Ḥijja 23 (31 October 644)–17 Dhū l-Ḥijja 35 (15 June 656), i.e. indeed twelve years.

[57] This refers to the struggle between ʿAlī ibn Abī Ṭālib and Muʿāwiya ibn Abī Sufyān between 35/656 and *ca.* 39/660 known as the great *fitna*, which ended in Muʿāwiya's victory following the battle of Ṣiffīn. See G.R. Hawting, *The First Dynasty of Islam* (Carbondale, 1987), pp. 24–33.

[58] This would be December 660–January 661. The chronology here is somewhat vague, but this falls within reasonable limits. Cf. *ibid.*, p. 30.

[59] Since the date of the beginning of his reign is not clear cut, it is difficult to determine how accurate this information is. According to this he reigned from Dhū l-Qaʿda 39 (March–April 660) to Rajab 60 (April 680).

[60] The author seems to have skipped the reign of Yazīd ibn Muʿāwiya from Rajab 60 (April 680) to 14 Rabīʿ I 64 (11 November 683), according to al-Ṭabarī, II, 428. The caliph who ruled for four months is Muʿāwiya ibn Yazīd, for the length of whose reign there are conflicting reports. Al-Ṭabarī (II, 432) cites two versions: one reporting three months, and the other forty days.

[61] He in fact ruled for nine or ten months, from 3 Dhū l-Qaʿda 64 (22 June 684) until Ramaḍān 65 (April–May 685); see al-Ṭabarī, II, 473, 577.

[62] It is interesting to note that ʿAbd Allāh ibn al-Zubayr is presented here as a legitimate ruler; this is unusual, although there are similar cases in Muslim historiography. See, for example, Muḥammad ibn Aḥmad al-Dhahabī, *Duwal al-Islām* (Hyderabad, AH 1364), I,

months.[63] After him rose 'Abd al-Malik ibn Marwān ibn al-Ḥakam, who ruled thirteen years and six months[64] and died. After him rose al-Walīd, his son, who ruled nine years and seven months.[65] Then rose Sulaymān, his brother, who ruled two years and eight months.[66] Then rose 'Umar ibn 'Abd al-'Azīz, who ruled two years and six months.[67] Then rose Yazīd ibn 'Abd al-Malik ibn Marwān, who ruled four years.[68] Then rose his brother Hishām,[69] who ruled nineteen years and eight months.[70] After him rose al-Walīd ibn Yazīd ibn 'Abd al-Malik, who ruled one year and three months;[71] after him rose Yazīd al-Nāqiṣ ("the defective")[72] ibn al-Walīd, who ruled five

---

31, claiming that at that time there were two caliphs, and that 'Abd Allāh ibn al-Zubayr was the greater of the two. The inclusion of Ibn Zubayr's name here could either be due to the fact that the Samaritans accepted his rule without question, or that the author's information originates in a Muslim source favorable to Ibn Zubayr.

[63]'Abd Allāh ibn al-Zubayr acted as caliph in Mecca from 15 Rabī' II 64 (13 December 683) until 17 Jumādā I 73 (4 October 692), which comes to nine years and one month.

[64]According to Islamic tradition he ruled from 27 Ramaḍān 65 (7 May 685) until the middle of Shawwāl 86 (first half of October 705), therefore, in fact, 21 years and one month, according to the Muslim calendar.

[65]Al-Walīd ibn 'Abd al-Malik ruled from 14 Shawwāl 86 (8 Ocober 705) until the middle of Jumādā II 96 (late February 715), that is, nine years and eight months, according to the Muslim calendar. But al-Ṭabarī himself (II, 1269–70) cites a version which counts the length of his caliphate as nine years and seven months.

[66]Sulaymān ibn 'Abd al-Malik ruled from 15 Jumādā II 96 (25 February 715) until 19 Ṣafar 99 (1 October 717), two years and eight months less five days, according to al-Ṭabarī, II, 1336.

[67]'Umar ibn 'Abd al-'Azīz ruled from Ṣafar 99 (10 September 717) until 20–25 Rajab 101 (5–10 February 720), that is, two years and five months. See al-Ṭabarī, II, 1361–62.

[68]Ruled from the end of Rajab 101 (February 720) until 26 Sha'bān 105 (28 January 724), that is, just about four years and one month.

[69]Ms. هاشم, instead of هشام.

[70]This is Hishām ibn 'Abd al-Malik, who ruled from the end of Sha'bān 105 (end of January 724) until 6 Rabī' II 125 (6 February 743). Al-Ṭabarī (II, 1728) cites several versions concerning the length of his reign.

[71]Al-Walīd reigned from 6 Rabī' II 125 (6 February 743) until 27 Jumādā II 126 (15 April 744), that is, one year, two months and 21 days. Still, al-Ṭabarī (II, 1810) also cites a tradition of one year and three months.

[72]There are two explanations concerning this title, one referring to the fact that he cut down on the people's pensions, and the other claiming that he was physically defective. For the sources explaining this title see Carole Hillenbrand, trans., *The History of al-Ṭabarī*, XXVI, *The Waning of the Umayyad Caliphate* (Albany, 1989), p. 126 n. 628.

The *Continuatio*'s knowledge of the title again raises the question of sources (cf. p. 49–50 n. 32 above), since criticism of Yazīd was an internal matter among Muslims that months.[73] Then rose his brother Ibrāhīm, who ruled two months and eleven days.[74] Then rose Marwān ibn Muḥammad, the last of Banū Umayya, who ruled five years and two months.[75] All [the years] since the [beginning of the] rule of Islam until this time were 131 years and three months.[76]

[**209**] In the days of Marwān a tremendous earthquake struck everywhere.[77] The houses came down upon their inhabitants and innumerable people perished; it was an immense earthquake, such as had never before been seen. Those of the people who survived remained outdoors for many days, because the earth kept moving and stirring beneath them. When God in His mercy willed that it should be so,[78] the people entered the cities and calmed themselves. After this, Banū ʿAbbās behaved in an unruly manner towards[79] Banū Umayya, and came forth in order to confront them in bat-

---

Samaritans in and around Nablus were unlikely to know first-hand. But Theophanes already refers to it in his *Chronographia*, I, 418:17. On his access to Arabic sources via the Syriac chronicle of Theophilus of Edessa, see Lawrence I. Conrad, "Theophanes and the Arabic Historical Tradition: Some Indications of Intercultural Transmission", *BF* 15 (1990), pp. 1–44, esp. p. 29 on the epithet *al-nāqiṣ*.

[73] Yazīd ibn al-Walīd died in Dhū l-Ḥijja 126 (October 744), that is, six months after his father's death. However, al-Ṭabarī also cites (II, 1874) a version citing five months and two days.

[74] Al-Ṭabarī's main sources report that he reigned for four months; however, he also cites a version (II, 1875) reporting that his reign lasted 70 nights, which would be equivalent to two months and eleven days.

[75] Marwān was given the *bayʿa* in Ṣafar 127 (December 744) and was killed in Egypt on Dhū l-Ḥijja 132 (July 750); this comes to five years and nine months. See *EI* ^{2}, *s.v.* "Marwān II"; F. Omar, *The Abbasid Caliphate* (Baghdad, 1969), pp. 126–27. See also al-Ṭabarī, III, 51, where the date of the *bayʿa* is not stated. Five years and two months would be Rabīʿ II 132/November 749, the date by which the armies of the Hāshimīya had managed to undermine Umayyad rule in Persia and Iraq, allowing for the proclamation of the ʿAbbāsid caliphate in al-Kūfa.

[76] Abū l-ʿAbbās ʿAbd Allāh ibn Muḥammad ibn ʿAlī ibn ʿAbbās al-Saffāḥ, the first ʿAbbāsid caliph, was sworn in, according to al-Ṭabarī, III, 23, on 13 Rabīʿ I 132 (31 October 749), which is the third month of AH 132. Al-Ṭabarī cites two other traditions claiming that it occurred in Rabīʿ II or Jumādā I.

[77] The sources disagree about the exact date of this earthquake, on which see Gil, *History of Palestine*, pp. 89–90 and additional references there; on the date see also Y. Tsafrir and G. Foerster, "The Dating of the 'Earthquake of the Sabbatical Year' of 749 CE in Palestine", *BSOAS* 55 (1992), pp. 231–35; I. Karcz and A. Elad, "Further Comments on the 'Sabbatical Year' Earthquake", *Tarbiz* 61 (1992), pp. 67–83.

[78] Ms. ... ولما اراد الله هذا برحمته ومن هذا دخلوا. Cf. Vilmar, p. 181:4–5: ولما اراد الله الهدوء برحمته دخلوا الناس الى المدن وهدءوا نفوسهم.

[79] For this sense of تجبّر see Kazimirski, *Dictionnaire*, I, 247.

tle. There was discord among the Muslims, some of them siding with Banū l-ʻAbbās while others sided with Banū Umayya, and a great and terrible war broke out between them. This was the war known as the "War of the Blacks" (*ḥarb al-kūshīyīn*).[80] Those who supported Banū Umayya were defeated, and were killed in a place...[81] [by] a man from Khurāsān known as Abū Muslim,[82] who had with him many troops. He rose in order to assist Banū l-ʻAbbās, until he seized the reign from Banū Umayya for them.[83] He confronted Marwān and defeated him, and Marwān was put to flight until he arrived in Egypt. Abū Muslim's men caught up with him and killed him in Egypt, taking his head[84] after[85] he had reigned for five years.[86] They returned and arrived [in Iraq], and Abū Muslim passed the rule to Banū l-ʻAbbās, who were of Banū Hāshim.

At that time the kingdom of Banū l-ʻAbbās became established **[210]** [as a] strong and mighty kingdom. They doubled the tax upon the land (*kharāj*) and raised the poll tax[87] and made its burden heavier; they levied *waṣriya*

---

[80]Kūshīyīn apparently comes from the Samaritan Aramaic כושיי = "blacks", pertaining to the black dress and banners which the ʻAbbāsid dynasty adopted as its symbolic colour. See M. Sokoloff, *A Dictionary of Jewish Palestinian Aramaic in the Byzantine Period* (Ramat Gan, 1990), p. 254, *s.v.* כושיי, esp. the reference to the Christo-Palestinian Aramaic dialect, which was very close to the Samaritan Aramaic dialect. Concerning the importance of the black colour in the ʻAbbāsid revolution, see M. Sharon, *Black Banners from the East II: Revolt—The Social and Military Aspects of the Abbasid Revolution* (Jerusalem, 1990), pp. 79–86.

[81]Here something seems to be missing in the text. Vilmar's text, p. 181:9–10, does not seem to be correct either, since قتلوا في مكان خراسان في رجل seems quite awkward and illogical. It is more probable to suppose that some words are missing here, e.g.: قتلوا في مكان [يسمى ... على يد] رجل من خراسان يعرف [بـ]ابي مسلم. In this case, the Paris Ms. would be more accurate.

[82]Ms. ابوا مسلم.

[83]Abū Muslim, a freedman of Persian origin, was indeed the central figure in the ʻAbbāsid revolution that started in Khurāsān. See *EI*[2], *s.v.* "Abū Muslim".

[84]For the story of Marwān's flight and defeat see al-Ṭabarī, III, 45–51; Abū Zakarīyā' al-Azdī, *Ta'rīkh al-Mawṣil*, ed. ʻA. Ḥabība (Cairo, 1967), pp. 133–37. For a description of the events see Omar, *The Abbasid Caliphate*, pp. 126–27. The story about his head being cut off and sent to Abū l-ʻAbbās appears both in al-Ṭabarī, III, 50; and in al-Yaʻqūbī, *Ta'rīkh*, ed. M.Th. Houtsma (Leiden, 1883), II, 414–15. See also Omar, *ibid.*, who cites Ibn Aʻtham al-Kūfī, *Kitāb al-futūḥ*.

[85]Ms. بعدا ملك. Cf. Vilmar, p. 181:12: بعد ان ملك.

[86]See above, p. 56 n. 75.

[87]The word used here is *jāliya*, a term equivalent to *jizya*. Vilmar, p. 181:15, reads:

(?)[88] from all their provinces and afflicted the people with it, levying the money and collecting it assiduously.

After Marwān rose ʻAbd Allāh, known as al-ʻAbbās, of Banū Hāshim, and he reigned four years and eight months.[89] After him rose his brother, known as Abū Jaʻfar,[90] who sent to Palestine a ruler[91] known as ʻAbd al-Wahhāb,[92] who was called Abū Shindī, and he afflicted the people much. . . .[93] ʻAbd al-Wahhāb despatched (?)[94] [a message] to the governor of Nablus (Nābulus)[95] [ordering] that he should burn the place of worship (lit. *qibla*) which Zeno, may his bones be ground to dust and no mercy [be upon him], built on the

---

وزادوا الجور على الرعاية (sic!), "and they increased the injustice upon the non-Muslim subjects". On the term *jāliya* see F. Løkkegaard, *Islamic Taxation in the Classic Period* (Copenhagen, 1950), pp. 140–41.

[88]This is an unclear word. *Waṣr* is a contract or certificate of land ownership; see Kazimirski, *Dictionnaire*, II, 1547. Perhaps *waṣriya* is a payment levied for the provision of such a certificate; I could not, however, find any verification of this assumption. Vilmar's text skips this sentence.

[89]See above, p. 56 n. 76. Four years and eight months, according to the tradition that he ascended on 13 Rabīʻ II.

[90]This is the second ʻAbbāsid caliph, Abū Jaʻfar ʻAbd Allāh al-Manṣūr ibn Muḥammad, who reigned from 136/754 to 158/775.

[91]The term used here is *sulṭān*.

[92]This is ʻAbd al-Wahhāb ibn Ibrāhīm al-Imām ibn Muḥammad ibn ʻAlī ibn ʻAbd Allāh ibn ʻAbbās ibn ʻAbd al-Muṭṭalib ibn Hāshim al-Hāshimī, al-Manṣūr's nephew, who was appointed by him to the post of governor of Syria and Palestine. Ibn ʻAsākir relates a tradition in the name of Muḥammad ibn Samāʻa al-Filasṭīnī that ʻAbd al-Wahhāb destroyed Palestine. According to Muḥammad ibn Samāʻa, al-Manṣūr invited two functionaries from Palestine and asked them about ʻAbd al-Wahhāb's rule; the first replied that although al-Manṣūr had given him the best contract ever given to anyone holding such a post, he continuously violated all the caliph's instructions, while the other replied, saying: "Your nephew left the land like this bird," and taking a plucked bird out of his sleeve. See Ibn ʻAsākir, *Ta'rīkh madīnat Dimashq* (Amman, 1989), XXXVII, 301–302 (= Ibn Manẓūr, *Mukhtaṣar ta'rīkh madīnat Dimashq*, Damascus 1988, XV, 270–72); see also al-Balādhurī, *Ansāb al-ashrāf*, III, pp. 127–28; Khalīfa ibn Khayyāṭ, *Ta'rīkh*, ed. A.Ḍ. al-ʻUmarī (Baghdad, 1967), pp. 445, 451, 454.

[93]Ms. وخبا نسله يرا لا نوع: the phrase is incomprehensible.

[94]Ms. و تحلا, which is unclear, but apparently a verb in the imperfect tense. Vilmar, p. 182:1, has ارسل.

[95]Ms. متولى نابلس.

mountain, from where the well of the Samaritans[96] could be observed;[97] this happened[98] (?) so that he would [have cause to] collect money from them on account of its burning.[99] A group of men were [there] alone at night, and they burnt it; they burnt the church whose light the Byzantines used to see at night,[100] and they killed five monks there. The Christians went around saying: "None but the Samaritans has burnt it!" Abū Shindī sent [an order], and the *ra'īs* was seized. There was a man there of Banū Nasāyta (?)[101] whose name was Yahnī (?)[102] ibn al-Malik; he besought him concerning the matter **[211]** of the *ra'īs*, and he released him into his custody. He[103] seized

---

[96]Ms. عرض منه نحب السامره; Vilmar, p. 182:3, reads: لجب السامره. This would be Jacob's Well, near Nablus. According to Samaritan tradition Joseph's tomb (*ḥelqat hasadeh*) was located nearby; in Zeno's days (see following note) the place was already considered a holy Christian site commemorating the meeting between Jesus and the Samaritan woman. See Geographical Appendix, *s.v.* 'Askar; cf. also below, n. 100.

[97]The events mentioned here are described earlier in the text. See Vilmar, pp. 180–82; Stenhouse, trans., pp. 240–41. After the Samaritan rebellion of 484, the emperor Zeno confiscated Samaritan places of worship on and around Mount Gerizim and established churches in their place. On top of the mount he consecrated a church to the Virgin Mary; a high tower with a signalling device was annexed to the church. For a summary of these events, see A.D. Crown, "The Byzantine and Moslem Period", in Crown, *Samaritans*, pp. 71–73.

[98]Ms. وحدنت; cf. Vilmar, p. 182:3, which has وحدث.

[99]It would have been very easy indeed to blame this subterfuge on the Samaritans, who had a long record of attacking and damaging Christian sites in their vicinity.

[100]Vilmar, p. 182:6, adds: من المدائن, "from the cities". See above, n. 97. The fact that this church, dedicated to St. Mary, continued to exist throughout the Muslim period and into the Crusader period is not attested elsewhere. All the sources referring to Nablus and to the see that continued to exist there during the early Muslim period mention the church located over Jacob's Well, where, according to tradition, Jesus met the Samaritan woman. See, for example, the *Commemoratorium de Casis Dei vel Monasteriis*, in T. Tobler and A. Molinier, *Itinera Hierosolymitana et descriptiones Terrae Sanctae* (Geneva, 1879), II, 302; the pilgrim Arculf (670s CE) in J. Wilkinson, *Jerusalem Pilgrims* (Jerusalem, 1977), p. 108; the pilgrim Willibald (726 CE), *ibid.*, p. 132. See also the *taktikon* published by G. Palamas in *A Short History of the Holy City of Jerusalem* (Jerusalem, 1862), 376–82 (in Greek).

[101]Other readings are: نسابتة, نسايتة, and نسايتا: see Vilmar, p. 182:8. The same is true for the additional Mss. checked.

[102]Or Yhyī: see Vilmar, *ibid.* The identity of this person is not clear. L.C. suggests that the name be read as يحيى.

[103]It is not clear whether this refers back to 'Abd al-Wahhāb, in which case it is a more detailed account of the short report given previously, describing more fully how the *ra'īs* was seized and how he was freed; or, alternatively, whether it refers to this Yhnī (Yaḥyā

the *ra'īs*, who was[104] Absabī ibn Dartā, who was invested with authority over the people; he afflicted him, shaved his head and set his fine at 3000 *dīnārs*. The Samaritans helped him, and he procured[105] [the money] and went free. In the days of the *ra'īs* Qarī Sabā[106] and the *ra'īs* Absabī[107] the domed building[108] was burnt down.

[Abū] Ja 'far ruled 22 years.[109] After him rose his son, who was called Muḥammad al-Mahdī, who ruled for ten years and a month and died.[110] After him rose his son, whose name was Mūsā,[111] and who reigned for one year and two months[112] and then died.

After this the *ra'īs* Qarī Sabā passed away,[113] and his son Nethan'el, who was a young boy, was appointed as his successor. Therefore, his nephew rose and was given the authority to rule the community.[114] He did not have the great Hebrew computation[115] with him, and instead he used the Greek computation.[116] He remained [in office] seven years and died, and his son

---

?) who freed the *ra'īs*, only to take him into his own custody and collect the fine from the Samaritans.

[104]The text is unclear here. It may include an unnecessary repetition: واخذ الرييس واخذه .... وهوا.

[105]For this sense of قام بـ see Dozy, *Supplément*, II, 422.

[106]Ms. قري سبا. Cf. Vilmar, p. 182:12, reading قراسبا.

[107]Ms. وابسبي, but the و here seems to be redundant. Cf. Vilmar, p. 182:12.

[108]Ms. قبّة. It is not clear what building is referred to here, whether a local Samaritan shrine or perhaps a Muslim or Christian shrine.

[109]From 13 Dhū l-Ḥijja 136 (9 June 754) to 6 Dhū l-Ḥijja 158 (7 October 775).

[110]18 Dhū l-Ḥijja 158 (19 October 754) to 22 Muḥarram 169 (4 August 785), indeed ten years and one month. See al-Ṭabarī, III, 451.

[111]Abū Muḥammad Mūsā al-Hādī ibn al-Mahdī.

[112]From 22 Muḥarram 169 (4 August 785) to 16 Rabī' I 170 (15 September 786), indeed a year and two months.

[113]Ms. انتقل, presumably in the sense of انتقل الى رحمة الله.

[114]For this sense of حكم في see Lane, *Lexicon*, I.2, 616.

[115]Ms. الحساب العبراني الكبير, probably referring to the Samaritan calculation system called חשבן קשטה, "true reckoning", or מחשב הימים, "reckoning of the days". According to this system, the beginning of the lunar month is not based on observation like the Muslim month, but is calculated by conjunction of the sun with the moon. The absence of this calculation means that precise dates in the Samaritan calendar cannot be calculated. See Powels, "The Samaritan Calendar", pp. 703–704.

[116]Ms. الحساب الرومي: this refers to the Julian calendar, which was used in order to

Yazīd rose after him in his place; he had no computation other than the one that his father had had, and he did not know how to add to it.[117] Then Nethan'el, son of Qarī Sabā, who had the correct Hebrew computation, rose in opposition to him, and they advertised[118] two papers, [one of] Nethan'el and [one of] Qaraqalā.[119] They were in a state of disagreement with one another, and the Samaritans fell into a great dissension over them, some being with Qaraqalā[120] and others with Nethan'el. They advertised [**212**] two papers [fixing the date] for the fast, Nethan'el's paper [prescribing] Monday and Qaraqalā's paper [prescribing] Tuesday. Half of the people of the villages supported one, while the other half supported the other. Those who were with Nethan'el fasted on Monday, and those who were with Qaraqalā fasted on Tuesday, and for everyone who fasted [on one day] there was another who did the contrary.[121] The Samaritans were greatly distressed by this matter, and the leaders of the Samaritans came together to the *ra'īs* Dartā and asked him: "How can the Samaritans be rid of this great misfortune?" [He replied:] "Look for men who are knowledgeable and fearful of God, may He be exalted, who will enter [into the matter] and will examine [the evidence] in favour of this [side] and that [side], and wherever the truth shall be found, we shall all uphold it." [So] Dartā chose four men, two who were followers of one and two who were followers of the other, and made them swear that they would not treat the truth lightly, wherever it might be; he told them that those who know it and reject[122] it would take upon themselves the sin of the world, and [that] "you will discover the truth among them.[123] He who has the truth on his side will have the whole nation with him." [So] they entered [into the matter] and inquired and found that the truth was with Nethan'el. All the

---

reckon the beginning of the year (*ibid.*, pp. 707–708). This would mean that he could determine the beginning of the year using the Muslim and Julian calendars, but could not correctly reckon the months according to the Samaritan system.

[117]It seems that the text should read احسن rather than حسن. Presumably, he did not know how to convert dates correctly to the Samaritan calendar.

[118]The verb used is اخرج. For this sense see Dozy, *Supplément*, I, 358.

[119]Ms. ورفلا. At the first occurrence of this name, the copyist seems to have been baffled and did not know where to place the points. This changes, however, in the next page to a definite reading of Qaraqalā.

[120]The scribe erred at first and the name therefore appears corrected in the margins.

[121]Here the text reads: وكلمن صام عملوا الاخر فى ضده.

[122]Ms. يريدون, but more plausible is Vilmar, p. 183:13, reading يردّون.

[123]I.e. among the four witnesses.

people endorsed him[124] and confirmed that the course[125] of his leadership was in accordance with the truth.

[213] During the year in which Nethan'el rose, there rose after him Mūsa, brother of Hārūn son of al-Mahdī of Banū Hāshim.[126] In his days there was a huge [swarm of] locusts, the like of which had never before been seen, and it ate all the vegetation and all the plants of the earth; it multiplied[127] upon the land, and its offspring emerged and covered the face of the earth from the sea to the Jordan [River]. It ate all of the vegetation and the plants on the land; nothing remained on the face of the earth, and the land was left barren.[128] The following year a dispute broke out amongst the Muslims, and there was great slaughter amongst them and of them;[129] they split into two factions, one called the Mudarānīm and the other ... (?),[130] and fought each other with great enmity and killed each other without mercy.[131] The Samaritans

[124]For this sense of شد معه see Dozy, *Supplément*, I, 735.

[125]The text here has وبسيرن اماته, which seems corrupt; Vilmar, p. 183:16, has وسيرة اماته.

[126]See above, p. 60 nn. 111–12.

[127]Ms. اشرص, "multiplied", "bred", as in Hebrew and Aramaic. Cf. below, Ms. p. 257:8.

[128]A locust attack that started in 784 is described by Michael the Syrian. According to him this was a pernicious attack that started in Edessa and Sarug, from whence it passed on to the Jazīra and afterwards to the West, where it devoured all the vegetation, including the cereals, vines and trees. It may well be that although this attack started in the days of al-Mahdī, it reached what Michael the Syrian (*Chronique*, III, 4) calls "the West" in the days of Mūsā al-Hādī.

[129]Ms. وقتال منهم وبهم. Cf. Vilmar, p. 184:3–4: وقتل منهم قتل عظيم.

[130]The names of the factions appear in the Paris Ms. only, and are omitted in Vilmar. The first name, although misspelt, seems to refer to the Muḍarīya; the second name is written بسين, and it is clear that the scribe did not know how to read it himself. It may be Yamanīyīn; see following note.

[131]This is actually the feud, or *fitna*, known as the "War of the Watermelon", which was part of a long series of outbreaks during the period under discussion between tribal factions known as the Nizārīya or Muḍarīya on the one hand, and the Yamanīya on the other. See P. von Sivers, "Military, Merchants and Nomads: the Social Evolution and the Syrian Cities and Countryside during the Classical Period 780–969," *Der Islam* 56 (1979), pp. 220ff. For a detailed description of this outbreak and its causes, see Ibn al-Athīr, *Al-Kāmil fī l-ta'rīkh* (Beirut, 1965), VI, 127–28. The main part of this war took place around 176/792–93; see *ibid.*; al-Ṭabarī, III, 624–26. Al-Ṭabarī mentions tribal enmity in Palestine and some skirmishes already in 174/790–91. See also Ibn Taghrībirdī, *Al-Nujūm al-zāhira fī mulūk Miṣr wa-l-Qāhira* (Cairo, 1929–72), I, 67–68, who mentions the year 171/787–78 as the year of the outbreak. Both Ibn al-Athīr and al-Ṭabarī emphasize that many people were killed during the course of this war.

and the others who lived in their vicinity were in great and fearful difficulty, [since] they entered the villages and plundered crops,[132] gold, silver, copper and woollen clothing. And so the written curse had come upon us: "Your ox shall be slain before your eyes and you shall not eat of it",[133] and the rest of the curse (lit. the whole curse). The people fled, and their villages were left empty because of the punishment and affliction that came upon them. If they caught a woman they did to her what the people of Sodom did; they brought **[214]** upon the people an affliction that could not be averted (?),[134] and the people stayed in the mountains and in the caves, after they had been deprived of all their belongings and had been left destitute[135] of everything.[136] Of the notables, he who had [someone] who would join him[137] gave him his money in exchange for his protection, while people who had no companion remained wandering in the mountains, caves, and wadis. When [the raiders] would enter, they would come upon nothing without taking it.[138] They burned the houses and the seed grain,[139] and did not leave anything unburnt, [so that] the whole region was reduced to ruin. They remained so about a year, and God made good on His vow[140] and scattered[141] them.

---

[132] Ms. العلال; read الغلال.

[133] Deuteronomy 28:31.

[134] Ms. بلا لا نحبت. Cf. Vilmar, p. 184:10–11: ودخل على الناس منهم بلايا ونكبة, "and they brought upon the people trials and affliction".

[135] Ms. وبقيوا كشف = وبقيوا كاشفين; cf. Vilmar, p. 184:12: وبقيوا عرايا من كل شيء.

[136] The harsh consequences that this war had for the local non-Muslim inhabitants are described in detail in a contemporary Christian hagiographical composition called the *Passion of the Twenty Martyrs*. The author of the passion speaks of a ferocious tribal war which broke out between some of the most noble Arab tribes in Palestine. The effects of this war were devastating: the roads became unsafe, town dwellers fled, leaving important towns like Eleuthropolis, Ascalon and Gaza deserted, and there were robberies, looting and fires everywhere. For the Greek text see the edition by A. Papadopoulos-Kerameus in *Pravoslavnii Palestinski Sbornik* 57 (1907), pp. 1–41.

[137] The text is somewhat garbled here: ومن كان له من كبار منهم كان يستند اليه يعطيه ماله ...; cf. Vilmar, p. 184:13–14: ومن كان له من الكبار منهم من يستند اليه يعطيه ماله ....

[138] The text here has: الا يصيبوا شي ياخذوه, which seems corrupt. The correct reading is probably: ولا يصيبوا شي الا ياخذوه.

[139] Ms. الدور والبدور; read الدور والبذور. Cf. Vilmar, p. 184:15: الذور والبذور. The reading الدور, "houses", which appears in our text, seems to be preferable here.

[140] Ms. تصدق, form V used in the sense of I (L.C.).

[141] Ms. افرق, form IV instead of I.

The next year a great rise in prices came upon the people, and a merciless calamity took place. They had already been stripped bare from without and from within:[142] from without [by] locusts, and from within by the enemy. Furthermore,[143] they took pains in order to secure the *jizya*, and the curse was fulfilled: "And you shall be delivered[144] into your enemies' hands."[145] Under Kisrā[146] the price of bread increased and the people suffered terrible hunger until satiety was forgotten, as is said [in the Scriptures]: "And you shall eat, and you will not be satisfied."[147]

It was said that a woman ate her son in a village called Arba'. The baby died, and when he passed away she took him, cut him up into pieces and cooked him. **[215]** Some people entered and saw his hand emerging from the cooking pot, and said to her: "What are you cooking?" She replied to them: "A hedgehog." They said to her: "Where did you get a hedgehog?" Looking into the cooking pot and detecting human flesh, they said to her: "What is this terrible calamity?" She said that her son had died, and that she took him and cooked him in order to eat him because of [her] gnawing hunger. The woman was a bedouin Arab who lived there.

God delivered unto the people extinction and death.[148] O, how many died on the road and were not buried! And the road (?) turned into a graveyard.[149]

---

[142]The script here is somewhat unclear: قد انكشفوا من برا ومن داخل (cf. Vilmar, p. 184:18–19).

[143]Ms. وابعد ويكدو في طلب الجزيه (sic); cf. Vilmar, p. 184:19: وبعد.

[144]Ms. وتصبرو; read وتصيرو.

[145]Deuteronomy 28:48.

[146]Presumably the name of a provincial or local official. Kisrā was a common Persian name; see F. Justi, *Iranisches Namenbuch* (Marburg, 1895), pp. 134–39.

[147]Micha 6:14.

[148]A devastating plague that occurred at the beginning of the caliphate of Hārūn al-Rashīd (r. 170/786–193/809) is mentioned by al-Balādhūrī, who says that the plague was so deadly that at times it wiped out whole households. As a result, lands and fields left uncultivated were redistributed by the caliph. See al-Balādhūrī, *Futūḥ al-buldān*, p. 158; also p. 144.

[149]Ms. وصارت الخاطي قبره, which is surely corrupt. Vilmar's text, p. 185:10, reads: وصارت السكة قبورا. قبره may be an error for مقبره or قبور; الخاطي is perhaps a distorted form of خطّ, "main road", or خطّة, a "region" or "district". L.C. suggests that the sentence may be read: وصارت للخاطي قبره, taking the implied subject to be السكك or الطرق and reading الخاطي as a colloquial form of الخاطئ, "sinner"; in this case the translation would be: "And [the roads] became the sinner's grave".

Mothers would dig pits and place ten or five [children] in them because they could not manage to bury [them separately]. So many of the Samaritans and the priests died and were not mourned as they should have been, or buried properly.[150] So many sons became separated from their fathers, and fathers separated from their sons, and they died without one knowing the condition of the other, whether he was hungry or dead. The appearance[151] of the people changed, and not a father remained who asked about his son, nor a son who asked about his father, nor a brother about his brother, and matters became worse and worse. Woe to him who saw this calamity with his own eyes, and blessed be he who is tried and is rescued from his trial and achieves relief.

[216] After this God extended His mercy and alleviated [the suffering]; He lifted [His] wrath from [His] servants, and sent prosperity upon the earth and satisfied the people, and the people ate and were satiated. Those few people who survived and went up to the mountain[152] on the Feast of Tabernacles (*ʿīd al-mizāl*) that was [celebrated] after the year of the perdition were like those who congregate in a small village synagogue.

After that, ...[153] ...the farmer [returned] crying, and there was much vegetation...,[154] and he did not have any beasts, and the people were crying

---

150 The following sentence is added in Vilmar, p. 185:14: الا البعض يدفن في حفيرة تراب من غير قبر ولا خشاب; for خشاب read خشب, "a wooden case" (Dozy, *Supplément*, I, 372), thus: "only a few [had the privilege] to be buried, [and this] in an earthen trench because there was no [proper] grave or a wooden coffin". Another version appears in BL Or. 1447, fol. 90v: من غير حجارة, "for lack of stones". For evidence of burial in wooden coffins in Palestine, see, for example, G. Hadas, "Nine Tombs of the Second Temple Period at 'Ein Gedi", *'Atiqot* 24 (1994), English abstract, pp. 1*–9*; Hebrew, pp. 1–75.

151 Ms. سحن, presumably an error or a plural of سحنة, "external appearance", "looks", "complexion". Cf. Ms. p. 253:1–2: وتغيّرت صور الناس من المرض.

152 There is a superfluous repetition here of the phrase: والقليل من الناس. Cf. Vilmar, p. 186:2–3, bearing: .... والقليل من الناس الذين طلعوا الجبل ... كانوا مثل ما.

153 Here there is a gap in the middle of the page of six lines. The following section appears only in Vilmar's text, p. 186:4–7, and is missing, in this form, in the Paris Ms., which bears, however, other additional material on this event: "...the rain arrived and mercy came, and the farmer returned [to his land] crying, because he did not have any beasts or seeds; and the seeds which he brought from the distant places, he ploughed with his shoulders, and with donkeys and mules; and they ploughed with the rest of the beasts." Here ends Vilmar's edition. From here onwards the text is attested only by the Paris manuscript Sam. 10, with no known parallels to the text.

154 Ms. والعشب كان كثير داجن. The last word, داجن, is not clear in this context. "Rain"

continuously (?),[155] and they fasted on Mondays and Thursdays. The nation's elders wrote to the Samaritans everywhere, and they came before God and offered up a great prayer; this happened on the mountain [**217**] on the first day of the month which was after the holiday of the seventh month.[156] The letters of the *ra'īs* reached[157] the villages, and the people went up to the mountain on Sunday, and there was a great prayer. On Monday and on Tuesday there was a great wail,[158] and the small children cried out and said: "O God of our righteous fathers, lift this affliction from us." And the Lord God, may He be exalted, heard their call for assistance with the invocation of the fathers, and He lifted the perdition from them, and removed the anger through His benevolence,[159] because He is God, full of benevolence, and is prone to mercy[160] and does not seek [to vent His] anger. The people could not pass along the roads [**218**] because of the stench of the corpses, until their bodies changed because of the smell.[161] Even though the plague was lifted from the cattle, people became fatigued as a result of the threshing; they could not obtain anything with which they could thresh, and they had to resort to threshing with donkeys, camels and other beasts,[162] and the same

(see Lane, *Lexicon*, I.3, 854; Dozy, *Supplément*, I, 425) would indeed be quite logical here if we are to assume that the syntax of the sentence is corrupt. Another possibility is "cereals", from the Hebrew *dagan*, which was adopted also by Samaritan Arabic, as evidenced by the trilingual Samaritan biblical glossary (Hebrew, Aramaic, Arabic) *Hameliz*. For evidence of this see Z. Ben Hayyim, *The Literary and Oral Tradition of Hebrew and Aramaic amongst the Samaritans*, II (Jerusalem, 1957), p. 446.

155 The word here is unclear, and is written بغيت with double dotting of the *ghayn*. Read بقيت?

156 The Samaritans adhered to the biblical order and names of the months. The first month was therefore Nīsan (= March–April), while the seventh was Tishrei (= September–October). The holiday of the seventh month would be the Feast of Tabernacles; the first day of the month afterwards would therefore be the beginning of Ḥeshvan (October–November), the season when rain is again expected.

157 Ms. ومضت وكتب الرييس الى الضياع; the و before كتب is redundant.

158 Here there is a gap of six and a half lines in the text, parallel to the one in the former page, although in this case there does not seem to be any text missing.

159 For this sense of احسان see Kazimirski, *Dictionnaire*, I, 128.

160 Compare قريب الثرى; see Lane, *Lexicon*, I.1, 336.

161 According to Galenic humoral doctrine, which prevailed everywhere in the medieval Near East, foul smells can upset one's bodily constitution and lead to unhealthy changes and illness. Cf. the extensive discussion in R. Parker, *Miasma*, Oxford 1983 (L.C.).

162 As opposed to an ox, the beast usually used for threshing and plowing. The lack of oxen for agricultural tasks was similarly cumbersome during the days of Ibn Ṭūlūn.

was true in the case of sowing.[163] The earth became contaminated[164] and the curse was fulfilled for us, in His words: "I will annihilate your beasts, and so much of the earth shall remain barren because of the lack of beasts, and the earth shall be contaminated by the corpses of the beasts."[165]

All of these hardships [came upon us] when we defied[166] our God, and all this took place in the days of Hārūn, the caliph of the Muslims, when the *ra'īs* was Nethan'el, the *imām* of Israel.[167]

After this, when Hārūn al-Rashīd was on his deathbed, he summoned his three children Muḥammad [al-Amīn], 'Abd Allāh [al-Ma'mūn], and [al-]Qāsim, and divided his kingdom amongst them.[168] He allotted Khurāsān to 'Abd

---

[163] See below, Ms. p. 251:5–7.

[164] The verb used here is تطمت, an Arabicised version of the Hebrew root נטמא, which appears also in the form تطمأت. See below, Ms. p. 249:10. It was adopted by the Samaritans from the Hebrew and thus does not appear in dictionaries of Arabic.

[165] This seems to be a combination of two or more passages; most probably Nahum 3:3 or Lamentations 4:14, with Leviticus 26:22, 30, or Ezekiel 32:13ff.

[166] Ms. اعصينا, form IV instead of I.

[167] This ending is almost identical to the one at the end of Vilmar's text. See Vilmar, p. 186. A description of an almost identical series of events is found in a Latin document describing the conditions of the Christians in Palestine during this period. This includes three earthquakes (not described by our source, possibly because they did not reach Samaria), a severe attack of locusts, a plague, the Watermelon War, and the drought, all in a short period of time. We sincerely hope that Prof. A. Linder of the Hebrew University, who found several Mss. of this document quite some time ago, will choose to publish it.

[168] Here follows a description of the succession arrangements made by Hārūn al-Rashīd, the main source for which is al-Ṭabarī, III, 651–67. The arrangements were in fact made by Hārūn on his *ḥajj* to Mecca in 186/802, and not on his deathbed, as reported here. During his stay in Mecca two documents were composed, attested in turn by al-Amīn and al-Ma'mūn, which were deposited in the Ka'ba for safekeeping. In these documents it was stated that al-Amīn was to succeed Hārūn al-Rashīd, but that the empire would be divided between him and al-Ma'mūn, al-Amīn controlling the western part, while al-Ma'mūn would be in charge of the eastern part, i.e. from Khurāsān and eastwards. Al-Qāsim was to be in control of the border regions (*al-thughūr wa-l-'awāṣim*); see al-Ṭabarī, III, 653. Al-Ma'mūn would succeed al-Amīn in his turn, while al-Qāsim would succeed al-Ma'mūn, if the latter did not decide otherwise (al-Ṭabarī, III, 667). It is probable that the provision for al-Qāsim was actually added only a few years later, in 805. See C.E. Bosworth, trans., *The History of al-Ṭabarī*, XXX: *The 'Abbāsid Caliphate* (Albany, 1989), pp. 184–85 n. 674, citing R.A. Kimber, "Hārūn al-Rashīd's Meccan Settlement of AH 186/AD 802," *University of St. Andrews, School of 'Abbāsid Studies, Occasional Papers* 1 (1986), pp. 55–79. On the subject of the succession, see F. Gabrieli, "La successione di Hārūn al-Rashīd e la guerra fra al-Amīn e al-Ma'mūn," *RSO* 11 (1926–28), pp. 341–97; H. Kennedy, *The Early*

Allāh, and from the border of Khurāsān onwards, all the land until Ifrīqiya,[169] he allotted to Muḥammad, and all of the coastline from one end to the other he allotted to [al-]Qāsim. He gave Muḥammad precedence as sovereign after him, [**219**] and ʻAbd Allāh after him and [al-]Qāsim after him, arranging them in this manner. He took[170] from them oaths and agreements and testimonies, and appointed chiefs (*mashāyikh*) throughout his kingdom[171] so that after this pact and [in the case of] its breach it would be available for all the people to deliberate upon it,[172] and upon his pact and his oath.[173] Hārūn ruled for 22 years and eleven months[174] and died.

His son Muḥammad took his place. He was neglectful of his kingdom[175] and adorned himself, cleaving to the boys,[176] dressing them as women,[177] adorning them with women's ornaments, sleeping with them, and clinging to

---

ʻAbbāsid Caliphate (London, 1981), pp. 123–26.

[169]North Africa, particularly the region which is today Tunisia.

[170]Ms. يعقل, which seems to give no sense in this context.

[171]This probably refers to the letter written by Hārūn to all the provincial governors, which included a copy of the contract made in Mecca and ordered them to have the document read out loud and placed in their *dīwān* and to report any incident regarding it. See al-Ṭabarī, III, 666.

[172]For تساعد على see Dozy, *Supplément*, I, 654.

[173]The verb here is unclear; read يتروا, in the sense of "consider" or "deliberate". See Lane, *Lexicon*, I:3, 1195. This sentence, as it appears in the Ms., is somewhat problematic; the translation is therefore tentative.

[174]According to the accepted tradition Hārūn ruled for 22 years, six months, and nine days, from 16 Rabīʻ I 170 (15 September 786) to 3 Jumādā II 193 (24 March 809). Although there are additional traditions (see al-Ṭabarī/Bosworth, *The ʻAbbāsid Caliphate*, p. 303 n. 1022), they all fall within a month of the accepted date given by al-Ṭabarī, which is cited here.

[175]The following information is attested by al-Ṭabarī, III, 804–805, who cites verses attributed to ʻAlī ibn ʻĪsā concerning al-Amīn's idleness, the central position of the different court functionaries, and the homosexual habits which prevailed in his court. See the translation by Michael Fishbein, in *The History of al-Ṭabarī*, XXXI: *The War Between Brothers* (Albany, 1992), pp. 58–59: "The Caliph's active homosexuality (*liwāṭ*) is a marvel, even more marvellous than is the vizier's passive homosexuality (*ḥulāq*). One of them buggers, the other gets buggered: such, by my life, is the difference of the cases. . . ." ʻAlī then goes on to describe the scandal which arose in the royal court. See also T. El-Hibri, "The Regicide of the Caliph al-Amīn and the Challenge of Representation in Medieval Islamic Historiography," *Arabica* 42 (1995), pp. 354–64.

[176]Ms. הנערים, Hebrew in Samaritan script.

[177]The Hebrew word for "women", הנשים, appears here once in transliteration in Arabic script (l. 6), and once in Samaritan (l. 7).

them;[178] throughout his reign he used to rely upon the officials to manage it.[179] God became angry with him and lifted fear of him from the people, and they turned upon him; a state of great turmoil, conflict and disorder pervailed, and it is said that [it prevailed] everywhere. The whole time from the creation of Adam to the reign of Muḥammad ibn Hārūn al-Rashīd was 5239 years.[180] [Then] the dissent among the [Arabs] occurred, and many from all of the country as far as [Jund] al-Urdunn[181] were killed; there was looting everywhere, many Samaritans—heads of villages—were killed, and the written curse was fulfilled: "A sword shall be in your midst."[182]

[220] [Then] Abū 'Awf, a man from [the tribe of] Judhām,[183] rebelled and came to Palestine. He came down to Sālim,[184] and when he was killed his companions ran away and the believers[185] fell into great strife. A man by the name of Mirāhā whose son was one of those killed[186] in Sālim rose from his army,[187] and many people went forth with him. They gathered in Zaytā[188] and continued on their way to Arsūf. They plundered and killed, burned villages, looted the synagogues and burned the meeting place of the

---

[178]The Ms. has ينعلف, probably to be read يتعلق, though in the given context it seems that the appropriate expression would have been يتعلق بهم, "clung to them", rather than يتعلق عليهم, "depended on them".

[179]I.e. to manage affairs of state.

[180]The text actually has "5000 years and 239 months", clearly a mistake. Read all as years this date is roughly correct. According to Abū l-Fatḥ the *hijra* dating begins in AM 5047 (see above, p. 50 and n. 31). The year 5239 would thus be AH 192, while al-Amīn in fact reigned from AH 193.

[181]It is more likely that the author is referring here to Jund al-Urdunn rather than to the river Jordan itself. Cf. below, p. 93, where there is a comparison between the application of the restriction in Palestine and its application in al-Urdunn.

[182]The use of وسط with على here is irregular, although the meaning is clear. This could refer to several Biblical passages, e.g. Leviticus 26:33, Ezechiel 6:3, 11:8.

[183]Ms. حدامى; read جذامي.

[184]See Geographical Appendix.

[185]Referring to the Muslims. In *SA* أ may be replaced by ىء. See Stenhouse, "Samaritan Arabic," in Crown, *Samaritans*, pp. 600–601; also Blau, *Grammar*, I, 169, for a case of ميمن. Note also the incorrect use of the case, الميمنين instead of الميمنون, and اختلفو instead of اختلف.

[186]Ms. المقيولين; read المقتولين.

[187]The Ms. reads جيسه, which could be corrected either to جيشه or to جنسه, as is the case in the next line.

[188]See Geographical Appendix.

Dositheans[189] in Arsūf [because] they could not enter into it. [Then] they returned and plundered anything they could [lay their hands on], and we were terrified by night and by day. After that Muḍar[190] and Qays[191] gathered in Caesarea and ransacked the villages and laid the world waste. Mirāhā came forth a second time, and went to the province of Caesarea;[192] the Kinānīyīn[193] emerged from Caesarea with a large army, Mirāhā fled before the Kinānīyīn, and they overtook them and killed a number of them. After that God, in His mercy, brought relief and turned the hardship into joy. Muḥammad [al-Amīn] sent officers and governors over the land, the people were at peace,[194] the wicked were scattered, and we returned to our homes.

After two whole[195] years Muḥammad [al-Amīn] was killed, his brother 'Abd Allāh came to power, and there was strife amongst the people **[221]** everywhere; his rule was of no avail, and the people did not obey him. The people fell into enmity and killed one another—O, how many of them were killed! There was strife and hatred amongst them, women and children were taken into captivity, and a group of the Samaritans was made to follow [into captivity]. [Thus] the curse came true: "Your sons and your daughters shall be given to another people while your eyes look on, and it shall not

---

[189]The text here is not clear. It may read مقالة الدستا[ن] بـ[ا]لارسوف, with مقالة perhaps to be taken as مقاولة, i.e. the "conference place" of the Dositheans. The Dustān or Dositheans were a sect that left the Samaritan mainstream probably in the first century CE. On the Dositheans see Jarl Fossum, "Sects and Movements," in Crown, ed., *The Samaritans*, pp. 299–357.

[190]Here spelt مدر instead of مضر.

[191]Ms. قبس; read قيس.

[192]Ms. بر قيساريه.

[193]Ms. الكاسن; read الكنانيين, which may refer to men from the tribe of Kināna. There is evidence for the presence of the Banū Kināna in Palestine, e.g. 'Alqama ibn Ḥakīm of the Banū Kināna, who served as governor of Palestine in the days of the caliph 'Uthmān. See Gil, *A History of Palestine*, p. 116; I. Hasson, "The Penetration of Arab Tribes in Eretz Israel during the First Century of the *Hijra*", *Cathedra* 32 (1984), p. 64 (Hebrew).

[194]Ms. وهذه الناس; read وهدن الناس (L.C.).

[195]Here two words are covered by an ink blot, perhaps ولتمام سنتين, "after two whole years", presumably from the time affairs were under control again in Palestine, since al-Amīn acceeded to the throne on 24 March 809 and reigned for four and a half years before he was killed on 26 September 813.

be in the power of your hand [to prevent it]."[196] Women were defiled,[197] and Samaritans and others of all the other nations were killed; villages were destroyed and emptied of their inhabitants, the land was not trodden upon by passers-by, and the people were in a state of misfortune night and day. Misfortune multiplied, and locusts came one year after another and ate [both] the tender green plants and those that were dry. [Then] there was a rise in prices, the people weakened and lost their property and their herds, and we were scattered[198] amongst the people and fled in fear of the sword. All of this, and more, [happened] because of the sins and the crimes that the people commited before Almighty God. They pursued[199] vanity, deviated from the truth and from doing good, and broke the precepts of Almighty God. Because of this, all these calamities came upon us; **[222]** but God, blessed be His name, did not see fit to break His pact with Abraham, Isaac and Jacob, peace be upon them, and He granted favour and replaced these calamities with relief.

The Muslims assembled and detained each person in his place, and there was hatred and evil amongst them. A man spilling blood amongst them became a common thing, and many people were apprehended. A man called Masrūr ibn Abū 'Āmir[200] [was in charge of] the whole district of Nablus[201] and security arrangements there; he liked the Samaritans, and the people obeyed him. He was a great warrior and did good, and all the Samaritans in his territory fared well. He chose himself a friend from Sinjil[202] by the

---

[196]Deuteronomy 28:32. The full text of the passage is: "Your sons and your daughters shall be given to another people while your eyes look on, and you will fail with longing for them all the day; and it shall not be in the power of your hand to prevent it".

[197]Ms. تطمت. This verb is an Arabicised form of the Hebrew טמא, "defiled". See above, p. 67 n. 164.

[198]Ms. تبدنا, in the sense of تبدّدنا. See Blau, *Grammar*, I, 169.

[199]Ms. رعبو; read رغبو.

[200]Ms. مسرورين وابو عامر; read مسرور ابن ابو عامر, who is mentioned again, Ms. p. 237:9–10.

[201]Ms. كل عمل نابلس وامنه; read [كان على] كل عمل نابلس وامنه.

[202]This appears in the text as Sinḥil, but it seems most probable that it is Sinjil (see also Ms. p. 237:10), in the centre of Samaria. If indeed this is Sinjil, then it seems to be an early mention of this village. Traditionally it has been accepted that the name stemmed from St. Gilles, the name of this settlement during the Crusader period (its Latin equivalent being S. Egidius). This is based on a Crusader tradition according to which this was the place in which Raymond de St. Gilles, one of the leading Crusader commanders, encamped on his way to Jerusalem. See *Rorgo Fretellus de Nazareth et sa*

name of Ra'āma. The Muslims hated[203] him[204] and said: "We will not be able to kill him except by cunning, and the only one who can get to him is his friend Ra'āma." So they conspired with [Ra'āma] against [Masrūr], and when he visited Ra'āma the latter went up to him while they were eating and killed him. The affliction returned, and from the group of Ra'āma[205] [people] were killed without number or count. The *ra'īs*[206] made an agreement with some bandits,[207] and they took him to Ra'āma and arrested him until they agreed upon a fine,[208] which the Samaritans took upon themselves.[209] [The *ra'īs*] went to his home safe; it was a day of great joy and delight for the community, and they thanked God profusely for the safe return of the *ra'īs*. All of this was the fruit of our divergence from the command **[223]** of God, our Lord.

After these troubles, locusts came and ate the wheat, the best crop of the land,[210] and ate the trees; there was a great rise in prices, and the [price of] wheat reached one measure of wheat (*qabb*) per *dīnār*, and the [price of]

---

description de la Terre sainte, histoire et edition du texte, ed. P.C. Boern (Amsterdam, 1980), p. 29; also V. Guérin, *Description géographique, historique et archéologique de la Palestine, Samarie* (Paris, 1875), II, 34–35. However, it may be this was a popular Crusader etymology that may have been based upon an earlier name in Arabic. This may be hinted also by the fact that Yāqūt, who is usually quite meticulous when it comes to the spelling of geographical names, spells Sinjil in two different ways: as *Sinjil* (III, 162; IV, 312), and as *Sinjīl* (III, 220). The latter form of spelling is also used by al-Harawī, *Kitāb al-ishārāt ilā ma'rifat al-ziyārāt*, ed. J. Sourdel-Thomine (Damascus, 1953), p. 24; this may well be due to the Crusader pronounciation of the name of the settlement, which gained in size and importance during this period. In his *Āthār al-bilād* (Baghdad, 1960), p. 203, s.v. Sinjil, al-Qazwīnī cites al-Iṣṭakhrī, who wrote in the tenth century, as saying that Jubb Yūsuf is found between Nablus and Sinjil. However, this citation is not found, as far as I could see, in the existing editions of al-Iṣṭakhrī. Nevertheless, this may serve as another indication for the existence of the name Sinjil before the Crusades.

203 It seems that here كروه stands for كرهوه.

204 I.e. Masrūr, as will immediately become clear.

205 Ms. دعى اثنين, "[who was] called 'two'" (?), seems quite out of context here.

206 The *ra'īs* was the head of the Samaritan community.

207 Above the word ناس there appears a mark signifying that an additional phrase written in the margin should be inserted here: خراميه واخذوه الى رعامه واعتقله حتى قاطعوهم.

208 Ms. حلمة, in the sense of حمالة.

209 Cf. Ms. p. 211:2–3.

210 The word الارض appears to have been stricken out by the copyist, but clearly belongs here (L.C.).

oil, five measures of weight (*aqsāṭ*)[211] per *dīnār*. But God was loving and no one was harmed,[212] because God spares in His mercy. He is merciful and compassionate, and will not cast a man away.

The following year the locusts struck and the people's possessions dwindled because of the high cost; as long as the trouble increased the dissent continued amongst the people, and the earth became impure[213] from the multitude of the killing and the discharge of dead bodies.[214] Many priests, priests' wives, and the children of the *ḥakākima*[215] and those in charge of precepts[216] and synagogues did not guard their honour.[217] When the daughter of the priest of 'Askar[218] neglected her honour, her father was not able to kill her because the people of [his] village made it impossible for him to do so; [so] he decided to send her away from him and [thus] kept the Word of Almighty God: "And remove it from your midst."[219]

---

[211]The *qisṭ* (= ξέστης, sextarius) was a measure for olive oil used in the Umayyad and 'Abbāsid periods. There were actually three measures called *qisṭ*: one contained 476 grams, another 1.07 kilograms, and another 2.14 kilograms. See *EI* [2], *s.v.* "Makāyīl".

[212]Ms. ولم ينظر احدا; read ولم ينضر احد, and cf. the similar phrases in the Ms., pp. 230:4, 243:3, 258:9–10. On انضر, see Dozy, *Supplément*, II, 4. Here, as elsewhere, the author probably means that no Samaritan was harmed.

[213]Ms. وتطمتمت, to be read something like وتطمأت, from the Hebrew טמא, the last two letters being repeated by mistake. See above, pp. 67 n. 164, 71 n. 197.

[214]According to Lane, *Lexicon*, I.4, 1713, صَلَب is "the watery humour, mixed with blood, that flows from the dead".

[215]This is the usual form that appears in Abū l-Fatḥ, rather than *ḥukamā'*. The *ḥakākima* were a group of seven men, learned in the Torah and its precepts (*aḥkām*), who were appointed to supervise over the priests and the people. According to Abū l-Fatḥ, this institution was established by the famous Samaritan leader Baba Rabbah (end of second century/beginning of third); the *ḥakākima* served as leaders of the Samaritan community and thereby weakened the position of the priests. See Vilmar, pp. 129–32; Stenhouse, trans., pp. 178–82.

[216]Ms. احكام, referring to the precepts of the Torah. See the note above; also Vilmar, pp. 128:14, 130:7; Stenhouse, trans., pp. 178 n. 766, 180 n. 783.

[217]As will become clear below, the point is that desperate circumstances led to a rise in prostitution.

[218]A village located on the outskirts of Nablus. See the Geographical Appendix.

[219]This is apparently a Biblical citation, although I could not find a passage with a similar wording. The expression من جملتك is the accepted Samaritan translation for מקרבך, "from your midst"; e.g. Deuteronomy 13:6, 17:7, where ובערת הרע מקרבך is translated as وتنقي القبيح من جملتك or وتنقي السو من جملتك. It may be that this is a free translation that

The Samaritans of ʻAskar had not been affected by anything because they were so strong, but they did not treat her charitably or take into consideration the fact that she had strayed on account of hunger. Since they did not treat her or others besides her charitably, God increased their misery in several ways, having confirmed their guilt, for God **[224]** will not show favour and will take no bribe,[220] but rather judges by truth and justice,[221] because God increases the hardship of whoever can do good yet does not do it, and makes him taste misfortune so that he will love God and rejoice. Then the people ate and were satiated by the grace of God, the roads were travelled and the people were heartened,[222] and the Samaritans from all places went up to Mt. Gerizim; they fasted and prayed and thanked God profusely and praised Him for His favour in having removed this misery from them and replaced it with joy and mercy.

After thirteen years of the reign of ʻAbd Allāh al-Ma'mūn, he sent a man known as Khālid ibn Yazīd[223] and with him a great army. The people were unaware of his approach until he suddenly appeared in Palestine.[224] All the Muslims were in great fear of him and despaired of their lives; the rebels

---

the author chose for this same phrase.

[220]Ms. رشا stands for رشوة. The phrase refers to Deuteronomy 10:17: "For the Lord... shows no favour and takes no bribe". يرفع وجه, lit. "show face", is a literal translation of ישא פנים.

[221]Ms. الاحكام حق وصدق, the syntax of which seems quite awkward here.

[222]Cf. لَبّ, according to Lane, *Lexicon*, I.7, 2642, "one who renders himself near to people by affection and friendship (or is friendly and affectionate to them)".

[223]This is Khālid ibn Yazīd ibn Mazyad al-Shaybānī, who was sent by al-Ma'mūn in 207/821–22 to assert his rule in Egypt, which was effectively ruled at the time by two rivals who controlled different parts of the country. On him and his family see P. Crone, *Slaves on Horses* (Cambridge, 1980), p. 170 no. 68. ʻUbayd Allāh ibn al-Sarī (*ibid.*, p. 75) controlled al-Fusṭāṭ and the south, while the north was ruled by ʻAlī al-Jarawī (for sources concerning his revolt see C.E. Bosworth, trans., *The History of al-Ṭabarī*, XXXII: *The Reunification of the ʻAbbāsid Caliphate* (Albany, 1987), p. 164 n. 494). Khālid did indeed engage in several bloody battles in Egypt before he was finally defeated, captured and turned out of Egypt by ʻUbayd Allāh in February 823. See al-Kindī, *Kitāb al-wulāt*, ed. R. Guest (Leiden, 1912), pp. 173–76. The dating of the invasion by Khālid ibn Yazīd to the thirteenth year of al-Ma'mūn's reign may refer back to the date of al-Ma'mūn's rebellion against al-Amīn, i.e. 194/810, thus bringing his period of reign to thirteen years. These two years are usually excluded: see al-Ṭabarī, III, 1140. This is also supported by the computation cited below, p. 80 n. 277.

[224]See al-Yaʻqūbī, *Ta'rīkh*, II, 555.

decided to flee and abandon all their possessions, but when they saw [Khālid] leaving for Egypt, they were safe again, as they had been before; they harmed the Samaritans and killed a group of them. Khālid passed through and made his way down to Egypt, and the Egyptians waged war against him; he was a great warrior, and he killed a great many of them in battle and besieged and afflicted them. **[225]** Then they took him prisoner, and when they captured him all his companions took to flight. The Egyptians detained him for some time, and when they let him go again[225] he went to his country. All the years from Adam to the arrival of Khālid ibn Yazīd in the land of Egypt were 5250.[226]

After four years 'Abd Allāh the king sent a man called 'Abd Allāh ibn Ṭāhir[227] accompanied by a great army, the like of which in might[228] and destruction had never been known in action against the rebels.[229] When he went forth from Baghdad he conquered the lands before him; God gave him victory and worked good deeds through him, and he crushed all the tyrants of the land. Upon his arrival at Ḥimṣ, Naṣr ibn Shabath[230] rose against him with a great army of brigands, so ['Abd Allāh ibn Ṭāhir] besieged Ḥimṣ and beleaguered Naṣr until he requested a guarantee of safety (*amān*)[231] and left Ḥimṣ. When he emerged, 'Abd Allāh seized and enchained him; he took all of his possessions and his children, and sent him to Baghdad. He came to Palestine in the first year after the Sabbatical Year,[232] in the month of Kānūn al-Awwal, in the year 212 of the reign of Islam,[233] and no one waged

---

[225]For this use of عاد see Blau, *Grammar*, II, 442.

[226]According to the computation of Abū l-Fatḥ the *hijra* took place in the year 5047 after Creation; therefore 5250 = 825 CE. This computation seems to be somewhat imprecise, since the author himself states several lines later that 'Abd Allāh ibn Ṭāhir arrived in Egypt four years after Khālid ibn Yazīd, in December 827. Cf. above, p. 74 n. 223, and also below, n. 233.

[227]'Abd Allāh ibn Ṭāhir was appointed by al-Ma'mūn in charge of the region between Raqqa and Egypt in 821–22. In 825–26 he managed to quell Naṣr ibn Shabath's rebellion, which is mentioned below, and proceeded to Egypt, where he succeeded in establishing al-Ma'mūn's rule.

[228]Ms. وراه. Cf. *CA*, وَزَأ, "strong", "sturdy"; Kazimirski, *Dictionnaire*, II, 1527.

[229]Ms. جواريح, *sic!*

[230]The leader of a group of Qaysī rebels who finally surrendered to 'Abd Allāh ibn Ṭāhir in 824–25. For parallels and bibliography see al-Ṭabarī/Bosworth, *Reunification*, 138–44.

[231]I.e. surrendered in return for an *amān*, a formal pledge of safety and protection.

[232]Ms. سنة السمطة, an Arabic form of the Biblical term שְׁמִטָּה.

[233]December 827.

war against him [there].

[Then] he went down to Egypt **[226]** and waged war against it; the rebel there was called Saʿīd ibn Sarī,[234] and he took him prisoner and conveyed him to Baghdad to the king.[235] He conquered the land to the frontier of Ifrīqiya,[236] God established mercy for the people in his heart, and he lightened the affliction which was upon them—except for what the rebels[237] did before him, [an affliction to which] there was no limit:[238] all the people[239] had left their places vacant, run away and strayed from their beliefs. [ʿAbd Allāh] ordered that anyone who paid[240] the *kharāj* would receive a certificate[241] so that no one could take anything further from him, as had been done previously. Because of that affliction[242] many people were ruined; each [governor] who came was such an oppressor that many people were ruined and innumerable families[243] perished, and towns and villages were vacated and fell into ruin. When relief came, a sadness came over anyone who had lost his family and relatives[244] during the times of the oppression and hardship.

After him, there was a king who conquered Palestine (?);[245] [he stayed] until he had appointed governors throughout the country, and then returned

---

[234]The Sarī mentioned here is ʿUbayd Allāh ibn al-Sarī (see above, p. 74 n. 223), who was indeed deported from Egypt to Baghdad, where he led quite a comfortable life. For sources and bibliography, see al-Ṭabarī/Bosworth, *Reunification*, pp. 160–61 n. 482.

[235]That is, to the caliph. According to al-Ṭabarī, III, 1093, ʿUbayd Allāh ibn al-Sarī was brought to Baghdad on 23 Rajab 211 (29 October 826).

[236]Ms. الي نحم افرىقيه; read: الى تخم افريقية.

[237]Ms. الخوارجى here seems to be a combination of the plural and the singular forms: خارجي and خوارج.

[238]This last part of the sentence is somewhat unclear, and the translation is therefore tentative.

[239]This description seems to regress to the previous state of affliction just mentioned.

[240]The term used here is وزن خراج; see Dozy, *Supplément*, II, 800.

[241]Ms. خط.

[242]Ms. سيت ذلك, instead of سيئة ذلك.

[243]Ms. قبايل.

[244]Ms. جماعه; read جماعته.

[245]Ms. سنين. L.C. suggests that this is a misreading of a badly worn فلسطين, "Palestine", which fits into the context very well.

to his land.[246] After his departure there revolted[247] a rebel called Ibn Firāsa. He was an evil man who hated the Samaritans; he wanted them to abandon their religion in favour of his own, **[227]** and punished them and filled the prisons[248] with them—men, women and children. He oppressed them with hunger and thirst, and many people died in the prisons. They had[249] to pay money[250] in order to be allowed to circumcise their sons on the eighth day; he who had money [had] the gentiles[251] testify for him that he had paid, and he returned a Samaritan.[252] Many people abandoned their religion, [still] many[253] [others] showed endurance and patience until relief came from God, who sent mercy because He is merciful and benevolent.

Chapter

The Muslims gathered once again in opposition to al-Ma'mūn, who was [called] 'Abd Allāh,[254] and killed the governor of Jericho (Rīḥā).[255] [Al-Ma'mūn] departed[256] for Jerusalem (Bayt al-Maqdis) accompanied by many soldiers.[257] When his nephew 'Alī was killed in Jericho, he ordered that many

---

246 It may be that this obscure statement refers to Abū Isḥāq Muḥammad ibn Hārūn al-Rashīd, who is referred to as " king" here because he was the future caliph al-Mu'taṣim. Abū Isḥāq did indeed serve as governor of Syria and Egypt after 'Abd Allāh ibn Ṭāhir, between the years 213–15/828–30; he personally quelled the revolts in Egypt and later returned to Baghdad. See al-Kindī, *Wulāt*, pp. 188–89; al-Ṭabarī, III, 1099–1100, 1101, 1103; al-Ya'qūbī, *Ta'rīkh*, II, 567.

247 Ms. نار; read ثار.

248 Ms. الحيوش; read الحبوس, a reading confirmed on the next line: ومات ناس كثير في الحبوس.

249 Ms. احاجو; read احتاجو.

250 Cf. Ms. p. 226:6: وزن خراج, and note thereto, p. 76 n. 240 above.

251 I.e. the Muslims.

252 Ms. שמרי. Presumably it is meant here that the child was circumcised.

253 Ms. اكثر, rather than كثر.

254 More precisely, Abū Ja'far 'Abd Allāh al-Ma'mūn ibn Hārūn al-Rāshīd.

255 Ms. ريحا, = ريحاء or اريحا; see Yāqūt, II, 884–85.

256 Ms. وخرجواج, with جوا crossed out, for وخرج.

257 There is no other evidence concerning al-Ma'mūn's personal presence in Palestine, and specifically in Jerusalem, apart from a tradition in Nu'aym ibn Ḥammād, *Kitāb al-fitan*, ed. L.I. Conrad (Wiesbaden, forthcoming), no. 1160. It seems likely that al-Ma'mūn passed through Palestine on his way to Egypt to quell the rebellion there. He arrived in Egypt on 10 Muḥarram 217 (16 February 832) and left 47 or 49 days later, towards the end of March. See al-Ṭabarī, III, 1106–1107; al-Kindī, *Wulāt*, p. 192; al-Ya'qūbī,

people be rounded up. He waged war[258] again against the dissenters, and God gave him victory; he killed 22 of their men and burnt the fortress in which they had taken refuge.[259] They waged war against him, and a group of them went on to Bayt Jibrīn and raised troops there. The king's brother,[260] **[228]** whose name was Ibrāhīm,[261] came accompanied by a great and mighty army and went to Bayt Jibrīn. He called upon them to offer them a guarantee of safety (*amān*), but they did not accept it. So he waged war against them[262] and fought them,[263] and overtook them and destroyed them; he seized their possessions and ruined their villages, and took many of the people [captive] in iron fetters and conveyed them to Baghdad. Now the evil man—that is Ibn Firāsa—ran away and was never heard of again. And God brought relief to him who persevered in his patience and his belief, because He is merciful and benevolent, and everyone returned to his place safe and sound.

Ibrāhīm, the king's brother,[264] departed and went on to Egypt, but they did not receive him favourably and waged war against him.[265] He killed

---

Ta'rīkh, II, 569. The information concerning his visit to Jerusalem is well-supported by the inscriptions on the copper plates found above the northern and eastern entrances of the Dome of the Rock, which bear his name and are dated to Rabīʿ II 216 (May–June 831). See M. van Brechem, ed., *Matériaux pour un corpus inscriptionum arabicarum*, 2B, II: *Jérusalem-Haram* (Cairo, 1925–27), pp. 246–55; K.A.C. Creswell, *Early Muslim Architecture*, I: *Umayyads* (Oxford, 1932), pp. 47, 56. See also above, pp. 31–32.

[258]Ms. اوفف حرب; read اوقف حرب. This seems to be a very irregular usage; the phrase واقف حرب is also used in the sense of "to stand up in battle".

[259]Ms. نختمو; read يحتمو.

[260]Ms. اخوا, instead of اخو. See Blau, *Grammar*, II, 317, 318, 320.

[261]Ibrāhīm ibn al-Mahdī was al-Ma'mūn's uncle and Hārūn al-Rashīd's brother; he was caliph for a short period of time between 5 Muḥarram 202 (24 July 817) and Dhū l-Ḥijja 203 (June 819), when he abdicated and withdrew from political life; see *EI* ², III, 987. This does not fit our context at all; in addition, since on the next page (Ms. p. 229) it is clearly mentioned that this so-called Ibrāhīm was proclaimed caliph after al-Ma'mūn, it follows that the reference is obviously to Abū Isḥāq Muḥammad ibn Hārūn al-Muʿtaṣim (see above, p. 77 n. 246; below, n. 264, p. 80 n. 278). The reading "Ibrāhīm" therefore seems to be a mistake.

[262]See above, n. 258.

[263]Ms. قتلهم; read قاتلهم. Perhaps the sequence of events was that he fought them, they fled, and then he overtook them and killed them.

[264]See above, n. 261.

[265]The presence of the future caliph al-Muʿtaṣim on this journey to Egypt, presumably accompanying al-Ma'mūn, is not mentioned anywhere else as far as I could see. It is not improbable, though, since he was in charge of Palestine and Syria at the time. See above,

a great many of them, destroyed their villages, and led their women and children and their dependents into captivity.[266] In addition to this, he took an enormous and fabulous amount of booty and appointed governors over the whole country. He returned to his country in the fifth year after the Sabbatical Year, in [the month of] Nīsān.[267] Al-Ma'mūn came to Damascus and built there very strong forts;[268] he arrived there in [the month of] Aylūl in the fifth year after the Sabbatical Year, which is the year 217 of the reign of Islam.[269] From Adam to the time of the arrival of al-Ma'mūn in Damascus was 5264 [**229**] years.[270] He left supervisors on his behalf, and they destroyed all the strongholds in which the remaining [rebels] had fortified themselves, and destroyed the citadel built by Zeno on top of the mountain.[271] They seized a group of dissenters, bound them in iron fetters and sent them to Baghdad.

Al-Ma'mūn remained in Damascus seven months;[272] from there he went to the land of the Rūm (Byzantium)[273] and there conquered many towns and villages. He returned to his land in the Sabbatical Year and ordered that the land be measured and the trees be counted, and this was done. He left in

---

pp. 77 n. 246, 78 n. 261, and below, p. 80 n. 278.

[266]Ms. سبا, instead of سبى. See Blau, *Grammar*, I, 190–91; also Stenhouse, "Samaritan Arabic," pp. 599–601.

[267]I.e. April 832. The fifth year after the Sabbatical Year is AH 217, as noted in the following sentence. This is the date of his departure from Egypt, as corroborated by al-Ya'qūbī, *Ta'rīkh*, II, 569, who reports that al-Ma'mūn left Egypt three days before the end of Ṣafar 217, i.e. on 2 April 832.

[268]This does not seem to be recorded elsewhere.

[269]September 832.

[270]This is based upon the computation that the *hijra* took place in AM 5047; see above, p. 50 and n. 31.

[271]See above, p. 59 n. 97.

[272]This would be already Ṣafar or Rabī' I 218 (April 833).

[273]Here the author seems to confuse two different invasions of Byzantium by al-Ma'mūn. The first invasion took place some time in AH 217 and included the long siege of Loulon, a fortress located northwest of Adana; this was a successful journey from which al-Ma'mūn returned in AH 218. The second invasion, which started on 16 Jumādā II 218 (9 July 833), was the one from which al-Ma'mūn never returned; he died in Byzantine territory on 18 Rajab 218 (9 August 833). See al-Ṭabarī, III, 1109–11, 1134–41; al-Ya'qūbī, *Ta'rīkh*, II, 570, 573.

Palestine a man who levied the land taxes,[274] called Abū l-Jārūd (?).[275] He oppressed the people and burdened them terribly, as none of those before him had done, and he sapped the people [until] towns and villages were ruined and emptied of their inhabitants. But God brought upon the earth peace from [all] this, satiety, and belief, and did not impede them.[276] ‘Abd Allāh al-Ma’mūn reigned for 22 years and died.[277]

Chapter

His brother Ibrāhīm[278] rose after him, and the people opposed him. A crowd gathered **[230]** and went up to Mt. Gerizim[279] on the Feast of Tabernacles, and [the enemy] came down in order to loot Nablus. The officer in charge (*za‘īm*)[280] left with his forces. The people of the town had acted against him earlier,[281] so the officer in charge (*za‘īm*) and his forces fled, and the enemy entered and looted and burnt many houses, and burnt the synagogue and the synagogues of the Dositheans.[282] But God had mercy, and none of the Samaritans were harmed.[283] They remained [there] looting for three days. [When] the king heard of it he sent two commanders, one called Ṣāliḥ

---

[274]Ms. يجلي الارض, in the sense of ياخذ جالية الارض, i.e. referring to one who collects taxes from non-Muslims? See above, p. 57 n. 87, and below, p. 82 n. 299.

[275]Ms. ابو الجرود, probably to be read as ابو الجارود.

[276]من هذا seems to belong to the word "peace" rather than "satiety", where it appears.

[277]Al-Ma’mūn's reign was usually counted from the time the war between al-Amīn and al-Ma’mūn ended, and is thus calculated as twenty years, five months and thirteen days (see al-Ṭabarī, III, 1140); the author of our text, however, seems to prefer a count which includes the two years of al-Ma’mūn's rebellion. This is corroborated by al-Ya‘qūbī, who says that "from the day he was acknowledged as caliph (سلم عليه بالخلافة) during the life of the Deposed (i.e. al-Amīn) until he died, there are 22 years, and from the killing of the Deposed there are twenty years, five months and 25 days". See al-Ya‘qūbī, *Ta’rīkh*, II, 574; also above, p. 74 n. 223.

[278]The reference here is without doubt to al-Mu‘taṣim, who ruled for nine years from 218/833 to 227/842; see above, pp. 77 n. 246, 78 nn. 261, 264. He, not Ibrāhīm, who is mentioned above, was al-Ma’mūn's brother.

[279]Ms. الى جبل הר גר[יזים].

[280]Ms. زعيم. Cf. Ms. p. 231:10.

[281]Ms. وكان اهل البلد قد عملوا عليه.

[282]See above, p. 70 n. 189.

[283]Ms. وما نظ; read وما انضرّ, and cf. Ms. pp. 223:3: ولم ينظر احدا for ولم ينضر احد, 243:3: وما انضر احد, 258:9–10: ولم ينضر احد من السامرة.

and the other called Ja'far, and they came to Tiberias (Ṭabarīya) and there killed a group of rebels and plundered their villages. Then they came to Beth Shean (Baysān) and there encountered a group of rebels seeking to loot it and killed a great many of them. [Then] the two commanders[284] went on and arrived in Ramla, and when the inhabitants of the land noticed this they mobilized great armies. The two commanders proceeded to Bayt Jibrīn and killed the rebels who were there. [When] they went up to Jerusalem on their way to Nablus, a group of rebels rose against them and attacked them in Wādī l-Jīb,[285] and [the commanders] killed a great many of [the rebels]. The Samaritans approached [the commanders] and took from them a guarantee of safety (*amān*), and [the commanders] told [the people of Nablus]: "We are responsible for the safekeeping of anyone who is in **[231]** the city, [but] we will kill whoever is outside it." They came to Nablus, and there they came upon rebels seeking to plunder it; they seized them and crucified them at the eastern gate of the city.[286]

The *ra'īs* Nethan'el died in the second year after the Sabbatical Year[287] in the month of Kāsālā'em,[288] and was buried in the grave which he had made for his son Yehoqīm,[289] whom he had wanted to appoint *ra'īs* in his lifetime. When he died he was buried there, and his grave is opposite the tomb of

[284] Ms. العايدين; read القايدين.

[285] Probably the northern tributary of the Soreq, the main stream draining the area of Jerusalem, running north–south near al-Jīb.

[286] Crucifixion in Islam was a criminal punishment in which the body of the criminal, either living or dead, was affixed to a beam or tree trunk and exposed for several days. It was imposed in various circumstances, usually in cases of cruel robbery or treachery. See *EI*^{2}, *s.v.* "Ṣalb".

[287] If the previous Sabbatical year ended in AH 218–19, as is stated above, then this must be AH 220–21 (835–36 CE).

[288] Kāsālā'em (כסלים, Hebrew Kislev, כסלו; see Powels, "The Samaritan Calendar", p. 709 n. 73) is the Samaritan parallel of Kānūn al-Awwal, or December 835. See Powels, "The Samaritan Calendar", pp. 710–11.

[289] Ms. יהקים. It appears that he was buried in the same grave with his son, who was already buried there.

Zeno,[290] close by the road that leads to al-Sārīn[291] and points thither, as was necessary because of the fear and desolation.[292] His priesthood (*imāma*) lasted for 50 years, and his grandson took his place.

The two commanders went on to Ramla, and people reverted to their former ways and gathered and came, intending to plunder Nablus once more. Word reached the officer in charge (*za'īm*) who was in the city, and his fellow officers came out with him;[293] the men of the city also came forth to wage war against them at close quarters (?).[294] They killed many of the dissidents; many of them were crucified, and the rest fled from the sword. Victory was given to the commanders,[295] and they conquered all the land of Palestine. They arrested the heads **[232]** of the bandits of 'Aqdīd,[296] chained them[297] and sent them in irons to Baghdad, and God brought security and welfare upon the earth[298]...the *kharāj* and the *jāliya*[299] and they oppressed the people terribly; people sold their possessions, and a head of cattle [sold] for one *dīnār* because of the hardship they were in, and five heads of sheep [sold]

---

[290] Abū l-Fatḥ reports in the *Kitāb* that Zeno built a tomb on top of Mt. Gerizim, south of the temple, and buried his son in it. He placed a cross on top of this tomb and ordered the Samaritans to kneel before it under penalty of death. See Vilmar, pp. 171–72. On the question of Zeno's personal presence in Palestine during that time see A.D. Crown, "Samaritans in the Byzantine Orbit," *BJRL* 69 (1986), p. 131, and additional references therein.

[291] Al-Sārīn may be Jabal al-Sīrī, a summit on the northwest side of the Gerizim ridge. The name appears earlier in the text; see Vilmar, p. 111ult (Stenhouse, trans., p. 153), where al-Sārīn is a place close by Nablus where the High Priest assembles the Samaritans.

[292] Ms. وما تلي كما تجب من الخوف والفرع; read وما يلي كما يجب من الخوف والفرغ (L.C.). It seems that the security situation was too bad to allow for erection of a tomb of his own.

[293] Ms. وخرج معه من اصحابه المقدمين; more coherent would be: وخرج بمن معه من اصحابه المقدمين.

[294] Ms. منا ربه; perhaps a misreading of مقاربة (L.C.).

[295] Ms. وجعل النصر القايدين; read للقاينين, unless وجعل is an active verb, in which the subject is God.

[296] Unidentified name.

[297] Ms. وقبروهم; read وقيدوهم (L.C.). This was usual practice.

[298] It seems that the scribe has skipped something here, since the sentence is discontinuous: وجعل الله في الارض امن وخير الخراج والجالية وضيقوا علي الناس كثير. It is hard to imagine that this should be read: "and God brought upon the earth security and the best of the *kharāj* and the *jāliya* and they oppressed the people", etc.

[299] The poll tax, more commonly known as the *jizya*. See Lane, *Lexicon*, I.2, 448. See also above, pp. 57 n. 87, 80 n. 274.

for one *dīnār*. But God conferred good in the end, and no one strayed from his faith. [In fact], they oppressed the Muslims more than they oppressed the Samaritans.[300] Due to God's love, the year passed without a single one of the Samaritans asking for assistance; blessed be He who changes but is not changed, for He does not forget the covenant of the righteous and does not abandon them, for he is God—their God.[301] Felicitations to he who leaves[302] the path of dissension and walks in the path of the truth.

When the *imām*[303] Pinḥas, son of Nethan'el, came into office, he annulled the system of the *ḥakākima*;[304] they were not invested with any authority, nor did they—or even the shaykhs of the Samaritans—exercise any. By my life, things could have turned out quite badly; but they did not come to such an end, or even take an iniquitous turn, since people acted in accordance with their command.[305] Praised be He who shows forbearance, and whom nothing escapes. We were forced to call upon judges without wisdom, who did not know true from false.

The synagogue of Nablus, which had burnt down, was in urgent need of the aid of Almighty God,[306] who aided the *ra'īs* Dartā, the head of the Samaritans. He went about **[233]** and raised [money] from the Samaritans and built it without wood, except for the middle building, and there was great joy and happiness among all the Samaritans. One of the *ḥakākima* saw in [his] sleep that they would perform the prayer and go up [to the mountain] on Monday on the holiday of Pentecost (*ḥajj al-sawābīʿ*). They went down from the mountain to the place of prayer[307] and stayed there until the evening,

---

[300] An interesting remark indicating that already in the first half of the ninth century there were permanent Muslim settlements in the area of Samaria, as opposed to wanderers, rebels and bandits.

[301] Ms. الههم, perhaps following the biblical expression כי אני ה׳ אלהיכם, "For I am God, your God", for example, as in Exodus 6:7, Leviticus 11:44, 19:2, 3, 4, 10, etc.

[302] Ms. يمرج عن الطريق, in the sense of "leaves the road [to pasture somewhere else]". See Lane, *Lexicon*, I.6, 2704.

[303] This is an alternative term for *ra'īs*, both used to designate the Samaritan High Priest.

[304] On the institution of the *ḥakākima* see above, p. 73 n. 215. See also below, pp. 89, 93, where this event is referred to again.

[305] Ms. ينولاه, for يناولونه or *SA* يناولوه? For this sense of ناول see Dozy, *Supplément*, II, 738. Ms. انه لسيت is perhaps a corruption of انه لسيئت or انه لسيّئة.

[306] Ms. اردت, instead of the correct ارادت.

[307] Ms. مصلا, instead of مصلّى. For the occurence of this change in *verba tertiae infirmae* see Blau, *Grammar*, I, 190–91; also Stenhouse, "Samaritan Arabic," pp. 599–600. Cases

and they did the same on Tuesday. The people remained in peace for five years.

The king Ibrāhīm[308] entered the land of Byzantium and devastated a large city of theirs called Amorium (ʿAmmūriya).[309] He aggravated[310] all the creeds,[311] just like his son Jaʿfar,[312] who provoked the hatred of all the people when he rose [to power] and reigned. Ibrāhīm ruled for nine years and died.[313] Before his death, Ayhūd (?)[314] came forth...[315] and rose against him. The beginning of his uprising[316] [was thus]: he came out to

---

of such change in nouns are apparently rarer.

[308]Again, actually referring to al-Muʿtaṣim.

[309]The most detailed description of this famous expedition, which took place in the summer of 838, is given by al-Ṭabarī, III, 1236–56. For translation and commentary see C.E. Bosworth, trans., *The History of al-Ṭabarī*, XXXIII: *Storm and Stress along the Northern Frontiers of the ʿAbbāsid Caliphate* (Albany, 1991), pp. 97–121. See also a detailed description of the conquest of Amorium in Ibn Manẓūr, *Mukhtaṣar*, XXIII, 215–17.

[310]Ms. يحرب, for which L.C. suggests يخوّف, "to fill with fear", with reference to Ms. p. 236:3–4.

[311]The word *umma*, pl. *umam*, is used in a similar manner in reference to Aḥmad ibn Ṭūlūn; see Ms. p. 251:11: وخافت منه كل الامم هو مد يد على كنايسهم, "all the religious communities were in fear of him, lest he extend [his] hand to their houses of worship". In this case it is quite clear that the reference is to members of other religious groups. *Umma* is also used in this manner in reference to al-Mutawakkil's decrees: see Ms. p. 239:5, 6.

[312]Al-Muʿtaṣim was succeeeded by his son Abū Jaʿfar Hārūn al-Wāthiq bi'llāh (r. 227–32/842–47), who was succeeded in turn by his brother Abū l-Faḍl Jaʿfar al-Mutawakkil (r. 232–47/847–61). Since al-Wāthiq is called Hārūn in the text, while al-Mutawakkil is referred to as Jaʿfar, it seems likely that the reference here is to al-Mutawakkil rather than to al-Wāthiq.

[313]See above, pp. 77 n. 246, 78 nn. 261, 264, 80 n. 278. Al-Muʿtaṣim did indeed reign from 218/833 to 227/842.

[314]Ms. ايهود, perhaps a name.

[315]Here there is a gap of two or three words in the text. From the following pages it becomes clear that the author is describing the rebellion of Abū l-Ḥarb al-Mubarqaʿ al-Yamānī at the end of al-Muʿtaṣim's reign and in the days of al-Wāthiq. A detailed description is given by al-Ṭabarī, III, 1319–22. Al-Yaʿqūbī, *Ta'rīkh*, II, 586, mentions that his name was Tamīm al-Lakhmī; he was called Abū Ḥarb, and his *laqab* was al-Mubarqaʿ. See also Ibn al-Athīr, *Kāmil*, VI, 522–23; Ibn ʿAsākir, *Ta'rīkh madīnat Dimashq*, XVIII, *s.v.* Rajā' ibn Abī Ayyūb al-Ḥiḍārī, pp. 94–95; H. Eisenstein, "Die Erhebung des Mubarqaʿ in Palästina", *Orientalia* 55 (1986), pp. 454–58; Gil, *History of Palestine*, pp. 295–96.

[316]Ms. تمرده.

the meadow[317] after the manner[318] of the bandits, and when a group [of them] had gathered around him, they came and plundered a village by al-Ṭawāḥīn[319] and came to Baṣalīyā.[320] [When] the governor (*wālī*) of Ramla heard of this, he left in his place[321] a commanding officer (*muqaddam*).[322] [Abū] Ḥarb fled to al-Shiʿr,[323] which is in Jordan,[324] and [the governor] was not strong enough to overcome him; he then returned to Ramla and went up to Baṣalīyā, leaving in charge the commanding officer (*muqaddam*), a man by the name of Ibrāhīm ibn Narfata.

[234] [When] the commanding officer arrived the rebels attacked him and killed many of his men; whoever fled was unharmed. The people were in great fear and assembled in Nablus. The chief (*zaʿīm*) of Ramla[325] came up to Nablus, and when he encamped outside it he was told: "If you want Abū Ḥarb, he is camped at ʿAqraba."[326] He set out at night and made his way towards him and waged war upon him in the mountains; a group of

[317]No doubt in reference to a specific place.

[318]Ms. زاي; read راى. L.C. understands زاي as the colloquial form of *CA* زي, which would give: "he came out to the meadow dressed as bandits dress".

[319]Literally, "the mills", located around the springs of Ra's al-ʿAyn, by the fort of Antipatris (Abū Fuṭrus), not far from Ramla; see *EI* 2, *s.v.* "Nahr Abī Fuṭrus". Ibn al-Athīr, *Kāmil*, VI, 523, mentions that the rebellion started in the vicinity of Ramla.

[320]Here the text reads بصليا; see Geographical Appendix. The reading يصليا two lines lower is an error.

[321]This should be خلى; see Stenhouse, "Samaritan Arabic," pp. 599–600.

[322]Apparently so that he could follow him and fight him.

[323]This refers to the biblical Mt. Seʿīr or the "land of Seʿīr" in the land of Edom, i.e. southern Transjordan, usually called al-Sharāt in the Muslim sources. The name *al-Shiʿr* for Seʿīr appears in the Samaritan Arabic translation of Genesis 36:8, 20, 30; see H. Shehadeh, *The Arabic Translation of the Samaritan Pentateuch*, I: *Genesis–Exodus* (Jerusalem, 1989). See also the Palestinian Aramaic translation of the Bible, *Targum Pseudo-Yonatan*, of Genesis 32:4, 36:8, where Seʿīr is translated as *Gabala*, i.e. the Byzantine district of *Gabalene*, Biblical Edom.

[324]Al-Ṭabarī (III, 1319) mentions that he hid in "one of the mountains in Jordan". The name mentioned here is not identified. In fact, al-Sharāt's status is not clear. There are geographers who claim it is part of Jund Dimashq, some say it is annexed to Palestine, while still others claim they are separate districts. See A. Elad, "Two Identical Inscriptions from Jund Filasṭīn from the Reign of the ʿAbbāsīd Caliph, al-Muqtadir", *JESHO* 35 (1992), pp. 337–38.

[325]Presumably the governor (*wālī*) who was pursuing Abū Ḥarb.

[326]Ms. فهوا نانزل في; presumably فهوا نازل في.

Muḥammad's companions was killed,[327] and [the others] returned to Ramla in disorder. The commanding officer (*muqaddam*) of Ramla had appointed over Nablus one of its people, Abū Nimr (?)[328] Mūsā ibn Hārūn, an oppressive man, and he went in flight to Ramla.

The rebel then asserted himself, and throngs of rebels gathered around him. They came to Qaryat Qūzā[329] and plundered [it]; [Abū Ḥarb] came to the district and collected from every village according to its ability, and came up to Nablus and descended upon it and demanded money from it, [but] they gave him nothing. Fighting broke out on Thursday, and people from both parties were killed. He passed the night in Sālim, and on Friday morning he appeared with a huge army, defeated the people, and entered Nablus, and killed. . . .[330]

[235] But suddenly,[331] God alleviated [the situation] through a man called ʿAlī ibn ʿAmbar with a small troop of cavalry (?).[332] When they heard that the army had arrived, Banū[333] Muḥammad were put to flight by the sword;[334] they clashed, and many on both sides were killed. The people rejoiced; but it was not over yet, for when it was night Ibn ʿAmbar left and departed to his place. The people left fleeing on the night of the Sabbath: fathers did not wait for their sons, nor sons for their fathers, such was the fear. Voices of priests, heads and dignitaries (*muqaddamīn*) [were heard] crying and screaming because of what had happened to them on that Sabbath. The inhabitants of the city fled from the sword. As for the *raʾīs*, he did not leave and was struck by the sword. He was taken down to Hebron (Khalīl), where he died and was buried, God aid his soul. When Abū Ḥarb saw that the

---

[327] This could be read either as وقَتَل or as وقُتِل. "Muḥammad" is probably Abū Ḥarb or one of his men, as becomes clear in the next sentences.

[328] Ms. للبنمر; perhaps ابو نمر (L.C.)?

[329] See Geographical Appendix.

[330] The scribe was apparently unable to decipher the text here. L.C. reads وقُتِل بجيرته والي هوا تجبّر, "and in a place nearby a governing official who was causing trouble was killed". Cf. above, p. 56 n. 79.

[331] See Blau, *Grammar*, II, 462.

[332] Ms. خبل; perhaps read خيل (L.C.).

[333] The Ms. here is not completely clear and appears to bear بنو; read بنو?

[334] The copyist seems again to have been at a loss, as at the bottom of the last page. Ms. هربله; read هزيمة, thus giving: انهزم بنو محمد هزيمة السيف. Cf. هربوا هروب السيف. It is not clear who the Banū Muḥammad mentioned here are; it can nevertheless be assumed that this is a part of Abū Ḥarb's army.

people had left their possessions and fled, he returned and entered Nablus, and burned and looted for seventeen[335] days. The looting persisted, and we were neglected throughout the land; thus the curse was fulfilled: "And he will send a sword behind them, and he will leave your country barren and your villages destroyed."[336] Nothing remained[337] of the curse, which did not take effect upon us.

The coward[338] left **[236]** and went on to Nīsā/Yansā (?)[339] and destroyed it; he continued to Baysān and levied from the people a great amount of money, and went on to ʻAtīl[340] and looted it. He turned to the south,[341] and many villages were plundered there; the people endured great hardship, and he was hated among all the creeds. We were overtaken by many calamities,[342] and terrible death came upon the people. O, how many left their place and did not return! Asasabī,[343] king of Israel,[344] pledged the Samaritans in oath[345] in front of Mt. Gerizim[346] and made it known that they would not eat with the Dositheans, drink with them, marry them or give [their children] in marriage to them.

As for Abū Ḥarb, he returned to Ramla and fought with [its people], who were not able to rid themselves of him. [When] the king Ibrāhīm[347]

---

335 Ms. سبعا عشر, probably influenced by حدا عشر or اثنا عشر. See Blau, *Grammar*, I, 238–39.

336 Leviticus 26:33.

337 Ms. ولم تبقا شى.

338 Ms. الجبانى, perhaps a misreading of الجبّان, "coward", i.e. he had dared attack only when they were defenseless (L.C.).

339 Unidentified name.

340 See Geographical Appendix.

341 The word *qibla* was used by the Samaritans both for Mt. Gerizim, or the "chosen place" (Vilmar, p. 65:2ff.; Stenhouse, trans., p. 85ff.), and simply for "south", as in Arabic (Vilmar, p. 26:5; Stenhouse, trans., p. 32).

342 Ms. وايد; read موائد. See Kazimirski, *Dictionnaire*, II, 1472.

343 Ms. اسسبى.

344 No doubt a reference here to the *ra'īs*, the leader of the Samaritan community.

345 See Kazimirski, *Dictionnaire*, II, 767; Hans Wehr, *A Dictionary of Modern Written Arabic*, ed. J. Milton Cowan, 3rd ed. (Wiesbaden, 1971), pp. 652, 775; Dozy, *Supplément*, II, 369.

346 Ms. הר גריזים.

347 I.e. the reigning caliph al-Muʻtaṣim. See above, pp. 77 n. 246, 78 nn. 261, 264, 80 n. 278.

heard [this], he sent a man named Rajā[348] with an army; when he was on his way, the king died and his son Hārūn[349] succeeded him. This Hārūn recalled Rajā[350] from the road and instructed him as to what he wanted and sent him [on his way].[351] He arrived in Damascus and found Ibn 'Abbās[352] besieging it. Rajā killed many of his chiefs[353] and destroyed all his estates.[354] He then crossed over and arrived in Mt. Lebanon (Lubnān).

[237] He came, and with him Aḥmad, to Ramla, and called upon the son of the commander[355] who had fled. When he arrived and encamped outside Lydda, Abū Ḥarb appeared[356] and seized horses from them; those who pursued him[357] could not catch up with him, and he reached Sālim and looted whatever had been deposited [there]. He [then] went up to 'Atīl[358] again, because he was determined to meet Rajā in Wādī 'Ārā.[359] When he arrived there, God, may He be exalted, did not bring about for him what he had wanted; [thus] he passed through Wādī 'Ārā and slept in Rāmīn.[360]

348 This is Rajā' ibn Ayyūb al-Ḥiḍārī. See Ibn 'Asākir, XVIII, 94–95; Ibn al-Athīr, *Kāmil*, VI, 522–23; al-Ṭabarī, III, 1320–22; spelt here Rajā.

349 This is Hārun al-Wāthiq ibn Muḥammad ibn al-Mu'taṣim, who came to power on 18 Rabī' I 227 (26 December 841). See al-Ṭabarī, III, 1329; *EI* 2, *s.v.* "al-Wāthiq bi'llāh".

350 The ر seems to be missing from the name here.

351 Al-Ṭabarī, III, 1319ff.; Ibn 'Asākir, XVIII, 94–95; Ibn al-Athīr, *Kāmil*, VI, 522–23, all placing the rebellion in the last year of al-Mu'taṣim's reign (227/841), while the other independent source, al-Ya'qūbī, *Ta'rīkh*, II, 586, places it at the beginning of al-Wāthiq's reign (227/842). Ibn 'Asākir expressly mentions this same fact that Rajā' was recalled by al-Wāthiq and given new instructions.

352 This is probably a distortion of the name of Ibn Bayhas, the leader of the rebels in Damascus. See al-Ṭabarī, III, 1320; al-Ya'qūbī, *Ta'rīkh*, II, 586; Ibn 'Asākir, XVIII, 94–95; Ibn al-Athīr, *Kāmil*, VI, 522–23.

353 Ms. وجا, presumably to be read وجهائه.

354 In this connection, "estates" seems preferable to "villages", since it refers to Ibn Bayhas' property. According to one of al-Ṭabarī's sources (III, 1322), Rajā' killed 5,000 of Ibn Bayhas' followers and two of his closest companions (*aṣḥāb*); Ibn Bayhas and Abū Ḥarb were taken prisoners and sent to Sāmarrā. Al-Ya'qūbī (II, 586) mentions only that Ibn Bayhas was taken prisoner.

355 Ms. ابن المقدم.

356 Ms. وجا; read جا.

357 Ms. من يكده. See Dozy, *Supplément*, II, 448.

358 See Geographical Appendix.

359 This sentence should be read thus: لانه كان معول على لقا رجا في وادي عار[ا]. See Geographical Appendix, *s.v.* Wādī 'Ārā.

360 See Geographical Appendix.

In the morning he came to Sālim, and on Thursday he went up to ʿAtīl, thinking that they would ask for [his] protection [so that] they could come out safe and sound. But they did not want to hear him. He warned them of the consequences,[361] then returned to Sālim and prepared himself. [Rajā] went after Abū Ḥarb,[362] and Abū Ḥarb confronted him, accompanied by Ibn Masrūr, the son of the man who had favoured the Samaritans and who was killed in Sinjil.[363] With them was a great host. [Rajā] warned them of the consequences,[364] and when they began to come forth he joined battle with them. God, may He be praised and exalted, gave him victory, and a great many of them were killed in ʿAtīl and its surroundings. He seized Abū Ḥarb and Ibn Masrūr and a group of their commanders (*muqaddamīhi*), bound them in iron chains [**238**] and sent them to the king.[365]

No one had expected that ʿAtīl would ever be purified[366] [until] the *ra'īs* Pinḥas—in his days and the days of the *ra'īs* Yōshaʿ the precepts (*aḥkām*)[367] were debased because they were annulled[368]—arrived from Afāzim.[369] [Now] this man was a *muftī*,[370] and he assumed responsibility[371] for the purification of ʿAtīl and made sure it was done properly, because it was one of the large villages. He purified [ʿAtīl],[372] though he had no experience in such things.[373]

Rajā went on to Egypt,[374] and [then] continued to his country, and we

---

361 Ms. واشهد عليهم, or more bluntly: "he threatened them". See Lane, *Lexicon*, I.3, 1610.

362 There seems to be no logical way to understand this sentence other than to presume that the scribe had omitted Rajā's name here by mistake. It should thus read: وخرج [رجا] ورا ابو حرب وخرج اليه ابو حرب.

363 See Geographical Appendix, and Ms. p. 222:7; also above, p. 71 n. 202.

364 See above, n. 361.

365 See above, p. 87 n. 347.

366 Ms. ظهر; read طهر, as becomes clear on l. 4: تطهير. The Samaritans considered any place where corpses were present unclean, and therefore in need of purification. See I.R.M. Bóid, "The Samaritan Halacha", in Crown, *Samaritans*, pp. 625–26.

367 This term appears earlier in the text. See above, p. 73 nn. 215–16.

368 Ms. ذلك الاحكام عنهم لانهم منعوا. This seems to refer to the annulment of the institution of the *ḥakākima* in the days of Pinḥas; see Ms. pp. 242–43.

369 Unidentified name.

370 *CA* مفت, an expounder of the law.

371 Ms. تولا, instead of the *CA* تولّى.

372 Ms. ظاهرها; read طاهرها, "purified it". See Kazimirski, *Dictionnaire*, II, 114.

373 Read the Ms. وما له منها خبر (L.C.).

374 The journey to Egypt took place, according to al-Yaʿqūbī, *Ta'rīkh*, II, 586, in 228/842–43.

returned joyfully to our homes safe and sound in the month of Nīsān, and sacrificed gladly and gave profuse thanks to Almighty God. After this the people suffered at the hands of the authorities;[375] they taxed the people heavily,[376] and because of the oppression the people came out and plundered all the way down to the bank of the Jordan.[377] Almighty God put mercy in the heart of the king in the month of the corn,[378] and he sent [an order] and annulled it.[379] All this took place in the days of Hārūn.[380] This Hārūn prohibited the Christians from sounding the *nāqūs*,[381] and he reigned for six years.[382] The Muslims prevented the Jews from worshipping,[383] even from afar.

We did not write down their recollection [of events][384] during this period, nor that of the kings of the land, **[239]** because we were preoccupied with our own affairs; there was no one left who had the zeal, or was interested in taking it upon himself,[385] except a few people from amongst all the groups of the Muslims.

---

[375]Ms. بيد السلاطين. Until the eleventh century, the term *sulṭān* implied any kind of ruler; see *EI* [2], *s.v.* "Sulṭān".

[376]Ms. وحببو; read وجبو. The reading would thus be: وجبو الناس جباية عظيمة.

[377]Ms. جيزة الاردن. A جيزة is the side of a valley, or a coast. See Hava, *Al-Farā'id*, p. 105; Kazimirski, *Dictionnaire*, I, 355.

[378]Ms. شهر الدحن; read شهر الدجن, as in Hebrew, "corn" (see Dozy, *Supplément*, I, 425; above, p. 66 n. 154)—the month of the corn; or perhaps دخن, millet or sorghum, which was already known in Palestine at that time; see A.M. Watson, *Agricultural Innovation in the Early Islamic World* (Cambridge, 1983), pp. 11–14. This may refer either to the month of sowing or of harvesting. شهر الدحن may also be "the rainy month". The "king" referred to is the caliph al-Wāthiq.

[379]I.e. he annulled the heavy taxes.

[380]I.e. al-Wāthiq; see above, p. 88 n. 349.

[381]A long resonant wooden plank which is struck in order to notify times of prayer. This restriction of al-Wāthiq is not mentioned elsewhere, as far as I know.

[382]18 Rabīʿ I 227–23 Dhū l-Ḥijja 232 (26 December 841–10 August 847), in fact, five years and seven and a half months.

[383]Ms. واليهود منعو المسلمين من سحدوا حتى من المبعد; for سحدوا read يسجدوا. The literal translation of this sentence would be: "the Jews prevented the Muslims from worshipping....", but this is most definitely unacceptable. A possible reading is واليهود مُنعو [من] المسلمين من [ان] يسجدوا. See the Introduction above, p. 34.

[384]Ms. دهنهم; read ذهنهم.

[385]Ms. نحلمه; read نحمله or يحمله.

From Adam to the death of Hārūn there were 5280 years.[386] He was succeeded by his brother Ja'far,[387] who afflicted the world with every kind [of affliction].[388] He at first ordered that people should wear distinguishing clothes,[389] except for the black and the blue, which he reserved for his faith. He ordered that there should be no scribe or public official (*'āmil*) except from his faith, and that there should be no one in charge of a fort or holding any kind of position except from his faith.[390] There were Christians[391] whom he cast out, and he appointed all the officials[392] from his faith. He ordered that no one should wear a garment with an embroidered edge (*ṭirāz*)[393] except the members of his faith,[394] and that no one should ride a horse [except the members of his faith]. He commanded that every *dhimmī* should wear a distinguishing sign front and back,[395] and that he should not sit in front

---

[386]The year AM 5280 = AH 233 (847–48 CE); see above, p. 75 n. 226. Al-Wāthiq's reign ended, in fact, in 232/847.

[387]Ja'far al-Mutawakkil, who reigned between 232/847 and 247/861.

[388]Al-Mutawakkil's decrees are described in detail by al-Ṭabarī, III, 1389–94. See also translation, notes and bibliography in J.L. Kraemer, trans., *The History of al-Ṭabarī*, XXXIV: *Incipient Decline* (Albany, 1989), pp. 89–94. Concerning the legal status of the *dhimmī*s under Islam see A.S. Tritton, *The Caliphs and Their Non-Muslim Subjects* (London, 1930); A. Fattal, *Le statut legal des non-musulmans en pays d'Islam* (Beirut, 1958). In general, the prohibitions that appear here are parallel to those in al-Ṭabarī. Two statutes, however, are missing. The first is the decree that one tenth of the houses owned by *dhimmī*s should be confiscated; this decree was most likely not enacted, since if it had been, in Palestine or at least amongst its Samaritan population, it is hard to believe that it would have gone unmentioned. The other decree not mentioned in our text concerns the prohibition against *dhimmī* children being educated in Muslim schools. In this case it may have been that the Samaritan population did not feel constrained by this decree—they had no interest in giving their children a Muslim education—and therefore did not mention it.

[389]Ms. غباران; read غيارات. In this context the reference is clearly to "clothes" rather than "signs", as Ms. p. 251:9, which may refer to badges as well.

[390]Ms. ولا يكون احد على حصن ولا يحمل كان الا من امته. Here the phrase ولا يحمل كان may refer specifically to a prohibition against *dhimmī*s bearing any sort of arms.

[391]Who held those positions.

[392]The word المستخدمين is partially obscured by an ink blot.

[393]See *EI* [1], *s.v.* "Ṭirāz".

[394]Ms. اهل ملته.

[395]According to al-Ṭabarī, this served as the distinguishing sign for the lower strata of society, who did not wear special mantles and hoods. The higher strata were distinguished, according to him, by the honey colour of their clothes. See al-Ṭabarī, III, 1389, 1392; al-Ṭabarī/Kraemer, *Incipient Decline*, pp. 89–90, 93.

on a velvet-like[396] sofa,[397] and that no one except the members of his own faith should have iron stirrups[398]—the rest [would have] wooden ones.[399] He ordered that every grave resembling[400] the graves of the members of his faith should be destroyed,[401] and the grave of the *ra'īs* Nethan'el was destroyed.

Before that occurred, he ordered that every *dhimmī* should afix to his door a wooden idol bearing the label of[402] "idol" (*wathan*).[403] **[240]** The Samaritans who resided in Nablus, may God remember them favourably, having presented the governor of Nablus with something (i.e. a gift),[404] asked him to grant them a delay so they could go down to Ramla, and he agreed to that. [Now] in Dājūn[405] there was a man possessed of dignity and power,[406] **[242]** whose word was accepted by the ruler (*sulṭān*), by the name of Abū

---

[396]Ms. حمال; read خمال. For this sense of the word, see W. Diem and H.P. Radenberg, *A Dictionary of the Arabic Material of S.D. Goitein's A Mediterranean Society* (Wiesbaden, 1994), p. 61.

[397]Undoubtedly during grand occasions and ceremonies, when these were reserved for those of honourable rank. For this sense of *martaba* see J. Sadan, *Le mobilier au proche orient medieval* (Leiden, 1976), pp. 54–55.

[398]See al-Ṭabarī, III, 1389.

[399]Ms. جديد; read حديد. See al-Ṭabarī, III, 1393, where it is also specified that the *dhimmīs* could only use wooden stirrups.

[400]Ms. يتشبيه; read يتشبه.

[401]Cf. al-Ṭabarī, III, 1390: وامر بتسوية قبورهم لئلا تشبه قبور المسلمين, "In addition, he ordered that their graves be made level with the ground so as not to resemble the graves of the Muslims" (trans. Kraemer, p. 91).

[402]Ms. وستميه, i.e. ويستميه, in the sense of تسمّى.

[403]See al-Ṭabarī, III, 1390, who calls these idols *ṣuwar shayāṭīn*, "images of devils". The reason given for this is cited by E. Ashtor, "The Social Isolation of *Ahl Adh-Dhimma*", in O. Komlós, ed., *Etudes orientales à la mémoire de Paul Hirschler* (Budapest, 1950), p. 80 (repr. in *The Medieval Near East: Social and Economic History*, London 1978): "if the houses of the *dhimmīs* will not bear distinctive signs the beggars approaching them will beg Allāh's mercy upon them and His forgiveness for their sins, and this—say the theologians—is absolutely forbidden". This was surely a restriction that was meant to be derogatory, since *shayṭān* and *wathan* were definitely negative terms.

[404]Ms. شي; read بشي (L.C.).

[405]A Samaritan settlement near Ramla. It is miscopied here as داحوس; later on, Ms. p. 248:2, the correct name appears. See Geographical Appendix.

[406]The correct reading is: وكان في داجون رجل قادر بجاه وقدرة. Concerning the term *sulṭān*, see above, p. 90 n. 375.

Yūsuf ibn Dhāsī,[407] may his memory be forever blessed.[408] He called on the governor and petitioned him, and [the governor] told him that it was not possible to annul the order of the king, but [said]: "Choose[409] for yourself an image which is not offensive." He chose the image of a candelabrum that we make; it was put in an envelope, and he stamped it[410] and sent it to the governor of Nablus. [The governor] commanded that a Samaritan should only make [an image] like that which Yūsuf ibn Dhāsī[411] made—[that is], a candelabrum. They rejoiced greatly in this and profusely thanked God, may He be praised and exalted. As for those [Samaritans] who were in [the province of] Jordan, this [concession] was not granted to them, and an image was made [by them] like the other peoples according to the law.[412]

In his days it was decreed that[413] a man shall not raise his voice in prayer, and shall not raise a voice in ...;[414] a funeral shall not be seen, and a *dhimmī* shall not lift his face to a Muslim's[415] face in order to speak or respond to him.[416]

All of these troubles came upon us in the days of the *ra'īs* Pinḥas and in the days of the *ra'īs* Yōsha'; we were prevented from [observing] the precepts (*aḥkām*),[417] **[243]** and the Samaritans remained like a herd without a shepherd—all the Samaritans did as they liked.

---

[407] Here "Dāsī", but later on the name appears as "Dhāsī"/"Adhāsī"; see Ms. pp. 243:5, 248:3, 253:7, and below, p. 99 n. 472. This seems to have been quite a distinguished family in Dājūn.

[408] Samaritan Aramaic: זכיר לטב עד לעלם.

[409] Ms. اختار لك, *sic*! See Blau, *Grammar*, I, 185. Or perhaps: "I will choose for you an image which is not offensive".

[410] For the use of اختم in this sense see Dozy, *Supplément*, I, 351.

[411] Ms. داسي. See above, n. 407.

[412] Ms. على الطريق; for this meaning see Kazimirski, *Dictionnaire*, II, 78.

[413] Here the scribe switches suddenly to Arabic in Samaritan script. The following is the transcription: لا يرفع احد صوته في صلاة ولا يرفع صوت في فنيقة ولا يرا جنيزة ولا يرفع ذمي وجهه في وجه جوي من ان يقول له ويجاو به.

[414] This word, written here quite distinctly in Samaritan script, is transcribed in Arabic as فنيقة. I could not find any meaning for it in Arabic or in other Semitic languages.

[415] The word used here is *goy*, in Hebrew, literally a man belonging to a different faith, a non-Jewish person.

[416] Ms. ויגאו به, implying ويجاو به, i.e. two words. But the correct reading is clearly ويجاوبه, "and to respond to him" (L.C.). Here ends the Samaritan script.

[417] See above, p. 73 n. 216. This event is mentioned above, p. 89.

On Saturday, on the first day of the Feast of Tabernacles, in the second hour, there was a great earthquake; but Almighty God's mercy sheltered [us], and no one was harmed. The people went up to pray on the Feast of Tabernacles in the seventh year of the reign of Ja'far.[418] In the third year after the Sabbatical Year, the governor of Ramla (*wālī*) seized[419] Yūsuf ibn Dhāsī and they[420] detained him. The poll tax[421] (*jāliya*) was multiplied, and he prevented him from going up to the mountain with the Samaritans. The governor of Nablus prohibited them[422] from raising their voices in prayer and from blowing the horn.[423] They prayed on that day, and on Thursday they went up and prayed in raised voices, and no one hindered them. But the Dositheans were prevented from [joining in] the prayer until they were excluded even from the recitation (?) of the book (i.e. the Torah).[424] The Samaritans continued to fare well throughout the days of Yūsuf ibn Dhāsī until his death, may God rest his soul. The Dositheans shouted[425] and clamoured[426] in a loud offensive[427] voice at his death. [As a result,] the *ra'īs* Pinḥas commanded that they should not give or take [anything] from them ever[428] **[244]** and that no one should eat with them or drink with them.

On Thursday, which fell upon the fourth day of Tishrīn, stars[429] were

---

[418]I.e. 239/853–54. Al-Suyūṭī, *Kashf al-ṣalṣala 'an waṣf al-zalzala*, ed. 'A.L. al-Sa'dānī (Fez, 1971), p. 26, mentions an earthquake in Tiberias that also occurred in AH 239.

[419]Ms. مسل; read مسك.

[420]Presumably the Muslim authorities, or the governor's officials.

[421]See above, pp. 57 n. 87, 82 n. 299.

[422]Here follows Samaritan script once more: من رفع اصواتهم فى الصلاه ولا يضربو ببوق (*sic!*).

[423]Literally "trumpet", here presumably the traditional horn or shofar.

[424]The sentence بل الدستان منعوا من الصلاه الي ما انتهوا من تلبية الكتاب is problematic. I could not find any specific reference to the term *talbiya* in Samaritan literature. However, since the term also acquired the meaning of "psalmody" (see *EI* ^{2}, *s.v.*), it may well be that this word was adopted for "recitation of the Torah". Another possibility would be the blessings before the reading; in this case, the blessings would be conceived as لبيك, a formula of presenting oneself before God.

[425]Ms. يعجو, which could be read either as يعتجو, which is irregular, or as يعيجو, in which case it would be a *mediae geminatae* behaving like *mediae infirmae*. See Blau, *Grammar*, I, 167.

[426]Ms. يغاغوا; cf. غاغة, a "mob", and hence the noise of clamour that a mob makes.

[427]Ms. بشفي; read بشعي.

[428]There is a superfluous repetition here: وامر الرييس فينحاس امر ان.

[429]The noun appears here in the plural, but both verbs are singular.

seen falling[430] at night from the east towards the west[431] and towards the south—a momentous event.[432] The [price of] flour reached two measures per *dīnār*; after four days there came a great sandstorm and the flour was sold... days....[433] After this, Almighty God blessed and conferred favour and relieved the world.

The *ra'īs* Pinḥas passed away, and his son ʿAbd'el took his place. [Then] there came a great rise in prices and three *uqqāt*[434] of flour were sold for a *dīnār*. Many people were compelled to take charity because of the pains in their stomach[435] and the hunger. How many left their faith as a result of the terrible rise in prices, and because they were exhausted by the *jizya*! Many sons and families who left the faith were lost. [But] God in His mercy watched over him who endured patiently, and comforted him with satiety and well-being.

During the reign of Jaʿfar there was a great event—a great wonder.[436] This was that Almighty God caused two towns with their inhabitants to be swallowed up, and their inhabitants were buried alive (lit. "remained") as they were [when the earth swallowed them up].[437]

---

430 Lit. "being thrown", ترمى instead of يرمى.

431 Ms. غروب; one expects غرب.

432 This meteor storm is mentioned in al-Ṭabarī, III, 1426; al-Yaʿqūbī, *Ta'rīkh*, II, 600, who report that this storm took place on 1 Jumādā II 241 (17 October 855). This is quite consistent with our text, which does not give the year (although it seems to be shortly after AH 239; see above, p. 94 n. 418) but reports that it took place on Thursday, on 4 Tishrīn. The Samaritans did not use the Babylonian month names adopted by the Jews after their return from the Babylonian exile, but adhered to the ordinal numbers in their ritual calendar; the Babylonian names, on the other hand, were employed for the Julian calendar (on this subject see Powels, "The Samaritan Calendar", pp. 703–705); the name Tishrīn here therefore refers to the month of October. Although the *Continuatio* specifies the date as 4 October, and not the 17th, it is no doubt the same event mentioned by al-Ṭabarī and al-Yaʿqūbī.

433 There seems to be some confusion on the part of the copyist here. The sentence reads: وبعد اربعه ايام جا سموم عظيم وابيع القمع ايام ومن بعد هذا انعم الله ...

434 Ms. افاب, for which L.C. suggests اقات, pl. of اقّة. As attested in Ottoman times, the Syrian *uqqa* was about 1.3 kilograms; see W. Hinz, *Islamische Masse und Gewichte* (Leiden, 1955), p. 24.

435 Ms. المغل, i.e. intestinal pains caused by the swallowing of earth while eating green herbs (in this case no doubt as a result of extreme hunger). See Kazimirski, *Dictionnaire*, I, 1133. L.C. suggests المقلّ, "destitution".

436 Here معجز rather than معجزة.

437 The last part of the sentence could also be understood as "they remained as they

[**245**] This Ja'far came to Damascus and built a fortress in it;[438] he remained there a short while and then returned to his city.[439] He counted the trees,[440] the shops, the taverns, the bath-houses,[441] the seeds,[442] and the presses. He counted the *jizya*[443] and annulled the appellations (*alqāb*), [ordering that] each person should be called by his [proper] name, and [so] increased the *jizya*.

In his days came a man called Qūmaṭī;[444] he arrived outside Nablus, and the governor (*muqaddam*) of Nablus came out to meet him and attacked him. The governor of Nablus was defeated and fled from the sword; there was killing,[445] and the army's camp was looted. Many of the Samaritans fled on that Saturday and [were in] fear of the sword. The Samaritans of Kafr Tiya,

were", i.e. unharmed. Suyūṭī, *Kashf*, pp. 26–27, reports that in Sha'bān 242/December 856 there was a series of earthquakes throughout the east, from Tunisia to Khurāsān, including Syria and Palestine.

438Ibn 'Asākir mentions that when al-Mutawakkil came to Damascus he built a huge fortress in Dārayyā (a village near Damascus, see Yāqūt, II, 536); see Ibn Manẓūr, *Mukhtaṣar*, VI, 87.

439Al-Mutawakkil moved his residence to Damascus on 21 Ṣafar 244 (8 June 858). As a result of the decision to move, he initiated several building projects. Al-Ṭabarī says only that "he gave orders for building in Damascus", while al-Ya'qūbī mentions the building of *quṣūr*; on the complexity of this term see L.I. Conrad, "The *Quṣūr* of Medieval Islam", *Al-Abḥath* 29 (1981), pp. 7–24. See al-Ṭabarī, III, 1436 (trans. Kraemer, pp. 151–52); al-Ya'qūbī, *Ta'rīkh*, II, 600. According to al-Ṭabarī, al-Mutawakkil disliked the conditions in Damascus and decided to leave. His stay there lasted two months and several days.

440See Ms. pp. 229:7, 249:1; also above, p. 79.

441Ms. حمايات, to which the reading حمامات seems preferable.

442Ms. والبدود; read والبذور, literally "seeds", but here perhaps referring to granaries or threshing floors.

443This survey, which was meant to reevaluate property and possessions, is possibly referred to by al-Ya'qūbī, *Ta'rīkh*, II, 599, who mentions that in 240/854–55 representatives of the vizirate claimed that the taxes of the lands of Damascus and Urdunn had to be reevaluated by the office of the *kharāj*; the payment due was then imposed upon each land.

444This may well be al-Qiṭāmī, a rebel from Banū Lakhm whom the governor of Jund Filasṭīn repeatedly failed to defeat, until finally he was defeated by a Turk named Muzāḥim ibn Khāqān, who is mentioned later on in our text. See Gil, *History of Palestine*, p. 299, who quotes al-Ya'qūbī, *Ta'rīkh*, II, 605. The *Continuatio* dates this rebellion to the days of al-Mutawakkil, while al-Ya'qūbī dates it to the rule of al-Musta'īn (248–52/862–66).

445Ms. وقتل قتل; read وقُتِل مَن قُتِل, lit. "those who were killed were killed", a common tautology expressing the notion of relatively moderate but unspecified casualties (L.C.).

[who] related the story, suffered with those who fled, but those who reached the coast were not harmed. They came to Bayt Ṣāma, but the Dositheans did not flee, for they had in mind a plan [against them]. They entered Bayt Ṣāmā on Saturday night, and seized Ibn Amtī, an upright[446] man, and those accompanying him; they piled straw around them and burned them, and killed seventeen men, good[447] people. They were defeated on Saturday; [some] of them were captured, and they destroyed and burned the fort.[448]

[246] The governor (*wālī*) of Ramla sent a man called Ashrakaṣī, a powerful man, and with him a great army. He went up to Nablus and continued to Bayt Ṣāmā, Zaytā, and Būrīn (?), and waged war upon Qūmaṭī. Ashrakaṣī killed many people from both sides. There came upon the people great misfortune, scarcity, affliction, and terrible fear, and the people fled from the sword to Ramla. [Then] from the east there came a man called Muzāḥīm,[449] and Qūmaṭī[450] departed and imposed himself[451] upon the governor (*muqaddam*) of [Jund] al-Urdunn. Then Muzāḥīm came and seized many men from Jordan...[452] the scarcity extended to Ifrīqiya, and they ate human flesh because of the lack [of food]. Then he[453] went down to Egypt, and Almighty God brought peace upon the earth, and everyone returned to his country.

Ja'far was killed at the hand of his son, and [his son] ruled after him for six

---

446 Ms. انسان سوا; read انسان سويّ. See Lane, *Lexicon*, I.3, 1479, رجل سويّ.

447 Ms. من ناس السور; read من ناس السوي/السواء. An alternative reading of السوء results in a completely different meaning: "wicked people". For this form of سوء, see also Ms. p. 247, in the margin.

448 This whole episode is written carelessly; it is difficult to discern which "they" is being referred to here. It may be the Dustān who are attacking Ibn Amtī, a bad man from al-Qiṭāmī's army, or perhaps al-Qiṭāmī's men who are attacking the Dustān, or just Samaritans living in Bayt Ṣāma who are considered here good people (or perhaps the Dustān are bad?). When Ashrakaṣī's army finally arrives, it is not explicit which the "both sides" are that he attacks and kills. If al-Qiṭāmī and his men defeated the Dustān or the Samaritans here, then Ashrakaṣī killed men both from them and from al-Qiṭāmī's army.

449 Ms. فزاحم; read مزاحم. See above, p. 96 n. 444.

450 The form قوطمي appearing here is closer to قطامي than the form قومطي which appeared above.

451 Ms. طرح روحه على مقدم الاردن; see Dozy, *Supplément*, II, 30–31. طرح روحه على فلان can mean either "to implore s.o.'s mercy" or "to impose o.s. upon s.o.". The latter meaning seems to be the more likely in this case.

452 Although there is no indication in the text, there must be something missing here.

453 Presumably Muzaḥim.

months.[454] Much befell him: the roads were emptied of travelers, adversity and fear increased, and al-Baṣra, [the] great city, was wiped out.[455] Many Samaritans were killed, and villages, women and children were plundered.

In the days of the *imām* ʿAbd'el the moon was seen on the Saturday at the beginning of the month, [**247**] and the computation of the fast was renewed.[456] ʿAbd'el was in office for sixteen years; he died and was buried in the fort of ʿAwartā.[457]

After that came a man known as Majmūra; he oppressed the people and collected money. In his days there was a terrible rise in prices, such as had never before been seen; the people were impoverished and stripped of their possessions, and withdrew from their homes on account of the oppression and the hunger.

Al-Mustaʿīn bi'llāh, brother of Jaʿfar, came to power[458] and ruled two and a half years; he was deposed and was called "the deposed among the sons of Hāshim". After him came to power al-Muʿtazz, son of Jaʿfar, who ruled three years;[459] after him came al-Muhtadī, son of al-Wāthiq, who ruled one year;[460] after him came to power al-Muʿtamid, who ruled 24 years.[461] He had a brother whose name was Abū Muḥammad; he seized him and because of

---

[454]Al-Muntaṣir participated in the conspiracy of the Turkish soldiers against his father, due to his fear of losing the title of heir apparent after having lost favour in his father's eyes. See *EI* [2], *s.v.* "Al-Muntaṣir"; Kennedy, *The Prophet and the Age of the Caliphates*, pp. 170–71. Al-Muntaṣir did rule for six months, between 4 Shawwāl 247 (11 December 861) and 25 Rabīʿ I 248 (29 May 862), when he died at Sāmarrā.

[455]This last sentence seems to refer to a longer period of time, as is also reflected in the next sentences. The most notable fact here is the destruction of al-Baṣra, which was, in fact, attacked and destroyed by Zanj rebels in southern Iraq in 257/871. This event was preceded by anarchy and disorder that characterised the period from al-Mutawakkil's murder onwards, through the reigns of al-Muntaṣir, al-Mustaʿīn, al-Muʿtazz and al-Muhtadī. See Kennedy, *The Prophet and the Age of the Caliphates*, pp. 171–81. This anarchy, caused by struggles against the Turkish mercenaries and amongst them, seems to be reflected in this sentence.

[456]Ms. وعاد [و] جدد الحساب الصوم.

[457]See Geographical Appendix.

[458]Al-Mustaʿīn ruled between 248/862 and 252/866, and was in fact al-Mutawakkil's nephew, a grandson of al-Muʿtaṣim. The information given here, claiming that he reigned two and a half years, is incorrect. On his abdication see al-Ṭabarī, III, 1642–43, 1645–56, where he is called *al-makhlūʿ* in several places throughout the verses.

[459]Ruled between 252/866 and 255/869. See *EI* [2], *s.v.* "al-Muʿtazz bi'llāh".

[460]Ruled between 255/869 and 256/870. See *EI* [2], *s.v.* "al-Muhtadī".

[461]In reality 22 years, between 256/870 and 279/892.

his[462] wickedness[463] put him in prison.[464] Then Aḥmad ibn Ṭūlūn's[465] men came forth and he descended upon Egypt with a strong force and took it over through cunning. There was a man there[466] known as Majmūra... governor in Ramla, a governor by the name of 'Īsā ibn Ḥabash ibn Ṭūbūn.[467] He[468] devised a cunning plan, came to Palestine, and entered Caesarea. 'Īsā left in his hands a man **[248]** named al-Kūnalī in Kafar Sālim.[469] He fought him, bound him in iron chains and brought him to Ramla.[470] In Dājūn[471] there was a man called Fils ibn Dhāsī[472] who was in 'Īsā's service, and he said to him: "What is the point of this man remaining in prison?", and he let him go.

---

[462] Abū Aḥmad's wickedness presumably.

[463] This seems to refer to al-Mu'tamid's brother, al-Muwaffaq, called Abū Aḥmad, who was the de facto ruler of the realm during most of al-Mu'tamid's reign. Abū Aḥmad did, in fact, prevent his brother, the caliph, from travelling to Egypt and detained him in the palace at Jawsaq. See *EI* 2, VII, 766; Kennedy, *The Prophet and the Age of the Caliphates*, pp. 175–76.

[464] The sentence missing in the text is provided in the margin.

[465] The scribe did not recognize Ibn Ṭūlūn's name, and in two places copied ابن طوبون instead of ابن طولون. On the next page the name appears correctly.

[466] Ms. كان فيها رجل, with فيها referring to Egypt. There is no gap in the text, but it appears to be discontinuous a few words later, where the text is suddenly speaking about a governor in Ramla.

[467] There seems to be considerable confusion here, and there are probably several words, maybe more, missing. "Majmūra", mentioned already above, seems to refer to Amājūr, who replaced 'Īsā ibn al-Shaykh as governor of Syria (including Palestine) in 871, after the latter had rebelled against the caliphs al-Mu'tazz, al-Muhtadī and al-Mu'tamid between 866 and 871. See Gil, *History of Palestine*, pp. 299–300; Hassan, *Tulunides*, pp. 46–48. The governor 'Īsā ibn Ḥabash mentioned in the same sentence may well refer, therefore, to 'Īsā ibn al-Shaykh. The addition Ibn Ṭūbūn is clearly a misreading of Ibn Ṭūlūn, as previously (see above, n. 465), and is probably part of the disorder in these sentences. Amājūr died in 878, and Palestine and Syria were then taken over by Aḥmad ibn Ṭūlūn.

[468] It is not clear whether this alludes to Amājūr or to 'Īsā. It may be that this sentence describes the entry of Amājūr to Palestine in order to crush 'Īsā's rebellion.

[469] Ms. بالفر سالم; read بكفر سالم.

[470] Ms. وحاربه; read وجا به (L.C.).

[471] Ms. داحون; read داجون. This site has already been mentioned, Ms. p. 240:3; see Geographical Appendix.

[472] Obviously a member of the same distinguished family mentioned previously (above, p. 92; Ms. p. 242:2, 6), who lived in Dājūn, near Ramla, and had connections in the *wālī*'s court in Ramla. The name appears there twice as Dhāsī, while here and on Ms. p. 253:7 it appears clearly as Adhāsī.

He departed to Egypt[473] and remained there two years. Outside the city[474] he built himself a castle[475] in the form of that built by ....[476] While he was digging he found money in a brazier;[477] he bought black slaves and others beside them, and established prisons. He continued to Barqa, besieged it and took possession of it, and appointed there a governor; he then continued to Alexandria, and its people submitted to him.[478] He wrote to Crete, on the frontier of Byzantium,[479] and received a reply [offering] their submission. He then conquered the west (i.e. North Africa) and returned to Egypt, and it flourished by the mercy of Almighty God. Affliction was replaced by relief, and the earth was generous in its fruit[480] and in everything that it bore;[481] the people ate and were satiated, and great satiety and well-being prevailed.[482]

After that the heavens held back the rain for three years, and the sky

---

[473]From what follows later it is clear that this refers to Aḥmad ibn Ṭūlūn, and not to ʿĪsā, as may at first seem.

[474]Ms. برا في; read برّا من.

[475]Ibn Ṭūlūn did indeed build himself a magnificent new palace north of al-Fusṭāṭ, which was called al-Qaṭāʾiʿ. Later, Saladin built there a citadel which still exists. See Hassan, *Tulunides*, pp. 48–49.

[476]Ms. الذي بنا صور/هيور. Alternatively, "In the form of the one he built in...."

[477]The word here is written بحموره. It is spelt exactly the same way as Amājūr's name was spelt twice before, yet Amājūr is completely out of context here. مجمرة, "brazier" or "fireplace", is the only similar word that could make any sense here. This story is recorded by al-Balawī, who reports that Ibn Ṭūlūn built the new mosque with money that he found on top of the mountain in a place called Tannūr Farʿūn (a *tannūr* is a circular earthen oven). See al-Balawī, *Sīrat Aḥmad ibn Ṭūlūn*, ed. M. Kurd ʿAlī (Damascus, 1939), pp. 56–57.

[478]When Yārjūj was given Egypt as apanage, he invested Ibn Ṭūlūn with authority over the whole of Egypt, including Alexandria, Barqa and the frontier districts which were not formerly under his jurisdiction. However, there seems to be no corroboration to the claim that he took them by force. See Hassan, *Tulunides*, pp. 45–46.

[479]Iqrīṭiya is one of several variants for Crete in Arabic. See *EI* [2], *s.v.* "Iḳrīṭish". Crete was in fact a continual skirmish ground between the Byzantines and the caliphate and during the period under discussion changed hands several times. See *ibid.*, III, 1083–84. However, although Ibn Ṭūlūn was engaged in several events along the Byzantine border, especially in Ṭarsūs (see Hassan, *Tulunides*, pp. 66–67), there is no evidence, as far as I know, of his involvement in Crete.

[480]Ms. علايها; read غلّاتها. Cf. Ms. p. 249:4: وانجبت الارض غلّاتها وثمرت الشجر, and Ms. p. 260:2: وانجبت الارض في غلّاتها.

[481]Lit. "and in everything in it".

[482]Ms. وحا; read وجا.

became like copper and the earth like iron[483] in the winter [for a long][484] time. [**249**] The springs dwindled, the trees and the vegetation dried up, the trees dropped their blossoms, and there was a rise in prices so great that it led to fatalities. [Then] Almighty God conferred favour and sustained the people.[485] After that Almighty God dispelled the grief of [His] creatures,[486] rain fell, the earth produced its crops generously, and the trees bore fruit; the [price of] wheat reached eight *uqqāt*[487] per *dīnār*, and God gave solace in His mercy and compassion.

[Afterwards] Yōsha', the *ra'īs*, passed away and his brother Yūsuf took his place; Madī, his father's brother, contested him and the people broke up into two parties: some were with Yūsuf, while others were with Madī. There developed a great dispute among the Samaritans. Madī paid money to the ruler (*sulṭān*) of the land,[488] and he rose and instructed and interpreted on the Feast of Tabernacles[489] without the consent of the Samaritans. Around him stood a group of the retainers of the ruler;[490] [they stood] around the Book of the Scroll,[491] [hence] the Book and the people became contaminated.[492] The people appealed for succor against him[493] and hated him, and he left

---

[483]Deuteronomy 28:23.

[484]Smeared ink has obscured one word.

[485]Presumably هدا and not هذا, as in the text, which gives no sense.

[486]For فرج عن in this sense see Lane, *Lexicon*, I.5, 2359, where he notes that فرج عنك is used as an abbreviated form of فرج الله عنك غمّك, "May God remove your grief".

[487]Ms. اواب; read اقات (L.C.). Cf. Ms. p. 244:7, and above, p. 95 n. 434.

[488]Ms. السلطان الارض *sic*! Concerning the term *sulṭān*, see above, p. 90 n. 375. This term was also used in the early period in abstract form; see Ms. p. 254:7, and below, p. 107 n. 550.

[489]Ms. عيد المظال, or Succoth in Hebrew.

[490]Ms. السلاطان; read السلطان. See above, p. 101 n. 488.

[491]Ms. كتاب المدرج, i.e. the Scroll of the Torah. See Vilmar, p. 58:12: لمدرج الكبير, the "great scroll". See also *ibid.*, p. 60:4: الكتاب الكبير, the "great book".

[492]The Samaritans were notorious for their fear of contamination by gentiles, and were known from early times as crying in public "noli me tangere". This is recorded by Epiphanius of Salamis, *Panarion* 30:2, 3 (ed. K. Holl in *Die griechischen christlichen Schriftsteller* XXV, Leipzig 1915, p. 334), who compares the Ebionites to the Samaritans on this matter. It is later mentioned in the Qur'ān in Sūra 20, vv. 87–97. On this subject see Fossum, "Sects and Movements," p. 348; I. Goldziher, "Lā Misāsa", *Révue africaine* 52 (1908), pp. 23ff.

[493]Ms. فيه, where one expects عليه. In this context استغاثوا الناس فيه can only be in the sense of "against him".

for Damascus. The letter of the heads of the Samaritans[494] was to be taken from them, and the ruler (*sulṭān*) ordered the seizure of a group of the Samaritans and incarcerated them until they agreed to pay a great sum of money, **[250]** which they divided among the villages according to their ability. They inflicted upon the people all sorts of punishments, and many of the people left their religion. He[495] departed again to the East in order to bring back with him the letters of appointment,[496] but Almighty God sent against him a black man who killed him. Word reached the ruler that the Samaritans killed him, [so] he seized the Samaritan leaders (*muqaddamī l-sāmira*) for punishment.[497] He exacted from them a large sum of money, the amount exacted from them coming to 15,000 *dīnārs*. The affliction wrought upon the Samaritans intensified, and they diminished both in their possessions and their faith; but Almighty God brought relief to whoever endured this patiently. [Then] the king (*malik*) died,[498] and there came [a time of] well-being, ease[499] and joy.

When Aḥmad ibn Ṭūlūn, king of Egypt, heard that the king[500] had died,

---

[494] Ms. كتاب روسا السامره, and below, كتاب الرياسة. This refers to the letter of appointment usually given by the caliph to the heads of the different religious communities. On this subject, see C.E. Bosworth, "Christian and Jewish Religious Dignitaries in Mamlūk Egypt and Syria: Qalqashandī's Information on their Hierarchy, Titulature, and Appointment", *IJMES* 3 (1972), pp. 59–74, 199–216. The words *ra'īs* (or *rayyis*) and *ri'āsa* were the accepted terms for the leader and leadership of the Jewish community (which in Egypt also included the Samaritans); see *ibid.*, pp. 70–71; S.D. Goitein, *A Mediterranean Society*, II: *The Community* (Berkeley and Los Angeles, 1971), pp. 23–40, 527 n. 41; M. Cohen, *Jewish Self-Government in Medieval Egypt* (Princeton, 1980), pp. 14–15. Another such document given to the Nestorian Catholicos was first partially published by A. Mingana, "A Charter of Protection Granted to the Nestorian Church in A.D. 1138, by Muktafi II, Caliph of Bagdad," *BJRL* 10 (1926), pp. 127–33; for a complete edition and translation of the text, see L.I. Conrad, "A Nestorian Diploma of Investiture from the *Tadhkira* of Ibn Ḥamdūn: the Text and its Significance", in W. al-Qāḍī, ed., *Studia Arabica et Islamica: Festschrift for Iḥsān 'Abbās* (Beirut, 1981), pp. 83–104.

[495] Presumably Madī.

[496] Ms. يحب; read يجيب. Cf. Blau, *Grammar*, I, 148, 179; II, 492–96.

[497] Here the text suddenly shifts to Arabic written in Samaritan script. The transcription is as follows: واخد منهم مال كثير [وكان قدر] ما اخذ منهم خمسة عشر الف دينار.

[498] Although the word *malik* usually refers to the caliph, in this case it apparently refers to the death of Amājūr, governor of Syria (and Palestine), who died, in fact, in the year 264/878, the same year noted here. It was indeed then that Aḥmad ibn Ṭūlūn took over Palestine. See above, p. 99 n. 467.

[499] Ms. somewhat unclear. Read راخية, in the sense of *CA* رخاء (L.C.).

[500] By *malik*, "king", the governor of Syria is meant.

he marched forth at the head of a great army of blacks and others and arrived in Palestine in the month of Ḥazīrān, in the fifth year after the Sabbatical Year, which was the year 264 of the reign of Islam.[501] The black soldiers brought ruin upon all the people and looted villages situated along the route; many women were defiled,[502] and great affliction came upon the people. He entered Ramla [**251**] and appointed a governor (*wālī*) there;[503] he then continued on to Damascus and conquered and ruled over it, conquered the rest of the country, and then reached Antioch. He besieged it for a long period of time, killed its ruler, looted its property, and killed many people there; he appointed a governor who ruled on his behalf, and great sorrow came upon the Muslims.[504] He returned with his army[505] and oppressed the people, and commanded that provisions be brought to him and to the troops who were with him wherever he was to be found, and that draught animals[506] [likewise be brought] to every camp. He sent[507] [his men] and seized the people's draught animals: they never would have believed that their draught animals would be taken from them, [so] they themselves let them go.[508] He oppressed the people in every way.

[501]The month of Ḥazīrān 264 = June 878. According to Muslim sources, Aḥmad ibn Ṭūlūn did indeed leave Egypt in April 878; see Hassan, *Tulunides*, p. 65.

[502]For the lack of concord here in the gender of a preceding verb to its feminine subject, وتطما نسا كثير, see Blau, *Grammar*, II, 281. For the verb تطمأ, see above, pp. 67 n. 164, 73 n. 213.

[503]This is Muḥammad ibn Rafīʿ, governor under Amājūr, whose appointment was reconfirmed by Ibn Ṭūlūn; see al-Kindī, *Wulāt*, p. 219.

[504]Ḥimṣ, Ḥamā and Aleppo did indeed accept Ibn Ṭūlūn's rule, while Sīmā al-Ṭawīl, prefect of Antioch, refused to do so. In response, Ibn Ṭūlūn beseiged the city for a long period until he finally captured it. According to al-Kindī, some local inhabitants who tired of the siege supplied him with information concerning its weak point. Antioch was taken, according to him, in Muḥarram 265 = September 878; Sīmā was killed and his property confiscated. There is no mention, however, of a great slaughter such as is described here. See al-Kindī, *Wulāt*, pp. 219–220; al-Maqrīzī, *Kitāb al-mawāʿiẓ wa-l-iʿtibār fī dhikr al-khiṭaṭ wa-l-āthār* (Bulaq, AH 1270), I, 320; Hassan, *Tulunides*, p. 66.

[505]He returned most probably to Palestine, on his way back to Egypt (see al-Kindī, *Wulāt*, pp. 219–20). Before he started on his way back he spent some time in Ṭarsūs: see Hassan, *Tulunides*, p. 66.

[506]I.e. beasts used for work and transportation.

[507]Ms. اسل; read ارسل.

[508]Presumably believing that they would be returned to them. Another possibility is: "and that they would be left in need of them" (L.C.). For this sense of صدق, see Kazimirski, *Dictionnaire*, I, 1323. Ms. يحلوهم; read يخلوهم.

In the second year a governor (*wālī*) came to [rule over] the people on his behalf and oppressed [them] in every way; he ordered that the *dhimmīs*[509] should wear distinguishing signs, engraved (lit. made) idols on their doors,[510] [ordered that] a *dhimmī* should not raise his head in the presence of a Muslim (lit. *goy*), that he should not raise his voice in prayer, and that he should not blow the horn. He also destroyed a synagogue of the Jews.[511] All the religious communities were in fear of him, lest he extend [his] hand to their houses of worship so as to put them to his own use.[512]

He prohibited the drinking of wine[513] and oppressed [them] in every possible manner, and his Muslim subjects[514] who were in the villages **[252]** behaved overbearingly towards the *dhimmīs*.[515] He plundered everything he found, and the curse written in the Holy Law[516] was fulfilled: "The sojourner who is among you shall mount above you higher and higher, and you shall come down lower and lower".[517]

In the days of his rule he sent an order to seize all the people from the villages [and take them] to Egypt. Amongst those who were seized was a group of Samaritans, whom he conveyed to Egypt in ships. He ordered that a fortress be built overlooking Jaffa,[518] and he took all the draught animals and impoverished the people[519] in every possible way—in their property and in their bodies. He restored al-Fusṭāṭ and renovated it, because it had gone

---

[509]Ms. الدمم; read الذمم, i.e. اهل الذمّة.

[510]Here the text shifts back and forth between Arabic script and Samaritan script. The transcription is as follows: وعمل على ابوابهم اوثان ولا يرفع ذمي راسه بين يدي جوي وصلاة لا يرفع فيها صوت ولا يضرب ببوق ودم نيسه ليهود وخافت منه كل الامم هوا مد يد علي كنايسهم بان يخدموهم وبطل شرب النبيذ وضيق بكل فن ورعية امته ... . Cf. the next two notes below.

[511]Ms. ودم نيسه ليهود; read وهدم كنيسة ليهود.

[512]Ms. يخدموهم, in the sense of يستخدموهم; see Dozy, *Supplément*, I, 354.

[513]The word used here is *nabīdh*; this is an alcoholic drink usually made of raisins or dates. It could, however, also mean "wine expressed from grapes" (Lane, *Lexicon*, I.7, 2757).

[514]Lit. those subjects who were of his religion.

[515]Ms. الدمم; read الذمم.

[516]I.e. the Pentateuch.

[517]Deuteronomy 28:43.

[518]See al-Balawī, *Sīrat Aḥmad ibn Ṭūlūn*, pp. 184, 351. This is also mentioned by Ibn Khaldūn; see Gil, *History of Palestine*, p. 308 and n. 74, quoting *Kitāb al-ʿibar* (Beirut, 1958), IV, 652.

[519]Ms. معر بالناس, = امعره, "he reduced him to poverty": see Lane, *Lexicon*, I.6, 2724.

to ruin, having changed hands (?)[520] a number of times. We lived in fear day and night, and all the people were in difficulty;[521] everyday life[522] became hard to bear, and all the people became poor and were stripped of all their amenities and possessions. All this took place in the days of Aḥmad ibn Ṭūlūn.

At that time he added to the oppression of the people in every possible way: he seized all the draught animals, and the people were compelled to use cows[523] in the mills. That wicked young man Aḥmad ibn Ṭūlūn arrived in the days of the *imām* El'azar, in the year 269 of the reign of Islam;[524] there descended upon the people an affliction that has not been known nor encountered, and excessive pestilence; **[253]** there was not one who did not mourn. The people remained[525] in affliction, and the pestilence lasted for six months. The people's looks altered as a result of the disease, and only a few people went up to the mountain (i.e. Gerizim) on the Feast of Tabernacles. After that Almighty God brought favour upon the world and remembered the covenant of Abraham, Isaac and Jacob. Above and beyond every other benefaction, Ibn Ṭūlūn was defeated;[526] he stopped in Damascus,[527] where fatal illness befell him, and was carried hurriedly to Egypt.[528] There was a governor in Ramla by the name of 'Abd Allāh ibn al-Fatḥ, and when he heard of [Ibn Ṭūlūn's] death he started oppressing the people[529] and exacted much

520Ms. في التقاق; perhaps في التقاف (L.C.).

521The colloquial style here is typical of this text, which seems to give a spoken account rather than a written one.

522Ms. الحيا الحاليه (*sic*!). This form of حياة may be due to an incidental omission of the *tā' marbūṭa*, yet it may also be the "correct" spelling, since similar cases do indeed occur in Christian Palestinian Arabic. See Blau, *Grammar*, I, 120–21.

523As opposed to draught animals, i.e. oxen, donkeys, or mules.

524I.e. 882–83 CE. On this occasion Ibn Ṭūlūn journeyed northwards to secure his rule in Ṭarsūs. See Hassan, *Tulunides*, pp. 82–83.

525Ms. وبمي; read وبقي.

526This refers to his failure to take over Ṭarsūs. After a long unsuccessful seige, Ibn Ṭūlūn at first withdrew to al-Maṣīṣa, where he fell ill. He then started on his way back to Egypt. See Hassan, *Tulunides*, pp. 90–91.

527Other sources (*ibid.*) refer to him passing through Antioch on his route back to Egypt; there is no mention of Damascus in any of the other sources.

528Ibn Ṭūlūn died in Dhū l-Qa'da 270/March 884.

529Ms. واخذ تضيق علي الناس; the use of form V of the verb rather than II in this sense is irregular.

money from them. He arrested Ibn Dhāsī,[530] pressured him [for funds] and exacted much money from him, and made up his mind to punish him. When Ibn Dhāsī learned of this, he fled to the mountains and caves and remained there.

Ibn Ṭūlūn was succeeded[531] by three sons: al-ʿAbbās, Khumārawayh,[532] and Abū l-ʿAshāʾir. Al-ʿAbbās was killed[533] by his brother Khumārawayh;[534] Khumārawayh[535] appointed[536] two sons,[537] one was ʿAbd Allāh, and the other Saʿīd.[538] When Ibn al-Fatḥ heard of this he fled to the East; the rulers

---

[530]Ms. ابن اداسى. Concerning this family, see above, pp. 93 and n. 407, 99 n. 472.

[531]كان is used here as an auxiliary verb of خلفه, which is a common feature of *MA*. See Blau, *Grammar*, II, 432.

[532]Apparently the copyist did not recognize the name. Here and elsewhere he chose to write جمار instead of خمار, which in fact seems to be some form of خمارويه.

[533]Ms. وقبل; read وقتل.

[534]Ibn Ṭūlūn had, in fact, 33 children, seventeen of whom were sons. The names mentioned here are three of eight names known to us. Khumārawayh was Ibn Ṭūlūn's heir and reigned from 884 to 896. Al-ʿAbbās, his first-born son, known as his hated son, tried to revolt against his father and failed. Abū l-ʿAshāʾir headed the Egyptian troops in the battle against al-Muwaffaq. On the successors of Ibn Ṭūlūn see Hassan, *Tulunides*, pp. 107–45.

[535]Following is the story of the hostilities between Khumārawayh and his men on one side, and two generals of al-Muwaffaq: the legal apanagist of Egypt, Isḥāq ibn Kundāj, who was in charge of al-Jazīra and al-Mawṣil at the time, and Ibn Abī l-Sāj, who ruled over al-Kūfa; these were joined by al-Muwaffaq's son, Abū l-ʿAbbās Aḥmad ibn al-Muwaffaq, who was to be the future caliph al-Muʿtaḍid. The latter group decided to challange Khumārawayh's rule, which was not legally sanctioned by the caliph. They began by taking over central cities in Syria such as al-Raqqa, Qinnasrīn, Ḥimṣ, Aleppo, and Antioch. In response, Khumārawayh sent his army. The first battle at Shayzar on the Orontes ended in the defeat of Khumārawayh's troops; then Damascus was also taken in February 885. The final battle, which took place at al-Tawāḥīn ("The Mills", Antipatris, near Ramla) on Tuesday, 5 April 885 (see Gil, *History of Palestine*, p. 308), ended in the victory of Khumārawayh's troops, headed by Saʿd al-Aysar, after the commanders of both sides fled from the battlefield. See al-Kindī, *Wulāt*, pp. 233–36; Ibn Khaldūn, *ʿIbar*, IV, 305–306; Hassan, *Tulunides*, pp. 109–14.

[536]Ms. وخلق; read وخلف. See below, p. 107 nn. 539, 541.

[537]Ms. ابيين; read ابنين, "two sons", although from the next sentence it is clear that these are *muqaddamūn*, i.e. supervisors or governors appointed over Palestine by Khumārawayh. He did in fact have two sons; however, their names were Abū l-ʿAsākir Jaysh ibn Khumārawayh and Abū Mūsā Hārūn ibn Khumārawayh. See Hassan, *Tulunides*, pp. 134–38, 139–45.

[538]In fact, the names of the generals sent by Khumārawayh were Abū ʿAbd Allāh Aḥmad ibn Muḥammad al-Wāsiṭī and Saʿd al-Aysar. It is recorded that the Ṭūlūnid troops were

appointed[539] by Khumārawayh ruled upon the whole land and appointed a governor (*wālī*) in Ramla who was called Iṣba', a mean man **[254]** who was from Bayt Fūrīk. He divided (?)[540] money among the commanders appointed[541] by Khumārawayh...[542] in Palestine, [so] they departed and left him in charge of Palestine. They departed to Shayzar[543] and waged war upon Shayzar against Ibn Abī l-Sāj and Ibn Abī Jūbāsh.[544] There was a great massacre there, and they returned to Damascus; they did not let them[545] in, so they came to Tiberias but could not stop. When 'Abd Allāh [al-Wāsiṭī] learnt that[546] the people had already[547] resolved to try to overcome him,[548] he went there (i.e. to Ramla) and left Sa'īd (i.e. Sa'd al-Aysar) behind. He came to Ramla, seized it, and appointed for that....[549] He received a letter from the government[550] that he should collect money, so he arrested Iṣba' and imprisoned him.[551] When Sa'īd heard [this] he pursued him in a great fury and killed 130 of the best of his officers (*muqaddamīn*) who were with

indeed first in Palestine before they continued northwards. See Hassan, *Tulunides*, pp. 110–11.

[539] Ms. خلو, but recognized as an error and crudely corrected; read خلّف.

[540] Ms. صار, possibly from صور, "turn towards", "divide"; see Lane, *Lexicon*, I.3, 1744.

[541] Ms. خلا, crossed out and crudely corrected; read خلّف.

[542] Ms. غرمه or عزمه. This is a very difficult sentence, and its reading is tentative only.

[543] Ms. سيجر throughout. In the Muslim sources this is spelt "Shayzar". Shayzar is a town on the Orontes, where a detachment of the Ṭūlūnid troops was indeed defeated. See above, p. 106 n. 535; and Hassan, *Tulunides*, p. 111.

[544] Ms. دجو باش. Concerning these events and persons, see above, p. 106 n. 535. The text here is faulty; the name of the second general is Isḥāq ibn Kundāj, as mentioned above.

[545] Although the text has له, it seems it should be لهم. In February 885 the caliph's army took over Damascus (Hassan, *Tulunides*, p. 111), and it is clear therefore why the Ṭūlūnid troops could not enter the city.

[546] Presumably بان الناس.

[547] Ms. قذ; read قد (L.C.).

[548] Ms. يسانقوا; read يسابقوا (L.C.).

[549] There seem to be a few words missing here: ... وجعل لذلك, probably a reference to an appointment.

[550] The term *sulṭān* is used here in its early abstract form; see *EI*^{2}, *s.v.* "Sulṭān", and above, pp. 90 n. 375, 101 n. 488. This probably refers to the caliph or to al-Muwaffaq or his son, since al-Wāsiṭī was inclined to be on their side at this stage.

[551] This part was copied by mistake and then crossed off on Ms. pp. 240–41. The text there has يخبى المال instead of يجبى المال and وسحبه instead of وسجنه. It seems, however, that the text here is preferable.

him, and also killed a great many of his men.[552] ʻAbd Allāh fled and came to his brother Hārūn.[553] The Muslims he met[554] in Damascus ...[555] and said to him:[556] "Ṭūlūn has died, and there is no one who will challenge you." He came to Palestine and wrote to Saʻīd that he should come and join him. When his letter reached Saʻīd and he read it, he sent it to Egypt to Khumārawayh and informed Khumārawayh. [Khumārawayh] set out for Palestine and arrived **[255]** at Ramla with an immense number of troops, [consisting of] blacks, Berbers and others. He camped at Ra's al-ʻAyn, which is the camping site for armies,[557] then sent to Iṣbaʻ and said to him: "Gather for me every bandit in the land". Then Ibn Abū Aḥmad,[558] brother of Hārūn, of Banū Hāshim, came with his troops and descended upon Ra's al-ʻAyn. The two sides fought there, and many from both sides were killed. Ibn Aḥmad al-Hāshimī fled, and ʻĪsā pursued him assiduously[559] all the way to Caesarea. A great misfortune came upon the people and the curse was fulfilled: "You will wear yourself out for it, and people you do not know will eat it".[560]

He oppressed the people in every matter, and many villages came to ruin. [When] Khumārawayh heard that Saʻīd had rebelled against him, he came to

---

[552]As far as I know, this story about the hostilities in Palestine between Khumārawayh's two generals is not found elsewhere.

[553]As becomes evident on the next page, the reference is to Hārūn ibn al-Muwaffaq, brother of Abū l-ʻAbbās Aḥmad ibn al-Muwaffaq, who was to be the future caliph al-Muʻtaḍid (see above, p. 106 n. 535). See al-Ṭabarī, III, 2040.

[554]Ms. لقه; read لقيه.

[555]Ms. p. 240pu reads: وقال له المسلمين لقه في دمشق وقال له ان ابن طولون قد مات; Ms. p. 254:10–11 bears المسلمين لقه في دمشق وقال له ان ابن طولون قد مات... lacuna.

[556]Here follows the story of al-Wāsiṭī's treachery. Having been sent together with Saʻd al-Aysar to Syria, he reported to al-Muwaffaq or to his son and advised him to march against Egypt since Khumārawayh was weak and incapable of defending himself. See al-Kindī, *Wulāt*, p. 234; Hassan, *Tulunides*, p. 110.

[557]Ms. العشاكر; read العساكر. Ra's al-ʻAyn is the Arabic name of Antipatris, also called al-Ṭawāḥīn, where the famous battle took place on 5 April 885; see above, p. 106 n. 535.

[558]Ibn Abū Aḥmad is identical with Ibn al-Muwaffaq, since al-Muwaffaq was known as Abū Aḥmad. See *EI* [2], III, 801.

[559]Ms. وكد, should be form II. For this sense of كدّد, see Kazimirski, *Dictionnaire*, II, 872.

[560]See Deuteronomy 28:33. As usual, this is a free citation. The passage, in fact, is: "A nation which you have not known will eat up the fruit of your land and of all your labours".

Ramla with a great army; once inside the city he seized[561] Sa'īd and killed him[562] and appointed Iṣba' governor of [Jund] Filasṭīn and [Jund] al-Urdunn. [Iṣba'] oppressed the people, seized property, stripped the people of their possessions, and took their towns;[563] many of the Samaritans abandoned their villages. There were five brothers, wicked people. . . [564] **[256]**. . . [565]

[257] This blessed book was copied (?) by the pious elder 'Abd Allāh son of the orthodox elder Ibrahīm (?) al-Qabāṣī, may Almighty God make him blessed. Amen, O Lord of the Worlds. Written on the blessed day of Monday, the sixth of the month of Jumādā l-Ākhar, from among the months of the year 969,[566] at the hand of the servant . . . .

Let him who finds any blemish correct the error
And exalt Him in whom there is no blemish.[567]

---

[561]Ms. احد; read اخذ.

[562]Sa'd al-Aysar, who was the champion of the battle of Ṭawāhīn and had gone on and captured Damascus, had apparently been disappointed that Khumārawayh had not responded with the appropriate appreciation, and therefore rebelled against him. See Gil, *History of Palestine*, pp. 309–10; Ibn Taghrībirdī and al-'Aynī (cited by Hassan, *Tulunides*, pp. 113–14) report that Khumārawayh killed him in person. This occurred in Dhū l-Qa'da 272/May 886. See Hassan, *Tulunides*, pp. 113–14; al-Kindī, *Wulāt*, p. 236; Ibn Taghrībirdī, *Al-Nujūm al-zāhira*, IV, 51.

[563]قراهم is translated here as "towns", since the usual term for villages is ضياع, as at the end of the sentence.

[564]Here the text is cut off.

[565]This page contains the word نجز (Ms. نحر), "it is finished", an invocation: باسم الله العظيم الرحمن الرحيم الحى القيوم, given twice, a brief note stating that this was written during the day on Wednesday, 27 Muḥarram. . . , and one paragraph of the chronicle, which is repeated on the next page.

[566]6 Jumādā II in fact fell on a Wednesday, while 6 Jumādā I fell on a Monday.

[567]Ms. هذا الدفتر المبارك برسم الشيخ التقي عبد الله ابن الشيخ السني [ابر]هيم القباصي الله تعالى يجعله مباركا عليه امين يا رب العالمين كتب في نهار الاثنين المبارك سادس شهر جمادى الاخر من شهور سنة تسع وستين وتسعماية على يد الفقير ... ومن وجد عيبا فسد الخللا فجل من لا فيه عيبا وعلا. This colophon, placed awkwardly in the middle of the text, was written in a non-book hand on Monday, 4 March 1560, that is, more than 36 years later than the colophon appearing at the end of the text on Ms. p. 264 (see below). It was written by a member of the same family, the colophon on p. 264 being written by Yūsuf ibn Ibrahīm ibn Hiba ibn Qabāṣ al-Sāmirī, while this colophon was written by 'Abd Allāh son of Ibrahīm (?) al-Qabāṣī. The name Qabāṣ appears also several other times on Ms. pp. 266–69 in the names of other family members mentioned in owners' and readers' notes. It seems, therefore, that after

Chapter

In the year 297 of the reign of Islam[568] there came a [swarm of] locusts; it multiplied[569] and destroyed the trees and the crops and the world was filled[570] with it—nothing remained that was not destroyed. [Then] the trees[571] bore fruit again, and God sent[572] welfare, mercy and satiety; flour reached twelve measures[573] per *dīnār*, and oil rose to five measures per *dīnār*.[574]

[**258**] In the month of Kānūn al-Thānī there was snow for three days, so great as had never before been seen; after that came locusts, the like of which had not been seen, and afterwards a rise in prices.

In[575] the year 369[576] of Islam, in the days of the *ra'īs* 'Abd'el and of the *ra'īs* Dartā, they agreed[577] upon the annulment of the reading in Aramaic[578]

---

having been copied by Yūsuf ibn Ibrahīm ibn Hiba ibn Qabāṣ al-Sāmirī, the book passed down in the family and other members left their notes in it.

I would suggest that the fact that this colophon appears in the middle of the text, on p. 257, is due to the fact that there was a lacuna in the original text, probably a section missing or badly damaged in the manuscript being copied by Yūsuf. In fact, the original text breaks off here and the next paragraph is clearly not an immediate continuation. This empty space was later filled in by a different hand, as can readily be observed. I would like to thank my *SLAEI* editor Lawrence I. Conrad and Ephraim Wust of the Manuscript Department in the Hebrew University for their aid in reading this colophon.

568 AH 297 = 909–10 CE.

569 Ms. اشرص, "multiplied", "bred". See above, p. 62 n. 127; also Ms. p. 213:3.

570 Ms. امتلت, instead of امتلأت.

571 Ms. الجنابن, pl. of جنبة, "every kind of tree that produces new leaves in the spring or summer". See Lane, *Lexicon*, I.2, 466–67.

572 Ms. ابعث, in the sense of بعث.

573 The measure specified here is *makūk*, a measure of grain and other dry ingredients equaling about 5–6 kilograms. See Kazimirski, *Dictionnaire*, II, 1137; Hinz, *Islamische Masse und Gewichte*, pp. 44–45.

574 This seems to refer again to the damage caused by locusts. See also a similar event above, p. 72 (Ms. p. 223:2–3), where the wheat is measured by قت and the spelling of the plural of قسط appears properly as اقساط.

575 The following text is problematic in several places; those parts of the translation that are tentative appear in brackets.

576 AH 369 = 979–80 CE. This seems quite unlikely, since on the former page the year was 297/909–10, and on the next page the events take place in the days of the caliph al-Rāḍī, i.e. between 322/934 and 329/940.

577 Ms. واقفو; read وافقو.

578 There is a correction here, which renders a clear reading difficult. At first glance the reading seems to be بالرومي, i.e. "in Greek". However, it seems most unlikely that

in the synagogue in all the places of the Samaritans. The assembly was in . . .[579] a convocation of the priests, the Samaritans and all the elders of the community. The *ḥakīm* stood and cursed whoever returned to pronouncing the reading [of the Scriptures] and other things [in this manner]. This was during the Feast of Pentecost, and [this manner of reading] was annulled. This was the doing of the *ra'īs*, a deed which pleased Almighty God and all the people.

The people were afflicted by misfortune, for a conflict broke out amongst them and there was a great dispute amongst them.[580] [But] Almighty God watched [over them] in [His] mercy, and not one of the Samaritans was harmed.[581] In [that] year[582] the governor (*amīr*) al-Rā'irī died, and [another] was instated in his place. Almighty God did the people great good through the hand of 'Abd Allāh[583] and drove the tyranny away from them. [Then] in Tishrīn[584] there came a great earthquake; it was a terrible thing, [but] Almighty God watched over His servants, and no harm came to any Samaritan.

[259] At that time the governor (*mutawallī*) of Egypt was a man called Ṭīlīn[585] (i.e. Takīn). He had a slave whom he especially cherished. The youth

---

in the tenth century Samaritans would be reading anything in Greek. A much better reading is بالرمي, "in Aramaic". A final shift from Aramaic to Arabic at this date seems quite logical: by this time the Samaritan community was speaking mostly Arabic and had given up Aramaic as a spoken language. This reading is supported by the fact that this seems to have been the form in which Samaritans pronounced the word "Aramaic". See Z. Ben Hayyim, *The Literary and Oral Tradition of Hebrew and Aramaic amongst the Samaritans*, I.1: *Recitation of the Law* (Jerusalem, 1961), p. 168 (in Hebrew). I would like to thank Prof. Ben Hayyim for his help in this difficult matter.

[579]Ms. المصه?

[580]It seems likely here that the great conflict was amongst the Muslims, since "not one of the Samaritans was harmed".

[581]Ms. ولم ينضر احد من السامره. Cf. above pp. 73 n. 212, 80 n. 283.

[582]It is not clear what year this is.

[583]According to the sequence of events described below, Abū 'Abd Allāh is to be identified with al-Rāshidī, governor of Palestine before al-Ikhshīd, and then again, after al-Ikhshīd transferred to Damascus. See below, p. 113 n. 593.

[584]This could be either October or November, depending on whether it is Tishrīn I or Tishrīn II.

[585]This may well refer to Abū Manṣūr Takīn ibn 'Abd Allāh, the Turkish governor who ruled Egypt on and off from 297/910 to 321/933. This seems quite suitable, since it comes just before the reign of Muḥammad ibn Ṭughj, the Ikhshīd, who ruled from 323/935. See al-Kindī, *Wulāt*, pp. 267–70, 276–78, 280–81.

broke out with leprosy (*waḍaḥ*), so [Takīn] assembled all the physicians, who gave [the boy] potions to drink and smeared him with ointments.[586] But the more they gave him to drink and smeared him, the sicker he became. [Then the doctors] told him that in Syria there were people [called] Samaritans, amongst whom there were priests who could attend to[587] this illness and pray over him[588] so he would recover. He then ordered that one of the Banū Sayba be brought to him; with him [came] one of his relations [589] from 'Ūskūn who was in his service. The name of Ibn Sayba was El'azar, and the name of his relation was 'Abd'el al-Falūk. When they examined the boy they said: "This is by Almighty God's will." [The Samaritan healer] remained at his bedside for two whole months, and the youth was cured by the will of Almighty God, and his[590] story became known among the nations. [The governor of Egypt] bestowed upon them much bounty, money, and robes of honour, and he wrote that they should be honoured in every place where they reside—when they come, during their stay, and when they leave—for a year and two months. They arrived on the Feast of Tabernacles, and the community was greatly delighted; they thanked Almighty God profusely for the benefactions which He had bestowed upon them, and for having conferred this favour upon them.

During [this] year there was snow in Egypt for three days, such as had never before been seen, **[260]** and many people perished on the roads. After that, Almighty God opened the gates of His kindness and mercy: it rained, and the earth produced its crops, its bounty and its trees generously. There came a reduction in prices of every kind, and the people were satiated and gave profuse thanks to Almighty God for the favour that He had bestowed upon them, for He is a powerful and merciful God and clement to His servants.

That year there came a violent wind on the night of the fast;[591] ships that were at sea broke apart, and countless numbers of people perished in

---

[586]The form لطوخات is unusual. For لطائخ and ملطخات as ointments, see Dozy, *Supplément*, II, 531.

[587]For this sense of نظر, see Kazimirski, *Dictionnaire*, II, 1288.

[588]The text reads يرقيه in singular, but it seems the reading should in fact be in plural, relating to the priests.

[589]A صهر was usually the father or brother of a wife, but could be any relative of the woman's family.

[590]The boy's or the healer's?

[591]This refers to the Day of Atonement, the only fast observed by the Samaritans, being of Biblical origin. See R. Pummer, "Samaritan Rituals and Customs," in Crown, *The Samaritans*, pp. 686–87; Powels, "The Samaritan Calendar," p. 731.

them. In that year locusts came forth and multiplied upon the earth; they ate all the vegetation and everything upon the land, and a great rise in prices followed.

Abū ʿAbd Allāh['s rule] in Ramla collapsed[592] and Ibn Ṭughj arrived from Egypt [to take up the post] of governor of Ramla.[593] His fellow officers (*aṣḥābuhu*) did harm everywhere in the land, and he remained seven months[594] and then departed for Damascus.[595]

[Then] Abū ʿAbd Allāh returned to Ramla, and a rebel by the name of al-Ḥiyātī[596] revolted and assembled vast forces and went to ...[597] on the feast day of the Muslims,[598] and he killed a great many of them; he violated[599] the women's honour and plundered the gold, the silver and everything that was in the house. He left but few of the people unharmed.

In the second year it was reported that a river had overflowed and ruined

---

[592]This translation of انكسر as "collapsed" (see Lane, *Lexicon*, I.6, 2611) rather than "was broken/was defeated" is based on Ibn Saʿīd's description that when al-Rāshidī got word of al-Ikhshīd's due arrival he fled, leaving his house furnished: ولما بلغ الراشدي امير الرملة مسير الاخشيد هرب وترك داره مفروشة. See Ibn Saʿīd, *Mughrib*, p. 8.

[593]On the following pages the rule of Muḥammad ibn Ṭughj, the Ikhshīd, in Palestine is described. The episode described here took place when the Ikhshīd escaped from Egypt, after having fallen from favour there, and received the governorship of Palestine (928–31); see Gil, *History of Palestine*, pp. 316–17. He thus took the place of the former governor of Ramla, named in the Muslim sources as al-Rāshidī, who is called in our text Abū ʿAbd Allāh—using, as usual, his *kunya* rather than his *laqab*. Hearing this al-Rāshidī fled to Damascus and received the post there. Then al-Ikhshīd, preferring the post of Damascus himself, took it over and al-Rāshidī returned to Palestine. This is recorded by Ibn Saʿīd, *Kitāb al-mughrib*, IV, ed. K.L. Tallqvist (Leiden, 1899), p. 8; and by ʿArīb ibn Saʿd, *Ṭabarī Continuatus*, ed. M.J. de Goeje (Leiden, 1965), p. 159, who says expressly that Ibn Ṭughj was appointed governor of Damascus in place of al-Rāshidī, who was given back the district of Ramla (i.e. Palestine) . On Ibn Ṭughj, see J.L. Bacharach, "The Career of Muḥammad b. Tughj al-Ikhshīd, a Tenth-Century Governor of Egypt", *Speculum* 50 (1975), pp. 586–612, esp. p. 590 for this specific episode.

[594]This fact is not mentioned, as far as I know, in other sources.

[595]Ibn Ṭughj was made governor of Damascus in Jumādā II 319/July 931. See Bacharach, "The Career of Muḥammad b. Tughj", p. 590.

[596]Ms. الحاتي. This reading is tentative, and the name does not appear again.

[597]The word here—presumably a place name—is unclear, and it is obvious that the copyist could not decipher it.

[598]Ms. في عند المسلمين; read في عيد المسلمين (L.C.).

[599]For this sense of نهب see Dozy, *Supplément*, II, 727.

many places, **[261]** and many people perished as a result of this destruction. That year there was bounty in everything and a reduction in prices such as had never before been seen.

In those days Ibn Ṭughj started gathering troops in Damascus and rebelled against the ruler (*sulṭān*).[600] Al-Qāhir [was deposed],[601] and his place was taken by the son of Ja'far, al-Muqtadir,[602] who was called 'Abd Allāh al-Rāḍī.[603] He wrote to Muḥammad ibn 'Alī, who was in charge of Palestine, that Ibn Ṭughj was planning to wage war against him in Palestine in the month of Āb, in the fifth year after the Sabbatical Year. Muḥammad ibn 'Alī's men came and attacked Ibn Ṭughj; Muḥammad ibn 'Alī was defeated, and he fled, taking everything he owned. He left and entered Egypt,[604] and Ibn Ṭughj ruled over the land of Palestine.

---

[600]Ms. وعصي على السلطان. This, it seems, is a reference to Ibn Kayghalagh, the ruler of Egypt whom al-Ikhshīd fought and defeated in August 935. This seizure was later legitimized. See Bacharach, "The Career of Muḥammad b. Tughj", pp. 593–94.

[601]The word السلطان is followed by a gap about one word long, then the word القاهره. The reference to al-Qāhira is strange here, since Cairo was founded by the Fāṭimid caliph al-Mu'izz only in 970. It is most likely that it is a result of the copyist's misapprehension, writing القاهرة instead of القاهر. The caliph al-Qāhir was deposed on 24 April 934. It is thus possible to complete the lacuna thus: وعصي على السلطان [وعزل] القاهر وقام بعده.

[602]The ر of المقتدر is missing in the text.

[603]The caliph al-Rāḍī was actually called Abū l-'Abbās Aḥmad al-Rāḍī and not 'Abd Allāh, and he reigned from 322/934 to 329/940.

[604]The episode described here seems to be a continuation of عصى على السلطان above. Muḥammad ibn 'Alī is, in all probability, Abū Bakr Muḥammad ibn 'Ali al-Mādharā'ī, who was in charge of the finances in Egypt—the most powerful position in the Egyptian court. The Mādharā'īs were a well-known family who served as high officials under the Ṭūlūnids in Egypt, and then under the 'Abbāsids, both in Egypt and in Syria. Abū Bakr Muḥammad ibn 'Alī served as director of finances in Egypt under the Ṭūlūnids (890–905), while his famous uncle, al-Ḥusayn ibn Aḥmad al-Mādharā'ī, called Abū Zunbur, served as director of finances in Syria.

Muḥammad ibn 'Alī returned to Egypt under the 'Abbāsids, and was again in charge of finances between 930 and 933. He actively resisted the Ikhshīd's attempt to rule Egypt and its legitimatization by the caliph al-Rāḍī. He did, in fact, base his claim upon a letter he had formerly received from al-Rāḍī. Muḥammad ibn Ṭughj fought him, defeated him, and had him arrested. See Ibn Sa'īd, *Mughrib*, pp. 15–16, 25; H.L. Gottschalk, *Die Madara'ijjun* (Berlin, 1931), pp. 103–105; idem, "Al-Mādharā'ī," *EI*², V, 953. Both Abū Bakr Muḥammad ibn 'Alī and his uncle al-Ḥusayn ibn Aḥmad had estates in Syria and in Palestine; an inscription dating from the days of al-Muqtadir grants al-Ḥusayn special privileges on his estate in Jund Filasṭīn. On this, see Elad, "Two Identical Inscriptions", pp. 301–60, esp. pp. 349–51.

It was a difficult year for all the Samaritans. Arab men from Jimsāfūṭ[605] assembled and killed five men of the Samaritans—four[606] who were from Ashkarū and one from al-Niḥāsa[607]—who were chiefs of their villages. [The Samaritans] were killed within the hour; it was said that they burned them, and there was great pain[608] among the Samaritans. After this, Ibn Ṭughj laid his hand upon the Samaritans. He began punishing them and took money from them; all the leaders of the Samaritans became impoverished, [**262**] and the people of the villages were stripped of all that they possessed. The affliction of the Samaritans, both the young and the old, continued everywhere. [Even] the pious man (*'abd*) was perplexed about the most sordid fate [decreed upon him] by heaven.[609] Oh, what sorrow and calamity! For ten days in the month of Tishrīn stars were seen falling from the sky; in their descent they coughed up fires, like immense lightning bolts, and they continued from the middle of the night until after sunrise, falling one after the other.

Ibn Ṭughj sent to Nablus an officer (*'āmil*) and with him a great army; he oppressed the Samaritans terribly and punished a group of them, and the synagogue became void of prayer in the days of...[610] on the road to Ramla...the corn[611] ...[612] in the synagogue because of the terrible evil and affliction that became evident...[613] during the rule...days...and after

---

[605]Ms. حمساڡوط, presently spelt Jinṣāfūṭ, is an Arab village in the centre of Samaria. The name is recorded already in documents from the time of Ramses II. See F.M. Abel, *Géographie de la Palestine* (Paris, 1938), II, 26. It seems that the copyist himself was not familiar with the place, since there are no diacritical points here. The obvious spelling error (Jinsāfūṭ instead of Jinṣāfūṭ) is based on oral rather than written transmission; see Introduction, p. 18.

[606]Ms. وواربعه; read اربعه.

[607]These are apparently names of places, although they bear no resemblance to any known place names in the area of Samaria.

[608]Ms. لحعه; read جعة, which appears to be an equivalent form of وجع.

[609]Ms. وحار العبد علي اقبح قضيه بالسما. This sentence is difficult, and the reading is tentative.

[610]From this point the text is incoherent, with lacunae in many places, where the text seems to have been illegible to the copyist.

[611]Or "leaves/stalks"; The word here is عصف; since the context is unknown it is difficult to determine the precise meaning.

[612]Ms. ولا ا الالوتيه.

[613]Once again the text is incoherent, and there seems to be no logical meaning, as if the copyist skipped over words he could not read but did not always leave blank spaces

this... Ibn al-Sabī and took much money from him; but God was benevolent towards His flock[614] and rescued [them]. [Then] there rose a Samaritan man, a priest[615] by the name of Kaydhāsh, may Almighty God have no mercy upon him and may He not be pleased with him; he served Ibn Ṭughj and was obedient[616] to him, and wrote down for him the names of the Samaritans who had money. Ibn Ṭughj took their money **[263]** and seized them and punished them in various ways. [But] Almighty God watched over them in His mercy, and Ibn Ṭughj dismissed and killed Kaydhāsh,[617] may Almighty God have no mercy upon him and may He not be pleased with him, and the Samaritans did not [want?[618]] for anything.

Glory be to the Almighty, who changes yet does not change himself; His glory shall not cease for ever and ever. He is the Almighty, the Beneficient, the Merciful, the Compassionate, the Giver of life and the Causer of death, the Bestower, the Almighty and Master of all things, the Crown of life whose crown shall be for ever and ever. There is no god but Him; may His name and the veneration of His majesty be exalted; He is sufficient for me, an excellent Guardian is He.[619]

[**264**] In the name of Yahweh:

This blessed book was finished with the aid of Almighty God, His favour and the goodness of His guidance on the blessed day of Thursday, the twentieth of the exalted month of Ramaḍān[620] in the year nine hundred and thirty, in the name of him who is copying [this work] for his own use, the most meek, most base, most despicable slave, who will confess [his] sins and shortcomings on

---

accordingly.

614 This should obviously be رعية or alternatively رعايا, since رعاة bears the meaning of "shepherds".

615 Ms. כהן.

616 Ms. سلس له. See Lane, *Lexicon*, I.3, 1404.

617 Since it is known that Ibn Ṭughj reigned until his death, it seems that اعزل here bears the sense of عزل.

618 There is a gap of one word in the Ms. here.

619 See Sūra III, v. 173: حسبنا الله ونعم الوكيل. This benediction was often used at the end of Islamic manuscripts.

620 The twentieth day of Ramadān 930 fell on a Friday. If it was indeed a Thursday (19 Ramaḍān), then it was 21 July 1524.

the Day of Judgment, the slave Musallam ibn Yūsuf ibn Ibrahīm ibn Hiba ibn Qabāṣ al-Sāmirī al-Yūsufī by descent, Mūsawī in his belief, may Almighty God forgive him, then his father, then he who reads it and invokes [God's] forgiveness upon the writer and upon the whole of the community of Israel in its entirety. [Let] the peace of Yahweh [be] upon Moshe.[621] The reader is asked not to rebuke the slave for his penmanship, since he is an apprentice; the words bespeak of their speaker. Praised be God, Lord of the Worlds, who does not neglect the wages of those who do good.

[621] This seems to be a transcription of the Hebrew שלום יהוה על משה.

ARABIC TEXT

(Bibliothèque Nationale Ms. Samaritaine n. 10, pp. 203–64)

203

ثالث عشر كراس

فصل

وكان في تلك الايام ثلاثة رجال منجمين يقولوا اما يجري الاول
من مصر سامري من عسكر والثاني كعب الاحبار يهودي
والثالث عبد الله نصراني من اللاذقية وكانوا الثلاثة يعرفوا صناعة
بعضهم بعض ونظروا في علو منهم ان ملك الروم قد زال وملك
اشعيل مبتدي وان قايم لهم قايم من اولادها شهر وعلامته في طهره
شامة صفرا في وسع الكتف واول ما يبتدي يخرج من الجزيرة ~~وحهام~~ مدينه
تسما مدينة الرسول فاجتمعوا الثلاثة وقالوا ان مات لنسير ننظر
هذا ان كان اياه ام لا فان كان هوه دبرنا ما نفعل به ولا سلمنا
من هولاي الذي تقدم ذكرهم مضوا الثلاثة ووصلوا الى مدينته التي
هو فيها فان لما اتوا اليه وزاره فقالوا من يقدم عليه واستقر بان يتقدم
كعب الاحبار يتقدم الى النبي صلى الله عليه فقال له محمد من انت فقال
رجل من مقدمي اليهود اصبت في توراتي ان يقوم من نسل اسمعيل

204

يملك في نفح الدنيا ولا يقف بين يديه احد وقال عبد الله مثله ه
اصبت في الانجيل ولم يكونوا اعرفوا شي الا حكومته فلما تقدم ه
ضمر مضر السامري قال له هل انت تدين بدين في شريعه وتملك بها
رقاب الكفار وتملك بها الدنيا ولنا نيل علامه بين اكتافك فقام
وكشف ظهره ونظر السامري في ظهره واتفق كعب الاحبار
لما سمع كلام ضمر مضر واتفق ايضا عبد السلام وفرح الرجل ايضا
بذلك وفرح بما سمعه من كلام [illegible] وقال اما الذي تفعل
مثل ما فعلوا اهو لاني كان قد اخذ عليه الاحد والميثاق قبل ما بشره
انه لا يدرهه على ما لا يريده فقال له ضمر مضر السامري عندي من هذا
حاجتي يعني الشريعه والدين فقال له جواب هذا ما خطابك
يا سامري في تمام الكلام وهي من كعب الاحبار انه بحيث ان يعمل
مثله وكل بليه ما لحقنا الا من اليهود الله يطالبهم وراح ه
ضمر مضر وبقي كعب الاحبار وعبد السلام وصار كعب الاحبار

بكاسه

205

يكاتبه وهو الذي رتب كل ما ترتب في كان ينك على كل فعل وغيره
ومن خليقة ادم الى ملك بيشغال خمسة الاف وسبعه واربعين سنه وبعد
هذا خرجوا على الروم محمد وكل جيوش العرب
وفتحوا الارض وكسروا الروم وقتلوهم وهربوا من بين ايديهم وكان الامام
الذي كان في تلك الايام عقبة بن العز ساكن في بيت تمامه
ولما خرجوا المسلمين وهربوا الروم من كل الشامره الذي كانوا على
ساحل البحر هربوا مع الروم من قدام المسلمين وكانوا انهم يعودوا
ولما جاوا الشامره يسيروا مع الروم الى زميهجا والى الرئيس عقبة
بن العز الى بيت تمامه لانه كان ساكن هناك وقالوا له انك
رجل مامون ونحن نودع مالنا الى ما نعود وكانوا يظنوا انهم
عايدين عن قريب فجمعوا اموالهم وجعلوها عنده واجتمع عنده مال
لا يحد ولا يعلم ما هو لهاولا القوم الذي ادعوا اهل قيسارية وارسوف
ومباس ويافا ولد وعسقلان وغزه وبقية الضياع المتفرده والذي

206

علي ساحل البحر من بعد هذا سار ازرو الي شرق صيده ولم يعودوا الي الآن
وهناك اقاموا ودخلوا المسلمين الي الارض كنعان وملكوها واخذوا سائر
المدن وسكنوا فيها وملكوا كل الاماكن وما بقي مكان الا واخذوه الا قيسارية
فانها عصيت وانتم اليهم لانها كانت الها ام المدن ومقدم عليهم
ونزلوا عليها وحاصروها سبع سنين قبل يفتحوها وكانوا الروم
يتحزموا البحر قبل ما يعرفوا المسلمين البحر وكان في حصن قيسارية
من الشام في زاوية الشام الا الي الغرب باب لطيف كانوا الروم
يدخلوا ويخرجوا منه والمسلمين ما يعلموا وسيره مصوح مفتوح
وخرج جوج منه كلب فلما راوه جاوا وراه الي الباب في ما عليهم وركبوا
القتل في المدينة واقاموا يوم كامل يقتلوا في السوق السفلاني وبقي
قبل يغلبوا الفوقاني لانها كانت مبنية مدينة فوق مدينة ومن قدر يهرب
في البحر هرب في من قام منهم وقتلوه ومن استسلم لهم سلم وافتحت هرب
المدينة وسكنوا فيها فلما فتحوها حلت هيبتهم علي سائر الاماكن هو

بي

207

بني اسمعيل الخياطين واكل الاما لكن ورتب الجزيه اربعه دراهم ومثلاه

شعير من سوى خراج الارض في الاسلام ما انتسا الى احد كل ما امر

كان يعرض على الناس الذهب عن جا اليه قبله ومن لا يجي ما يغصبه وقام

عشر سنين في ملكه وكل العمال الطايعين له ومنه انتقلت مملكته الى اقاربه

بني اميه على ما اوصاهم لم يزيدوا ولا ينقصوا ولا اسوا الى احد وقام

منهم تسعه عشر ملك اولاد [illegible] محمد عاش ثلاثه وستين سنه ثلاث

واربعين سنه لم يتعرض الى احد بشي وعشر سنين حروب وعشر ه

وقام ب ..... سنين [illegible] وملك ومات بعده [illegible] بدعي

ابي بكر الصديق وملك سنتين وثلاث شهور وقام من بعده عمر بن

الخطاب وملك عشر سنين وسبع شهور وفي السنه السابعه فتحت ه

نيسابور وقتله رجل يعرف ابو لولوه عبد الرجل نيسابور الي وقام بعده

عثمان بن عفان وملك اثني عشر سنه وقتل ووقع الخلف في المسلمين

واقاموا اربع سنين وتسع شهور في الخلف وقام بعد ذلك معاويه

208

بن ابي سفيان ثم ملك عشرون سنة وثمان شهور ثم قام بعده ابنه معاوية
ابنه ملك اربع شهور ومات ثم قام بعده مروان بن الحكم وملك اربع
شهور ومات ثم قام بعده عبد الله بن الزبير وملك ثمانية سنين وخمس
شهور وقام بعده عبد الملك بن مروان بن الحكم وملك ثلاث عشرة
سنين وست شهور ومات ثم قام بعده الوليد ابنه وملك تسع سنين
وسبع شهور وقام سليمان اخوه وملك سنتين وثمان شهور وقام
عمر بن عبد العزيز وملك سنتين وست شهور وقام يزيد بن عبد الملك بن
مروان وملك اربع سنين ثم قام هشام اخوه وملك تسع عشرة سنة وثمان
شهور وقام بعده الوليد بن يزيد بن عبد الملك وملك سنة واحدة
وثلاث شهور وقام يزيد الناقص بن الوليد وملك خمس شهور وقام
ابرهيم اخوه وملك شهرين واحد عشر يوم وقام مروان بن محمد
الآخر من بني امية وملك خمس سنين وشهرين كل منذ ملك الاسلام
والى هذا الوقت مائة واحد وثلاثون سنة وثلاث شهور وجاء في

ثم

209

ايام مروان زلزله عظيمه كبيره في كل مكان ونزلت الدور علي سكانها
وفني من الناس ما لا يحصي وكانت زلزله عظيمه لم يري مثلها ومن سلم
من الناس اقاموا في البراري ايام كثيره ما كانت تطرب وتلعب بهم ولما
ولما اراد الله هذا برحمته ومن هذا دخلوا المدن وهدا نفوسهم
وبعد هذا اتحبروا بني العباس علي بني اميه وخرجوا الي لقاهم
ووقع في المسلمين الخلف منهم مع بني العباس ومنهم مع بني الاميه ووقع
بينهم حرب عظيم هايل وهو الحرب المعروف بحرب الكوشيين وانهزموا
الذي كانوا في عون بني اميه وقتلوا في مكان رجل من خراسا ن
يعرف ابو مسلم ومعه عساكر كثير نقام في عون بني العباس
حتي ياخذ لهم الملك من بني اميه والتقا مع مروان وكسره وانهزم
مروان حتي وصل الي مصر ولحقوه رجال ابو مسلم وقتلوه في
مصر واخذوا راسه بعدما ملك خمس سنين وعادوا جاوا ودفع
ابو مسلم الملك لبني العباس من بني هاشم حينيذ ثبت ملكه في

210

العباس ملك اغريزة قوية واضعفوا الخراج في الارض وزادوا في
الله الجالر وثقلوا مشقتها وجبوا من كل اعمالهم وضريبة وضيقوا
على الناس فيها وجبوا المال وجمعوه جدا وقام من بعد مروان
عبد الله يدعي العباس من بني هاشم في ملك اربع سنين وثمان شهور
وقام من بعده اخوه يدعي ابو جعفر وارسل الى فلسطين سلطان
يدعي عبد الوهاب بن عبد الله ابو اشندي وضيق على الناس جدا وخا
نسل الاربوع وخلا عبد الوهاب الى متوليا بالشجر والقبلة الذي بنا اهلها
ريفون يشحون عظامهم لا يحتمل على الجبل عرض منه تحت السامرة وحرث
حتى يجبي منهم مال بسبب حرقها وخلا جماعة رجال في الليل واحرقوها
واحرقوا الكنيسة الذي كانوا الروم ينظروا الضو عليها في الليل
قتلوا فيها اشبع خمسة رهبان نصارا والنصارا يقولوا اما الله
احرقها الا السامرة وارسل ابو اشندي اخذ الرئيس وكان
هناك رجل من بني نشاية ويقال له يهني بن الملك وسالوني معني

الدين

.211

الرئيس وخلاه وسلمه اليه واخذ الرئيس واحد من هو [illegible] .

بن ذو تر وكان متولي رياسة الامور ضيق عليه وحلق راسه وقاطعه على

ثلثه الاف دينار واعانوه الشامرة وقام بها وتخلص في ايام قري شبا

الرئيس واستبى الرئيس واحترقت القبة جمعوا ملك اثنى عشر سنة

قام بعده ابنه يدعى [illegible] . المهدي وملك عشر سنين وشهر

ومات وقام ابنه بعده واسمه موشي وملك سنة وشهرين ومات

وبعد هذا انتقل الرئيس قري شبا وخلف ابنه [illegible] . صغير

وقام ابن اخوه وتحكم في الامر ولم يلي الحساب العبراني الكبير الا الصغير الا

يعمل بالرومي واقام سبع سنين ومات وقام ابنه يريد يكون مكانه وما

وما يعرف حساب الا الذي كان مع ابوه وما احسن يدبر وقام [illegible] .

بن قري شبا مقابله وكان الحساب العبراني الصحيح معه واخرجوا

بطاقتين [illegible] . و[illegible] واختلفوا ووقعوا الشامرة معهم

[illegible] في خلف عظيم منهم مع [illegible] . ومنهم مع [illegible] . واخرجوا

212

البطاقتين للصوم بطاقة تشال الاثنين وبطاقة قولا الثلثا
وكانوا رجال الضباع نصفهم مع هذا ونصفهم مع هذا فالذي
كانوا مع [illegible] قاموا الاثنين والذي كانوا مع قولا صاموا
الثلثا وكلمن قام عملوا الاخر في ضده ولحق السامره في هذا لحق
عظيم واجتمعوا امقدمي السامره الي [illegible] الريس وقالوا له
كيف نخلوا السامره في هذه البليه العظيمه تنتظر رجال عارفين
خايفين الله تعالي يدخلوا ويكشفوا الذي مع هذا ومع هذا فان كان
الحق فما كلنا معه واختاروا [illegible] اربع رجال
اثنين من اصحاب هذا واثنين من اصحاب هذا واستحلفوهم ذرثا
انهم لا يخفوا الحق حيث كان ويقال لهم الذين يرتدون علمه انهم
متقلدين انتم هذا العالم وانتم تكشفوا الحق بينهم واين من كان الحق
للحق معه كانت الامر كلها معه ودخلوا وكشفوا فاقام ابو
الحق مع [illegible] وشكل الشعب معه وبشيرن اما متد الحق

وكان

213

وكان في السنه الذي قام احمد بعده . قام بعد يونس اخوا هرون بن المهدي
من بني هاشم وجراد عظيم جا في ايامه مثل المطر اسبله واكل كل الخضير
وكل عشب البر واستقر في الارض وخرج شوصه وغطا وجه الارض
من البحر والي الاردن واكل كل ما علي الارض من خضير وعشب فلم
يبقي شي علي وجه الارض وبقيت الارض خاليه وفي السنه الاخري وقع
في المسلمين خلف وقتال بينهم وبينهم وصاروا فرقتين ولحد يقال لهم
مدرانين واخر يقال لهم سسن وكانوا يخرجوا ليحاربوا بعضهم
بعض بعضا وبعطيهم ويقتلوا من هاولاي ومن هاولاي بلا رحمه
وكانوا السكان منهم من الشام وغيرهم في شده عظيمه واهاليه
يخلوا الضياع وينهبوا الغلال الذهب والفضه والنحاس والكسوه
وقام علينا الوعيد المكتوب بزنا بدنح بين يديك ولا ياكل منه جميع
الوعيد هربوا الناس وخلوا ضياعهم خاليه مما كان يجري عليهم
من العقاب والبلاوان لحقوا امرا . يعلموا انها افعال اهل سنم ودخلوا

علي الناس منهم بلا لاسنه اقاموا الناس في الجبال وفي المغاير من بعد
ما انكشفت الناس من كل ما يملكوا او تفيو كشف من كل شي فمن كان له
من جاز منهم كان يستند اليه بعطيه ماله ويحميه وناس لم يكن له ما حب
يبقي تايه في الجبال والمغاير والاوديه وكانوا لما صاروا ايدخلوا الا
يصيبوا شي ياخذوه ويحرقوا الدور والبلاد ولا يبقوا شي الا يحرقوه
وخربت الديار واقاموا كذا لقرب سنين وتصدق الله وافرق بينهم
وفي السنه الاخري جا علي الناس غلا عظيم ودخل علي الناس بلا
ما فيه رحمه وكانت الناس قد انكشفوا من ٢ او من داخل من البر
الجراد ومن داخل العدو وابعد يدور في طلب الحربه وقام الوعيد
وتصير في يدي اعاديكم عند كسرتي قوي الحرب الخبر وجاعت الناس
الجوع الشديد الهابل حتي نسي الشبع كما قيل ما كلوا اولا
تشبعوا فقال ان امراه اكلت ابنها في ضيقه فقال لها ازبع
مات الطفل فلما مات خذته قطعته وطبخته ودخلوا له

الناس

215

الناس ونظروا ابدا طالعه من القدر وقالوا لها ايش تطبخي قالت تنفذ
قالوا لها من اين لك تنفذ ونظروا الى القدر فاذا بها لحم انسان
وقالوا لها ايش البليه هذه العظيمه قالت ان ابنها مات واخذته
وطبخته حتى تاكله من قوه الجوع وكانت الامراه بدويه من العرب ساكنه
هناك وارسل الله على الناس بالموت وما اكثر من ماتوا في فناء
الطريق وما قبروا وصارت الخلايق قبره وكانت الامم تحفر الحفره
يجعلوا فيها عشره وخمسه مما كانوا الا يلحقوا يدفنوا
وما اكثر من سامري وكاهن ماتوا وما بكيوا كما يجب لحاله
الكبر ولا دفنوا كما يجب وما اكثر من بنين ابعدوا عن اباهم واباء بعدوا
عن بنيهم وما تروا ما عرفوا احد منهم حال الاخر كمثل كان من الموت
والجوع وانقلبت سحن الناس وما بقي انسان يسال عن ابن ولا ابن يسال
عن ابي ولا اخ يسال عن اخوه ويريد يتعظ الويل الذي ينظر بنفسه
هذا البلا وهنيا لمن يسحن ويخلص من امتحانه ويصل الفرج

216

وبعد هذا ابسط الله يتحمد وفرج وارفع السخط عن عبيده وارسل
النجاح في الارض واشبع النفوس واكلوا الناس وشبعوا والقليل من الناس
الذي بقي والقليل من الناس طلعوا الجبال في جج الظلال الذي بعد
شدة الموت كانوا اشل ليجتمع في كنيسة ضيعة صغيرة وبعد لما ماه

فلاح ما لي الا العشب كان كثير دلجز وما كان لهم بهايم وبقيت الناس لما
باكلين نصوصو الاشين والخبيش وكبتوا شيوخ الشعب السامرة في
كل مكان نطلعوا بين يدي وصلوا صلاه عظيمة وكان ذلك في الجبل

الجميع الله

جدا

2.17

في باش الشهر الذي بعد عيد الشابع ومضت كتب الريس الى الضياع
وطلعوا الناس الى الجبل في يوم الاحد وكانت صلاة عظيمة وصراخ
عظيم كان يوم الاثنين والثلثا

وجعلوا الاطفال يصرخوا ويقولوا يا الاه ابانا الازكيا ارفع
عنا هذا البلا تشفع المولى الله تعالى معونتهم بذكر الاباء ودفع الموت
عنهم وانعدا السخط بالحسانه لانه الاه كثير الاحسان قريب الرحمة
لا يرغب في السخط وكانت الناس لا يستطيعوا ان يعبروا في الطرق

218

اجسامهم

من روايح النبايل حتى انهم تغيرت الجماسهم من الرايحه وارتفع الموت
عن البهايم وتعبت الناس في الدراس ما كانوا يقدروا على شي يدرسوا
عليه والجاحوا ايدرسوا على الحمير والجمال وساير البهايم وفي الزراعه
ايضا وبطلت الارض وقام علينا الوعيد بقوله واني بهايمكم وما
اكثر ما بار من الارض من قلة البهايم وظهيت الارض من نبايل البهايم
كل هذه الشدايد لما اعتقينا ربنا كل هذا كان في ايام هرون
خليفة المسلمين وكان الرئيس لهم ... امام اسرايل

فصل

وكان بعد هذا الحاضر لما حضرت وفاة الرشيد هرون
اخبروا اولاده ثلاثه ... محمد وعبد الله وقاسم وقسم المملكه
عليهم وجعل خراسان لعبد الله ومن خراسان وجاي
كل الارض الى افريقيه جعل لمحمد كل ساحل البحر من الطرف الى
الطرف وجعل القاسم وجعل محمد المقدم في الملك بعده وجعل

عبد الله

عبد الله من بعده وقاسم من بعد الكل ورتبهم على مثل هذا وعمل

منهم ايمان وعهود وشهادات وجعل مشايخ في كل مملكته ان من

بعد هذا العهد وجحد يوجد منه كل الناس يتساعدوا عليه

ويتبروا من عهده وقسامته وملك هرون اثني وعشرون سنه

واحد عشر شهر ومات وقام محمد ابنه في مكانه وكان مطرح للملاه

وحسن لنفسه يلازم [illegible] يلبسهم لباس حشم ويزينهم بزينه

[illegible] . وينضجع معهم وينعلع عليهم وشكل اهله على الاستادين

بدؤه وغضب الله عليه وازال الهيبه عن الناس وانعكست الناس

عليه ودخل على عسكر كبير واخلافه عسكر وقتل في كل الاماكن

وكان التاريخ من خليقة ادم الى قيام محمد ابن هرون الرشيد خمسة الاف

سنه ومايتي وتسعه وثلاثون سنه ووقع الخلف بينهم وقتل كثير من

ساير البلاد الى الاردن والنهب في ساير الاماكن وقتل سامره

كثير مقدمي ضياع واقام الوعيد للكتوب واشتغلتم شبعه خرج

221

ابو عوف رجل حرامي وجا الي فلسطين ونزل في شلم ولما قتل هو و
اصحابه واختلفوا المسلمين خلف كثير وخرج من جيشه رجل من
يعرف براهيم وكان ابنه من المقتولين في شلم وخرج معه جيش كبير
واجتمعوا الي نيتا ومضوا الي الدشوف ونهبوا وقتلوا واحرقوا اضياع
ونهبوا الكنايس واحرقوا مقاله الشبابك الدشوف ما قدروا يدخلوها
ورجعوا ونهبوا كلما قدروا عليه وكانخاف الليل والنهار واجتمعوا
بعد ذلك مدينه وقبس الي قيساريه وخرجوا ونهبوا الضياع
وخربوا الدنيا وخرج براهيم ثانيه ومضى الي قيساريه وخرج
الكناسين بجيش كثير من قيساريه وهرب براهيم من بين يدي
الكناسين فلحقوهم وقتلوا منهم جماعه وبعد هذا ابرح الله
برحمته وغير الشك بفرج وادنا محمد مقدسيين ولا علي
الارض وهذه الناس تبددوا اهل السوا ورجعنا الي بيوتنا
ول... سنين قتل محمد وقام اخوه عبد الله ووقع الخلف بين الناس

بال

في كل مكان وبطلت سلطنته وما سمعت الناس منه وكانوا
الناس يوقعوا الشر ويقتلوا بعضهم بعض وما اكثر من قتل بينهم
وكان الخلف والبغضة بينهم والسبي في النسا والاطفال
واتبع جماعة من الشامرة وثبت الوعيف بتوك وبنا تل بصير وا
لشعب اخر وعيسا كما طرة ولبس قدرة لك وبطلت نسا او قتل
شامرة وغيرهم من كل الامم وخربت ضياع وخليت من سكانها
وانقطعت الارض من يسلك فيها وكانت الناس واقعين في البلا
خايفين ليل ونهار وكثرت الشدايد وخرج الجراد سنه بعد سنه
واكل الرطب مع اليابس وجا الغلا وضعفت الناس وعدموا
مالهم وماشيتهم وتدنا بين الشعوب هرنا هرو في السيف كل
هذا واكثر منه من كثرة الخطايا والذنوب الذي فعلوا الناس بين
يدي الله تعالى وعبدوا الباطل وبعدوا من الحق وفعل الخير
وبطلوا امرا يض الله تعالى بسبب ذلك لحقنا هذه الشدايد

222

كلما ناديوا الله تبارك اليهم بطل علامته مع ابرهيم واسحق ويعقوب
عليهم السلام وانغم واخلف هذه الشدة بفرج واجتمعوا المسلمين
ومسكوا كل انسان مكانه وكان بينهم البغض والشر ومن كان
سفك الدم بينهم شي جملة ومسك رجال كثير ورجل يقال له
مسرور بن ابو عامر كلهم ربطوا بالحبل وامنه وكان يحب السامرة
واطاعوه الناس وكان رجل حرب عظيم ويفعل الخير وكل السامرة
الذي في خوف معين واتخذ له صديق من شغال السهر رعا مده وكرهوه
المسلمين وقالوا اما نقدر نقتله الا بمكر ولا نقدم عليه الا صديقه
رعا مده وحالفوه عليه فلما نزل عند رعامر وهم على الطعام قام
اليه رعا مده وقتله وعاد البلا وقتل من جماعة رعامر دعى اثنين
بلا عدد ولا احصا واتفق الرئيس ما تبع على جملة قاموا بها السامرة
وراح الى داره سالم وكان عند الطايفة يوم فرح وسرور عظيم وشكروا
الله كثير على سلامته وهذا كله ثمر الخلاف الذي خالفنا امر
الله

223

رابع عشر كراس

الله ربنا وبعد هذه السنة جا جراد واكل القمح وهو اعشب
الارض واكل الشجر وجا غلا عظيم وبلغ القمح قبة بدينار والزيت
خمس اقساط بدينار ويجب لله ثم ينظر الحال الان انه يرحم برحمته
وهو رحيم رؤوف لا يهوي الشخص وخرج الجراد في السنة لما
الثانية وضعفوا الناس من احوالهم من الغلا كلما زادت الشدة
زادوا الناس خلاف وتظلمت الارض من كثرة القتل والسلب وكانت
كثير يتذللوا ونساكا امنوا اولادهم كانه ومقدمي الحكام وحايش
ولما تبدلت بعسكر هن عسكر ما قدروا ابوها بقتلها من سبب
اهل اهل القرية انهم ما مكنوه من قتلها راى ابعادها عنه
وحفظ قول الله تعالى وبعد اليه من جلسته وسامره عسكرهم
الم يحصل لهم شي لانهم كانوا قادرين ولم يفعلوا معها خير لانها
تبدلت من الجوع ولما لم يفعلوا معها خير معها ولا مع غيرها زاد
الله البلا عليهم وعلى عدة انواع وثبت عليهم لان الله لا يرفع

224

وجبه ولا ياخذ شا الاحكام حتي وصيق لان من قدر علي عمل خير
ولا يعملونه زاد الله الشده عليه واذا تم طعم البلا وحب الله وفرج
واكلوا الناس وشبعوا من نعم الله انسلكت الطرق ولبثوا الناس
فطلعوا السامره من كل مكان الي [illegible] وصاموا وصلوا
وشكروا الله كثيرا وحمدوه علي تفضله الذي ازال عنهم هذه
الشده بالفرج والرحمه من قبله وبعد ثلثه عشر سنه من ملك عبد الله
المامون ارسل رجل يعرف بخالد بن يزيد ومعه جيش عظيم ولم
يعلموا به الناس الا وهو الي فلسطين وخافوا كل المسلمين منه
خوف شديد وايسوا من الحياه وكانت الخوارج عولوا علي انهم
يهربوا ويخلوا جميع ما يملكوه فلما راوه طالع الي مصر عادوا
الي امنهم كما كانوا واسوا الي السامره وقتلوا منهم جماعه
وعبر خالد والجيش الي مصر وحاربوه المصريين وكان
رجل حرب عظيم وافنا منهم بالقتل خلق عظيم وحاصرهم وبلاهم

حمده

225

جمعه وتقدم فغزوه بعسكر عظيم واستاسروه ولما اخذوه انطلق مع

كل اصحابه واعتقلوه المصريين ثمانية عادوا اخلوه وراح الي

بلده وكان كل السنين من ادم الي يحيى خالد بن يزيد الي ملك مصر

خمسة الالف سنة ومايتي سنة وخمسون سنة وبعد اربع سنين

ارسل عبدالله الملك رجل اسمه عبدالله بن طاهر ومعه جيش

عظيم ولم يعمل مثل ما تقدم على الخوارج وراه ومضي بين يديه الاملا

خرج من بغداد فتح البلاد الذي بين يديه واعطاه الله النصر

وفعل معه الاحسان وكثر كل جبابرة الارض وجا الي حمص

وقام عليه نصر بن شبث بجيش كبير جوارح وحاصر حمص وضيق

على نصر حتى استامن نصر وخرج من حمص فلما خرج قبض عليه

عبدالله وقيده واخذ جميع ماله واولاده وسيره الي بغداد وجا

الي فلسطين في اول سنة الشمطي في شهر كانون الاول في سنة

مايتين واثنى عشر سنة لملك الاسلام ولم يجا به احد ونزل الي مصر

226

وحاربها وكان الخارجي الذي فيها يقال له سعيد السرتي في اسره بن ح
وحمله الى بغداد للملك بفتح البلاد التي الى جهة افريقيه وجعل
الله في قلبه رحمه للناس وخفف عنهم البلا الذي كان عليهم سوي
من الذي كان يفعله الخوارجي قبله لانه ما كان فيه شده كانوا كل
الناس خلوا اماكنهم خاليه وهربوا وناس خرجوا من مداهبهم
وامر بان من كان يرد نزل خراج يأخذ خطه حتى لا يقدر احد يأخذ منه
منه شي اخر مما كان يفعل قبل ومن سنة ذلك فعل كذلك خلق كثير
كانوا كل من جا جبار حتى هلكت الناس وبنيت قبايل بلا
عدد ومنهم نزلوا خليزا دخروا ولما جا الفرج اتى احزان
على من كان بعد اهله وجماعته في زمان الجور والشده وقام
وقام بعده ملك في نحو سنين حتى ربت فلاه في ساير البلاد وعاد
شار الى بلاده وبعد مشبره نادر متمرد يقال له بن فراسه وكان
انسان شر يبغض النصاره ويرتد منهم يخرجوا من دينهم الى

دينهم

227

ذيبه وملا وعابهم وملا الجيوش منهم رجال ونسا واطفال

وضيق عليهم بالجوع والعطش ومات ناس كثير في الجيوش والحاجر

حتى علوهم

يزنوا مال ... لوا اجتنبوا اولادهم في اليوم الثامن ومن

كان له مال كانوا ... يشهدوا عليه انه انفق وعاد

... وخرج خلق كثير من ذيبهم وما اكثر من خلد وصبر

حتى جا الفرج من الله وبعث الرحمة لانه رحيم رووف

فصل

وعادوا المسلمين اجتمعوا علي خلف المامون الذي هو اعبد

الله وقتلوا والي ريحا وخرجوا الي بيت المقدس ومعه عسكر

كثير وقتل ابن اخوه علي ريحا وارسل وجمع خلق كثير وعاد

اوقع الحرب مع المخالفين واعطاه الله النصر وقتل منهم اثني

وعشرين رجل واحرق الحصن الذي كانوا اجتمعوا فيه وخربوه

ومضوا جماعة منهم الي بيت جبرين وتجيشوا فيها وجا الخوا

الملك واسمه ابرهيم ومعه جيش كبير عظيم ومضى الى بيت جبرين
ونادى لهم بالامان وما يقتلوا او وقف الحرب منهم وتسلمهم ولحقهم
وبلادهم واخذ اموالهم وخرب ضياعهم واخذ منهم ناس كثير
في سلاسل حديد وحملهم الى بغداذ والرجل الان ٥٩. الذي هو
ابن فراشه هرب ثم بعد يسمع له خبر والذي صبر على نفسه وعلى
مذهبه فرج الله له لانه تحصن ووقف ورجع كل انسان الى بلده سالم
وعبر احرز الملك ابرهيم ومضى الى مصر وما قبلوه وحاربوه وقتل وحاربوه ا
منهم قتل عظيم وخرب ضياعهم وسبا نساهم واطفالهم ومن تبعهم
وفعل ذلك اخذ نهب عظيم هايل يجعل ولا على كل الارض وعاد
الى بلده في السنه الخامسه من السلطان نيسان فجا المامون الى
دمشق بناها فبناك حصون عظيمه جدا ونزل فيها الى المنزل.
سنه خمسين من السلطه وهو وهي سنه مايتين وسبعه عشر سنه لملك
الاسلام ومن ادم الى حين وصول المامون الى دمشق خمسه الاف

ومايتين

227

وما بقي اربعه وستين سنه وخلا مقدمين من عنده وهدموا
جميع الحصون الذي كانوا الباقيين يحصنون فيها وهدموا القلعه
الذي كانوا يبنون على الجبل واخذوا جماعه من المخالفين وسلسلوهم
في سلاسل حديد وحملوهم الى بغداد وبقي المامون في دمشق سبع
شهور وسار من هناك الى بلد الروم وفتح هناك مدن
وضياع كثير وعاد الى البلد في سنه السمطه وامر بمساحه الارض
وعدد الشجر وفعل ذلك الدخلا في فلسطين وجعل على الارض يقال
له ابو الجرود وضيق على الناس وثقل عليهم جدا مما لا يفعلوا
الذي كانوا قبله واضعف الناس وخربت مدن كثير وضياع
وخليت من سكانها وجعل الله في الارض سلام وشبع من هذا
ومذهب فلم يعترض وملك عبد الله المامون اثنين وعشرين سنه
ومات

فصل

وقام بعده اخوه ابرهيم وخالفوه الناس واجتمعوا الخلق

230

وطلعوا الي جبل ٩٢٩ في تخ الخليل ونزلوا ونهبوا نابلس وخرج
الزعيم ومعه جماعه وكان اهل البلد قد عملوا عليه وهرب الزعيم
وجماعته ودخل الغز ونهبوا دور كثيره واحرقوها واحرقوا
الكنيسه وكنايس الرهبان وجعل الله رحمه وما نطسا منهم وبقيوا
ثلاثه ايام ينهبوا وشفع الملك وارسل قايدين اسم الواحد جانم صالح
واسم الاخر جعفر زجاطريه وقتلوا هناك جماعه جوارح
ونهبوا اضياعهم وجاز الي بيسان واصابوا هناك جماعه من
الجوارح ايضا نهبوها وقتلوا منهم قتل كثير وعبروا العابدين
وجاز الي الرمله ولما نظروا اسكان الارض جمعوا جيوش كبير ومعهم
الغايبين الي بيت جبرين وقتلوا الجوارح الذي كانوا هناك
وطلعوا الي القدس جايين الي نابلس وحربوا عليهم الجوارح
واقاموا معهم الحرب في وادي الجيب وقتلوا منهم قتل كثير
وطلعوا الناس اليهم واخذوا منهم امان وقالوا لهم من كان في

البلاد

231

البلد علينا جغظه ومن كان في البر نقتلوه وجاوا الى نابلس واصابوا
هناك حوايج بريد فانهبها واخذوهم وصلبوهم على باب
المدينه من الشرق ومات الزبيشر [illegible] في السنه الثانيه
من السلطه في شهر [illegible] وقبر في القبر الذي عمل لابنه
[illegible] . الذي اراد يقيمه زبلس في حياته ولما مات تقبر فيه
هناك وقبره مقابل قبر زبيرون قريب من الطريق الذي
ينزل على السائرين في ما يلي كما يجب من الخوف الفزع وكانت
امامته خمسون سنه وتقدم في مكانه ابن ابنه ومضوا الغايبين الى
الرمله ورجعوا اناس كما كانوا والغجوم جاوا الى مدينة شيمبرا
نابلس ثانيه ووصلوا الخبر الى الزعيم الذي كان المدينه وخرج معه من
اصحابه المقدمين نحو واحتوا رجال المدينه معهم الى الحرب مناربه
وقتلوا المخالفين وقتل كثير وصلب منهم كثير وبقيتهم هربوا هروب
السيف وحبل النصر الغايبين فيجوا من فلسطين ومضوا وسا

232

حرامية عقديد وتبروهم وارسلوهم بالحديد الى بغداد وجعل الله في
الارض امن وخبت الخراج والجالية وضيقوا على الناس كثيرة وكانت الناس
يبيعوا املاكهم وراس البقر بدينار من الشدة التي كانوا فيها وخمس روس
غنم بدينار واحسن الله الخلاص ولم يخرج احد من دينه وكانوا
يضيقوا على المسلمين اكثر من السامرة وحسب الله وجارت الشدة وما
استنصر من السامرة احد سبحان من يغير ولا يتغير لانه ما ينشا عهد
الانكيا الا انه لا يتخلا عنهم انه الله اللهم فهبنا لمن على طريق الخلاف
فيسلك طريق الحق وكان لما تقدم الامام [illegible] ابن تنال
وطلطرنيقه الحاكم لا يتولوا امر ولا سولاه ولا شيوخ السامرة لعمري
انه لشيت وما جرى الامر فيه ولا الفسا ثلاثهم كانت قانيعملوا بامرهم
فسبحان من يمهل ولا يفوته فوت واحتجا نعي حكام بلا احكام
ولا يعرفوا الحق من الباطل وكنيسة نابلس التي احرقت اعادت شرعه
بعون الله تعالى اعاد الكنيس دوثان بنابلس السامرة وداو

عمرج عزج

اجا

233

٢

وجبا السامره وبناها بالاخشاب الابيض الوسطاني وكان من ع
فرح عظيم وسرور علي كل السامره وناتي واجتمعين الحكاكه
في اليوم بان يقيموا الصلاه ويعلوا يوم الاثنين في فج السوابيع
ونزلوا من الجبل الي الصلا وماروا الي العشا وكانوا نعموا الي يوم
الثلثا وبقيوا الناس في سلام خمس سنين وللملك ابرهيم دخل
الي بلاد الروم وخرب لهم مدينه كبيره يقال لها عموريه وكان يحرب
كل الامر ما كان مثل جعفر ابنه لما قام وملك كان يبغض جميع
الناس وملك ابرهيم تسع سنين ومات وقبل موته خرج ايمود
وخرج عليه وبنايه مرده خرج في المرج علي راي
اللصوص فلما صار له جماعه جاوا ونهبوا ارتيه علي الطواحين
وجاوا الي بصليا وشمع والي الرمله وخلا وراه مقدم وهرب
حرب الي الشعر الذي علي الاردن ولم يقدر عليه وعاد الي الرمله
وطلع الي بصليا وخلا المقدم وراه رجل اسمه ابرهيم بن زرقه

239

ونزل القدم وخرجوا عليه الخوارج وقتلوا من رجاله ناس
كثير ومن هرب سلم وخافوا الناس خوف شديد واجتمعوا
الي نابلس وطلع زعيم الرملة الي نابلس ونزل خارج منها وقيل
له ان كنت تريد ابو حرب فهوا نازل في عقربة وقام في الليل
مضي اليه واوقع معه الحرب في الجبل وقتل من اصحاب محمد
جماعة ورجعوا الي الرملة مستدين فاقام مقدما علي نابلس
رجل من اهلها البشر موسي بن هرون رجل جبار ومضي
الي الرملة هارب فعبر الخارجي فاجتمع له جيوش كثيرة خوارج
وجاوا الي تربة تورا ونهبوا ونزل الي العمل جبا من كل ضيعة
٥ علي قدرها وطلع الي نابلس ونزل عليها وطلب منها مالا لم
يلتفتوا اليه شي فقام الحرب في يوم الخميس وقتل منها ولاي ومن
ها ولاي وبات في شالم واصبح يوم الجمعة في جيش عظيم وهزم
الناس ودخل الي نابلس وقتل حضرته والي هو اخير واذا قد

سهل

235

شمل الله برجل يقال له علي بن عمر بن تليل فلما سمع ان
قد دخل العسكر وانهزم بنو محمد هرب منه الى السيف فتصادموا وقتل
منهم جماعة من بعضهم بعض وخرجوا الناس الا انه ما تم الا
لما كان في الليل خرج بن عمر ومضى الى مكانه وخرجوا الناس
هاربين في ليلة السبت لا اب يعبر لابنه ولا ابن يصبر لابوه
من الخوف كانهم زوكاسا رعد ومقدمين اصواتهم بالبكا والصراخ
مما جرى عليهم من سبب السبت واهل البلد هم وبنوا هربوا
هربوا بالسيف فاما الرئيس فانه لم يخرج فضرب بالسيف وتولوا به
الى خليل ومات وقبر هناك رحمه الله رحمة ولما راى النحرب
ان تركوا الناس مالهم وهربوا رجع ودخل الى نابلس واحرق
ونهب ستة عشر ايام واقام النهب تبذلنا في سائر البلاد
وتام الوعيد وارسل خلفهم شيعة ازل بلاد خاليه وتركها كل
خرابه لم استقاشي عن الوعيد الا ثبت علينا كله وخرج الجابي

236

ومضى الى بيسا وانتفهما ومضى الى بيسان وجا من الناس
مال كثير ومضى الى عتيل ونهبها وتعدى الى القبلة ونهبت
هناك ضياع كثيرة وكانت الناس في الشدة وكان بعضه
بكل الامر بتلقشا وايد كثيرة وموت عظيم ووقع في الناس وما
اكثر من خرج من مكانه ولم يرجع واشتبى ملك اسرايل
تطغ عمه بن نكيه ٩٣٩٩٣٢٦٢٦٢ على السامرة وبينهم انهم
لا ياكلوا مع الدسنان ولا يشربوا ولا يتزوجوا منهم ولا يزوجوهم
فاما ابو الحرب عاد الى الرملة واقام معهم الحرب فلم يقدر واعلى
الخلاق منه وشبع الملك ابرهيم وارسل رجل يسمى رجا ومعه
جيش ومضوا في الطريق مات الملك فقام ابنه في اثره هرون
هذا هرون دجا من الطريق ووصاه بما اراد وارسله
نجا الى دمشق واصاب بغاش كثير هنا وقتل رجال
وجا قتل كثير وخرب كل ضياع عمه وعبر وجا ونزل في لبنان

وكان

237

وكان هو واولاده احمد وجا الي الرملة ودخل الي ابن المقدم الذي
هرب بلاجا ونزل علي الدجا ابو حرب واخذ منهم خيل ولم
يلحقه من يكذه وجاء الي الشام ونهب منها لما كان ابو الجاموذ وقع
وطلع الي عجلون يانسه لانه كان معول علي الغار حاني وادي
غار فلما جاءه انفعل له الله تعالي مالزاد وعبر وادي عارا وبات
في رامين واصبح جا الي الشام وطلع في يوم الخميس الي عجلون وظن
انهم يستامنوا ويخرجوا اسالمين [illegible] يستغنوا منه واشتد عليهم
وعاد الي الشام واعتد وخرج وزا ابو حرب وخرج اليه ابو
حرب وخرج معه بن مشرور بن الرجل الذي بعث الشام ره
وقتل في شهل منهم خلق عظيمه واشتد عليهم وساروا
يقتلوا واوقع معهم الحرب واعطاه الله سبحانه تعالي النصر
وقتل منهم في عجلون وغيره لما قتل كثير جدا واخذ ابو حرب
وابن مشرور وجماعه من معه وشدهم في قيود الحديد

238

ثم سلمنا الى الكلاب فلم يطمع احد بان يكون لعيش طمع ابدا رجاء

ودخل منا ناس فاذم الرئيس منحس الذي في ايامه وايام

الرئيس ~~[illegible]~~ ذلك الاحكام عنهم لانهم سخوا ومعنى هذا

الرجل وتولا تطهير غسل وتحمل ادركنا الا انها كانت من الضياع

الكلاب وطاهرها وسالة منها خبز ومضى رجا الى مصر ومضى

الى بلاده وعفنا الى بيوتنا سالمين في شهر نيسان نفرح

وتهنا نسر ونزور وشكرنا [illegible] الى الشدة الكثيرة ومن بعد هذا

تشتغوا الناس في السلاطين وتحبوا الناس جنايه عظيمه خرجت

الناس نعبروا الى جيرة الاردن من الظلم وجعل الله تعالى في

قلب الملك في شهر الدحن رحمة وارسل وبطل ذلك كل هذا كان في

ايام هرون هذا هرون منع النصارى من ضرب الناقوس ومد

ست سنين واليهود منعوا المسلمين من سجدوا حتى من

المتعبد ما كتبنا منهم في جزء المدة ولا ملوك الارض لاتنا

اشتغلنا

739

اشتغلنا بانفسنا ولا يبقى من له همه ولا يبحث عليه الا الحادث
للجماعات كل المسلمين من ادم الى موت هرون خمسه الاف
ومايتي وثمانون سنه وقد بعث اخوه جعفر وابلا العالم بكل نوع
وامر في ذلك بان يلبسوا الناس الغيار الا الاسود والازرق
فانه افرده للامشيد امر بان لا يكون كاتب ولا عامل الا من امته
ولا يكون احد على حصن ولا عمل كان الا من امته وكانوا
نصارى طردهم وجعل كل المتعبد من من امته
وامر بان لا يكون ثوب عليه طراز الا على اهل ملته ولا
يركب على سرج وامر بان يكون علامه على كل ذمي من خلف وقدام
ولا يجلس مقدم على مرتبه حال ولا يكون وكان جديد
الا لاهل ملته والقبه خشب امر بان يعمل على كل قبر نيشه قبور
اهل ملته وهدم تربة الرئيس في سنه ٢٤٧ . وقبل هذا كان امر بان
يعمل كل ذمي على بابه من خشب بستميه شي وقاموا

240

الناس المقيمون بنابلس ذكرهم الله بالإحسان وحلوا
لأن والي نابلس شي وسألوه بهم أن يأتي نزلوا الرملة ففعل لهم ذلك
وكان في داخوس رجل قادر بجاه وقدرة وكلامه مقبول
وأرسل إلى ... مع ابن ابي النساج ومع ابن ابي دجوباس
وقتل هناك ناس كثير وعادوا إلى دمشق وما فتحوا الله وجاءوا
إلى الطاهرية ولم يقدروا يحكموا فلما علم عبد الله بن الناس بن علي ولوا
بما نقلوا عليه مضى إلى هناك ... لا استغيثه جاء إلى الرملة
ومشكلا وجعل لذلك جاه كان من السلطان يحيي الحال
وتبع على صبح وتعجب فلما سمع الحجة بعض شديد وقتل
من مقدميه مائة وثلاثون من خيار من كان معه وقتل أيضا
من رجاله كثير وهرب عبد الله ووصل إلى أخوه هرون
وقال له المسلمين لقد نحن دمشق وقال له أنا ابن طولون تقدمت
وما هناك أحد يلقاك وجاء إلى فلسطين وكتب إلى المسلمين

تتغيدهم

خلق

وشقاما

241

يجي اليه لما وصل كتابه الى الشجد وقراه ارسل الى مصر الى الخازن ونصب
جار وسار الى فلسطين ووصل الى الرمله في جيوش عظيمه سودان
برابر ومن ساير الناس ونزل على راس العين التي الذي هي منزل
العساكر وارسل الى اصبغ وقال له اجمع لي كل بحري في الارض
وجا ابن ابو احمد اخو عمرون من بني هاشم ومن معه ونزلوا على
راس العين وادوا وتقعوا هناك الحرب بينهم وقتل جانب كبير ما
من هاولاي ومن هاولاي وهرب ابن احمد الهاشمي وعيسى ما
بنامه ووصل الى قيساريه وبقي الناس بلا راي قام الوعيد اجمعه ما
وبعث عليها كل عام الا نعرفهم وضيق على الناس في كل شي
وضاع كثيره خربت وشهد جار ان شعبه عاصي وجا جار الى
الرمله بجيش كثير ولما صار داخل المدينه اخذ جار السعيد قتله
وجعل اصبغ والي فلسطين والاردن وضيق على الناس واخذ
الاموال وكشف العام من اموالهم واخذ غرامهم وكثير من السامره

242

~~خلوا من ضياعهم وكان هناك شخص اخوه منه~~

مقبول عند السلطان يقال له ابو يوسف ابن داسي [illegible]

[illegible] فدخل الى الوالي برسالة وقال له ان

امر الملك ما يبطل بل اختار لك صورة لا تضر فاختار صورة منارة

نعملها وجعلت في لغانه واختم عليها وانفذها الى والي نابلس وامر

بان لا يعمل سامري الا كما عمل يوسف بن داسي منارة وفرحوا

كثير بذلك وشكروا الله سبحانه تعالى على ذلك كثير فانه الذي

كانوا على الاردن فانهم لم يهنيهم ذلك وعمل صورة مثل الشعوب

على الطريق وامر في ايامه بان لا [illegible]

[illegible]

[illegible]

[illegible] بها في ايام الريس فنحس

وايام الريس يوشع لحقنا هذه الشدايد كلها ومنعنا الاحكام تـ

النقيرا

243
خامس عشر دائر

وبقيوا السامره مثل الغنم بلا راعي وكل السامره ما اراد فعل ولما
كان في يوم السبت في يوم عيد الاول المظله في ثاني ساعه جات
زلزله عظيمه وظللت رحمة الله تعالى وما انضر احد وطلعوا
الناس يصلوا الى عيد المظله في السنه السابعه من ملك جعفر
في ثلثه سنين من الشطه مسلو الى الرمله ليوسف بن داسي ومنعوه
وكثرت الجاليه منعه من طلوع الجبل مع السامره
ومنهم والى نابلس [illegible] الصلاه
[illegible] وصلوا في ذلك اليوم ويوم الخميس
طلعوا وصلوا باصوات مرتفعه وما منهم احد الا الدستان
منعوا من الصلاه الى ما انتهوا من تلبيه الكتاب ولم يزل الودا
السامره في خير كل ايام يوسف بن داسي الى موته نيح الله
روحه وكانوا الدستان يعبروا ويناغوا بصوت عالي بشفعه
بموته وامر الرئيس نفيس امران لا يعطوهم شي ولا ياخذوا

244

منهم ولا ياكل احد منهم ولا يشربوا منهم ولما كان في اربعة من
تشرين يوم الخميس في الليل روي في السما كواكب ترمي من
الشرق الى الغرب والى الجنوب امر عظيم وبلغ القمح مدين
بدينار وبعد اربعة ايام جا سموم عظيم وابيع القمح ايام ومن
بعد هذا انعم الله تعالى برحمته وتسيق وفرح العالم وانتقل
الرئيس يحيى ومات قام عبد يلان ابنه موضعه وجا غلا عظيم
وابيع القمح لسه امداد بدينار واحتاج كثير من الناس اخدوا
الجيد من الغلا في الجوع وما اكثر من خرج من دينه من عظم
الغلا ومن الكدي في الجزية وهلك بنين وبنات كثير من
جوع من الذهب في من صبر اشرف الله عليه بالرحمه وفرج الله
له وما الشبع والخير في ملك جعفر كان امر عظيم ومن معجز عظيم
وذلك ان خسف الله تعالى بقريتين على سكانها وبقي سكانهم عمرها

تمت

هذا

هذا جعفر جا الى دمشق وبنا بها حصن وبقي فيها مدة قليل وعاد منها
الى بلده وعمل السجن والحوانيت والفنادق والحيات والحايات
والبيوت والمقاصر واحصا الجزية وبطل الالقاب ونادى
كل انسان باسمه وزاد في الجزية وفي ايامه جا رجل يقال له قوميطي
وجا الى الطاهر بنابلس وجرح مقدم نابلس في قفاه واوقف معه الحرب
وانكسر مقدم نابلس وهرب هروب السيف وقتل قتل وذبح عسكره وانهزم
كثير من السامرة في يوم السبت فخوفهم من السيف وسامرة
لقريته ذكر والخبر انضم مع من هرب والذي وصلوا الساحل
سلموا وجاوا الى بيت صامه ولم يعربوا الاسنان لانهم جابوا على
نفوسهم بشي يقوموا به ودخلوا الى شعاما في ليلة السبت
واخذوا ابن امتي لبنان شوا وكل جماعته وجمعوا عليهم القش
واحرقوهم وقتلوا اسبعة عشر رجل من ناس الشور وانهزموا
يوم السبت وسبي منهم وهدو الحصن الذي كان لهم واحرقوه

بالنار وارسل الى الرمله رجل يسمى رجل جبار ومعه
جيش عظيم وطلع الى نابلس ومضى الى بيت ماما والى ربنا والى يبرين
واوقع الحرب مع نومطي وقتل اشر كثير من هاوراي ومن هولا ي
خلق كثير ودخل على الناس بلا عظيم وضيق وشده وخوف
شديد وهربوا الناس الى الرمله لهربا بالسيف وجا رجل يقال
له فراح من الشرق ومضى نومطي وطرح روحه على مقدم الاردن
وجا امراه وقبض رجال كثير من الاردن والعدم الى افريقيه
واكلوا لحم الناس مما ضيق عليهم ولنحدر الى مصر وجعل الله تعالى
سلامه في الارض وعاد كل انسان الى بلده وقتل جعفر على يد ابنه
وملك بعده ست شهور وجا عليه كثير وانقطعت الطرق ممن
يسلك فيها وكثر الغلا والخوف وهلكت البصره مدينه
الكبرى وقتل كثير من الساكنه ونهبت ضياع ونسا واطفال
وفي ايام عبد الله الامام راى القمر في يوم السبت راس الشهر
واعاد

247

وعاد جدد الحساب الصوم تقدم قبل بست عشر سنه
ومات وقبر في حمص عن ورتما وبعد هذا جا رجل يعرف بمحموره ها
وضيق على الناس وجمع للمال وجا في ايامه غلا شديد
ما لا يرى مثله وافتقر الناس وانكشفوا من اموالهم وخلوا
من منازلهم من العدو والجوع وقام المستعين بالله اخوا
جعفر وملك سنتين ونصف واعزل وسمي المخلوع من بني
هاشم وقام بعده المعتز بن جعفر وملك ثلثه سنين وقام بعده
المهتدي بن الواثق وملك سنه واحده وقام بعده المعتمد وملك
اربعه وعشرين سنه وكان له اخ واسمه ابو احمد وقبض
عليه احمد بن طولون وقتل بمصر بيد شديده وملكها بمكر ها
وكان فها رجل يعرف بمحموره مقدم في الرمله مقدم اسمه ها
عيسى بن حنش بن طولون في حسب حساب بكر وجا
الي فلسطين ودخل الي قيساريه وخلا عيسى رجل بان يليه

وحصل في ايام المستعين
... وجوع جدا

248

يقال له الكونتلي ما الفرنسا وجا به واسره في سلسله حديد
وجا به الي الرمله وكان في داخون رجل يقال له
فلش بن اداسي حكيم مع عيسي فقال له ايش الفايده في مقامه
هذا في السجن فاطلقه من السجن ومضي الي مصر واقام سنتين
وسال ان يرا في المدينه ويحصن على شكل الذي باصور وهو يحفر
اصاب مال مجوزه واشتري ماليك وجوار من عنده وجعل
حبوش ومضي الي زقه وحاصرها وملكها وجعل فيها والي ومضي
الي سكندريه واطاعوه اهلها وكتب الي افريطس في تخم بلاد
الروم وجا الجواب بالتسليم وفتح الغرب الي مصر وعمر فيه وعادى
الله تعالي وغير الشي بالفرج وانجبت الارض في علا بعادي
كل ما فيها واكلو الناس وشبعوا وجا شي كثير وخير
كثير وبعد هذا ثلاث سنين انحبست الارض السما من المطر
وصار السما كالنحاس والارض كالحديد في ايام الشتا

زمان

219

زمان ونشفت العيون ويبست الشجر والعشب في طرح الشجر ثمارها

النوار وجا غلا عظيم حد الى ان ما كان فيه موت وتصدق

الله تعالي وهذا النقوش وبعد ذلك فرج الله تعالى عن الخليقه للخلايق

ونزل المطر واخصبت الارض غلا الانعام وثمر الشجر وبلغ القمح ثمان

اماب بدينار وفرج الله برحمته ورافته وتوفي يوشع الريس وقام

يوسف الريس اخوه في مكانه وقام [illegible] . اخو ابوه في منازعه

وصاروا الناس فرقتين منهم مع يوسف ومنهم مع [illegible] . ودخل

بين الشامره خلف كثير ودفع [illegible] . السلطان الارض مال

وقالوا ودرس ونشر في عيد المظال تغيير راى الشامره ووقف

حول جماعه من غلمان السلطان حول كتاب المذبح وقطعوا

الكتاب والناس واستغاثوا الناس فيه ونعصوه ومضي الي دمشق

وكتاب ذو شان الشامره يوخذ منهم وارسل السلطان وقبض

علي جماعه من الشامره وجعلهم في السجن حتى قاطعوا علي مال

كثير وقسموه على الضياع على اقدارهم وحسنوا الناس بامور
العقاب وخرج كثير من الناس من دينهم وعاد ومضى
الى الشرق عند كتب الرياسه وارسل الله تعالى عليه واحد اسود
قتله ومضى الخبر الى السلطان ان الشامره قتلوه واخذ مقدمي
الشامره للعقاب [illegible] وكان قدر
[illegible] واشتد
الشده على الشامره واقتص من اموالهم ومن دينهم ومن صبر على
نفسه فرج الله تعالى له ومات الملك وجا بعده خير وراحه وفرج
ولما سمع احمد بن طولون ملك مصر ان مات الملك خرج في جيش عظيم احمد بن طولون
سودان وغيرهم وجا الى فلسطين في شهر حزيران في السنه الخامسه
من السمطر وهي سنه مايتين اربعه وستون سنه لملك الاسلام واهلكوا
السودان كل الناس ونهبوا ضياع الذي كانت على الطريق
ولطا منها كثير وجا على الناس شده شديده ودخل الى الرمله

[illegible]

251

وجعل نيابا والي وعاد سار الي دمشق ... وفتحها وملكها وفتح سايره

البلاد ووصل الي انطاكيه وحاصرها مده طويليه وقتل ملكها ونهب

مالها وقتل فيها قتل كثير وجعل فيها والي من قبله واخذ والمسلمين

... كثير وعاد هو وجيشه وضيق علي الناس وامر بان يحمل

له الي كل مكان يكون فيه مونه له ولمن معه من العسكر والطعام

لا يكل منه ... واسل واخذ طعام الناس وكانوا الناس ما يصدقوا

يوخذ طعامهم وحلوالهم بنفوسهم وضيق علي الناس بكل نوع وفي

السنه الثانيه جا للناس والي من قبله وضيق بكل نوع وامر

بان يلبسوا الاسم غيارات وعمل علي ابوابهم [illegible] ولا يرفع

[illegible] يبني بيكه [illegible]

صوت ولا يضرب بيسوق ... ميشنو ليعود وخافت منه كل الامم

هو امد يد علي ... بان يخدموه [illegible]

وضيق [illegible] الذين كانوا في الضياع ... الذي

252

تجبروا على الدم ونهب كل ما وجد وقام الوعيد المكتوب في السيرة
المقدسة للجبار الذي في جلالته يتعالى عليك ان تجد فوق درجة منا
وانت تنحدر سفلا اسفلا في ايام مملكته ارسل اخذ جميع الناس من
من الضياع الى مصر واخذ فيهم جماعة من الشامرة واطلقهم الى مصر
في السفن واوصى ان يبنا حصن على ما فاو واخذ جميع البهايم ومعه للباس
بكل نوع في مالهم واحتشامهم وبنا مصر وجددها لانها كانت خربت
في النفاق عدة دفعات فكان يخاف ليل ونهار وفي الشدة كانوا الناس
كلهم وثقل حيا الحالية وافتقرت الناس كلهم وانكشفوا من
احوالهم وماتوا الهم كل هذا في ايام احمد بن طولون وفي ذلك الوقت
زاد في الضيق على الناس بكل فن واخذ جميع البهايم واحتاجت
الناس يستعملوا البقر في الطواحين في ايام [illegible] الامام
جا احمد بن طولون الشاب السو في سنة تسعة وستون ومايتين
سنة للملك الاسلام وحل بالناس بلا الا يعرفه لا يجد وموت زايد

زاد

253

ولا احد لا يبكي ويعي الناس في بلاوا شتم الموت شنت شعور وتغيرت
صور الناس من المرض ولم ينطلع الي الجبل الا قليل من الناس
في ج للظال وبعد ذلك فتح الله تعالي علي العالم وذكر محمد ابرهيم
واسحق بن يعقوب وبعد هذا خبر انكسر ابن طولون ونزل في دمشق
ومرض مرضة الموت وحمل علي بغل الي مصر وكان في الرملة
والي اسمه عبد الله بن الفتح وسمع بموته واخذ تضيق علي الناس
وجبا منهم مال كثير وقبض علي ابن اداسي وضيق عليه اخذ منه
مال كثير وعول علي انه يقتله فلما علم ابن اداسي ذلك هرب الي الجبال
والمغاير وبقي هناك وكان بن طولون خلفه ثلاث بنين العباس
وجاز وابو العشاير وقبل العباس بن اخوه جاز وخلف الجاز
ابنين اسم الواحد عبد الله والاخر سعيد فلما سمع بن الفتح بذلك
هرب الي المشرق وملكو المقدمين الذي خلفوا جاز كل الارض
وجعلوا علي الرملة الي يقال له اصبع وكان انسانا شريرا وكان

254

من بليت فور ريك وصار فلس عند المقدمين الذي خلا الحجاز عمره في
فلسطين ومصرا وخلوه متولي في فلسطين ومصر الي ان صار واوقعوا
الحرب علي شيحه مع ابن ابو الساج ومع ابن ابو دجوباش وقتل
هناك قتل كثير وعادوا الي دمشق وما انتصروا وجاوا الي طبريه ولم
يقدروا ايحلوا افلما علم عبدالله بن الناس تتعولوا اساتوا عليه
ومضي الي هناك وخلا سعيد وجا الي الرمله ومسكها وجعل لذلك
جا كتاب السلطان يجبي المال وقبض علي اصبغ وسجنه
فلما سمع سعيد جا الحقه بغضب شديد وقتل من مقدميه ميه وثلاثين
من خيار من كان معه وقتل ايضا من رجاله خلق كثير وهرب
المسلمين. لقيه في دمشق
عبدالله ووصل الي اخوه هرون
وقال له ان ابن طولون قد مات وما هناك احد يلقاك فجا الي
فلسطين وكتب الي سعيد يجي اليه ولما وصل كتابه الي سعيد وقراه
ارسله الي مصر الي جماز وبخبر حماز وسار الي فلسطين ووصل الي

الرملا

255

الرمله في جيوش عظيمه سودان وبرابر ومن ساير الناس ونزل
علي راس العين الذي هي منزل العساكر وارسل الي اصبغ وقال
له اجمع لي كل خراجي في الارض وجا ابن ابو احمد اخو
هرون من بني هاشم ومن معه ونزلوا علي راس العين واوقعوا
هناك الحرب بينهم وقتل خلق كثير من هاولاي ومن هاولاي
~~ومن هاولاي~~ وهرب ابن احمد الهاشمي وكذ عيسى وزراه ووصل
الي قيساريه ورحل بالناس بلاد واقام الوعيد احمد وتبت عليه ياكله
عالم لا تعرفهم وضيق علي الناس في كل شي وضياع كثيره خربت ومع
جمازان سعيد عامي وجا جماز الي الرمله بجيش كبير ولما صار
داخل المدينه احد جماز لسعيد قتله وجعل اصبغ والي فلسطين
والاردن وضيق علي الناس واخذ الاموال وكشف العالم من
امرالهم واخذ قراهم وكثير من السامره خلوا من ضياعهم وكان
هنالك خمس اخوه ناس شيوا

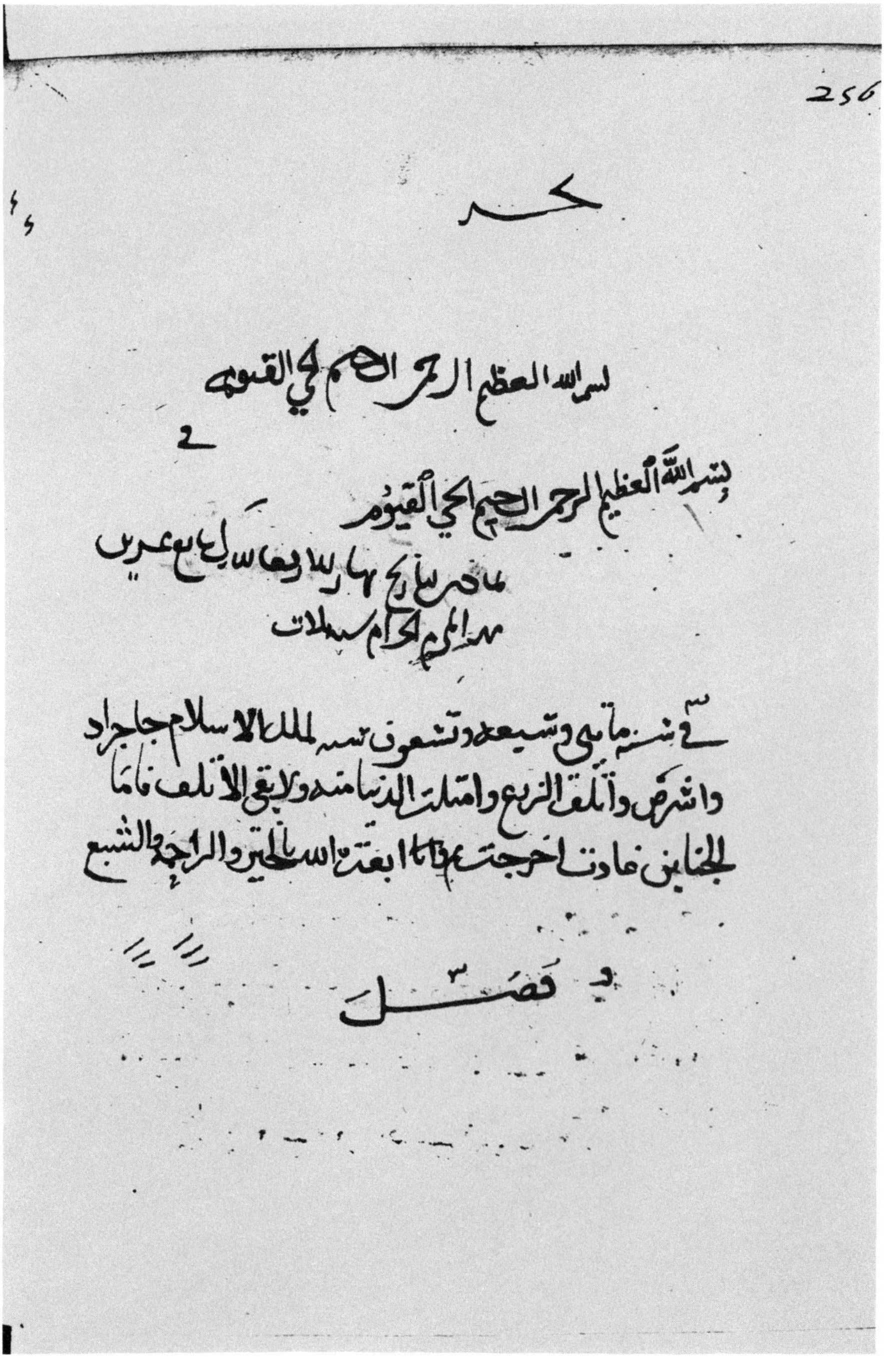
256

حـر

بسم الله العظيم الرحمن الرحيم الحي القيوم

2

بسم الله العظيم الرحمن الرحيم الحي القيوم

[illegible] بن عمرين

ما جرى بتاريخ نهار [illegible]

من المحرم الحرام [illegible]

في سنة ماتين وتسعة وتسعين سنة للملك الاسلام جا جراد

واشرص واتلف الزرع وامتلت الدنيا منه ولا بقي الا تلف ناما

الجانبين عادتنا اخرجته عنا ابعده الله بالخير والرحمة والشبع

فصل

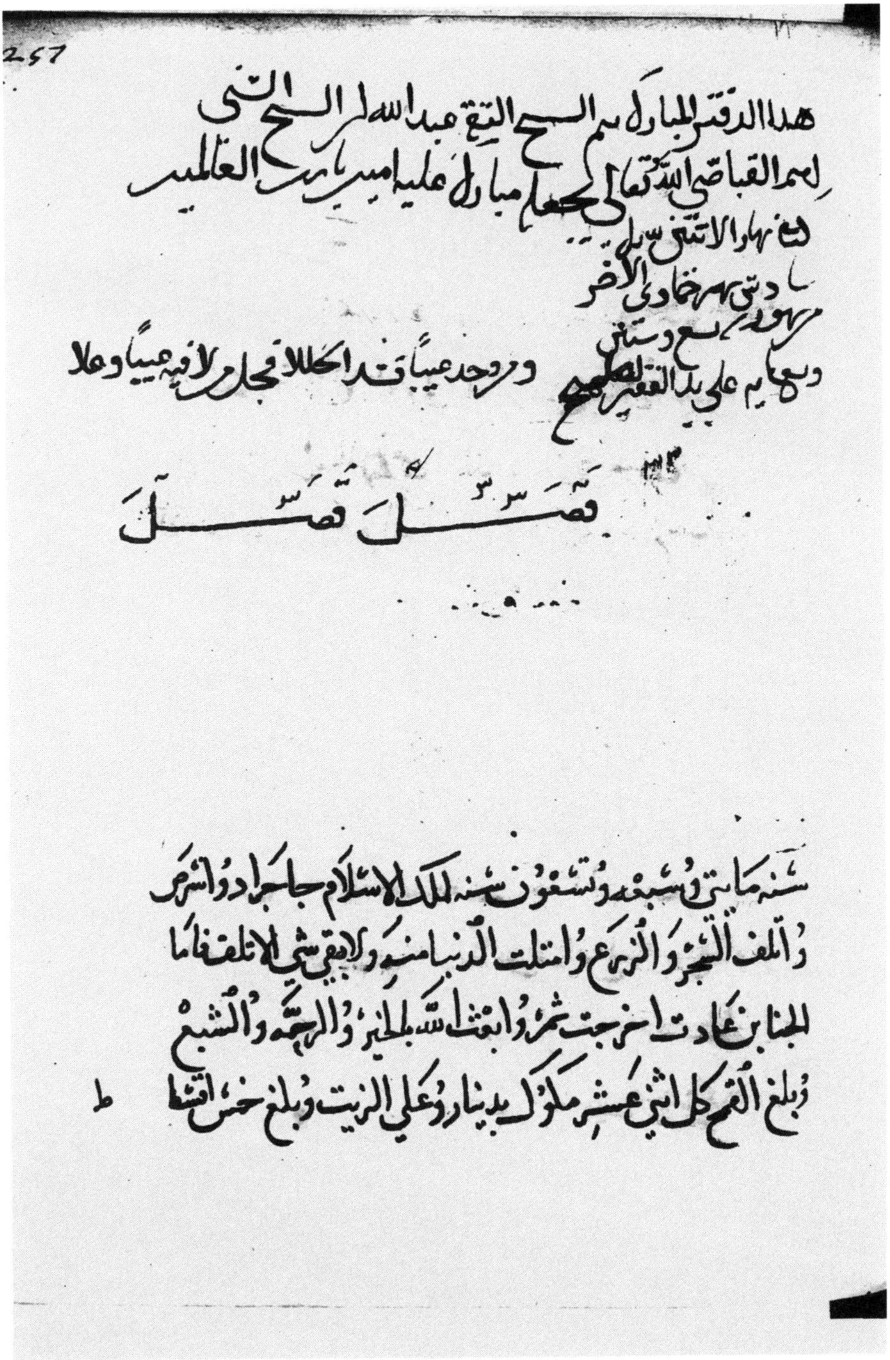

هذا الدفتر المبارك برسم الشيخ الفقيه عبد الله ... الشيخ
... القباضي الله تعالى يجعله مبارك عليه امين يا رب العالمين

سنة مايتين وسبعة وتسعون سنة الملك الاسلام جا جراد واشر
واتلف الشجر والزرع وامتلت الدنيا منه ولا بقي شي الا تلفه اما
الجنان عادت اخرجت ثمر وابعث الله بالخير والرحمة والشبع
وبلغ القمح كل اثني عشر مكوك بدينار وعلي الزيت وبلغ خمس اقسط ط

258

بدينار وجا في كانون الثاني جليد ثلاث ايام ما راي شي اعظم
منه وجا بعد ذلك جراد لم يري مثله وجا بعده غلا في سنة ثلثماية
وتسعة وستين للاسلام في ايام الرييس عبد يال الرييس درتا واتفقو
على تبطيل القراه بالترومية في الكنيسة في كل ما وقف السامرة وكان
الاجتماع في المصر جمع الكاهنة والسامرة وجميع شيوخ الطايفه
ووقف الحكيم ودعي على من يعود يتلفظ في قراها وغيرها وكان ذلك
في عيد الفصح وبطل وذلك كانت تفعله فعلها الرييس ارضاها
الله تعالى في جميع الناس ولحق الناس شره وذلك ان وقع فيهم
خلف منهم وبهم خلف عظيم واشرف الله تعالى بالرحمة ولم ينظر احد
من السامرة وفي السنه مات الامير الراعي وجعل في اثره
واحسن الله تعالى على يد عبد الله الي الناس احسان كثير وازال
الظلم عنهم وجات زلزله عظيمه في تشرين وكان امر
عظيم ونظر الله تعالى لعبيده ولم يلحق سامري شي في ذلك الوقت

وكان

١

257

كان متولي مصر رجل شريف يتلين في ذلك مملوك وكان عزيز عنده

وظهر على الغلام وضع وجمع جميع الاطبا واسقوه ادويه ها

ولطخوه باللطوخات وكان كل ما اسقوه ولطخوه زاد وقالوا

له ان في الشام اقوام شامي فيهم كاهنه ينظروا هذا المرض

ونتيسه ويبرا فارسل الى احضر واحد من بني شيبه ومعه صبي من

عمر سكون يخدمه وكان اسم ابن شيبه ٩٧٥٠٢٤ . واسم صبيه ط

عيديك الغلوكي ولما نظروا الصبي قالوا هذا بامر الله تعالى

وقام علاجه مده شهرين كامله وشفي الغلام بمشيئة الله تعالى

وارتفع ذكره بين الامر ونالهم خير كثير مال وخلع وكتب باكرامهم

الى كل مكان فيه مقامهم في طلوعهم وفي مقامهم ونزولهم سنه

وشهرين في نزلوني ح المطالك وفرحت الطايفه فرح شديد وشكروا

الله تعالى كثيرا على انعامه الذي انعم وتفضل عليهم بهذه النعمه

وفي السنه جا في مصر ثلاثه ايام بجليد لم يرا مثله هلك خلق

2.60

كثير في الطرق وبعد ذلك فتح الله تعالى ابواب احسانه ورحمته
ونزل المطر وانبتت الارض في غلاتها وخيرها وشجرها وجا الرخص
بكل نوع وشبعوا الناس وشكروا الله تعالى شكرا كثيرا على ما انعم به انه الله
قادر رحيم رؤوف بعباده في تلك السنه خرج ريح عاصف في ليلة الصيام
وانكسرت السفن التي كانوا في البحر وتلف فيها خلق كثير
بلا عدد وخرج الجراد في تلك السنه وانتشر في الارض واكل العشب
وجميع ما في البر وجا غلا كبير وانكسر ابو عبد الله من الرمله وخرج
وجا ابن طغج من مصر والي على الرمله واسروا اصحابه لكل مكان الارض
واقام شي شهور ومضى الى دمشق وعاد ابو عبد الله الى الرمله وخرج
خارجي يقال له الساني في جمع جيوش عظيمه وسار الى بلمه في
عند الساحل وقتل فيهم قتل عظيم ونهب الستور والذهب والفضه
وكل ما كان في البيعه ولم يسلم من الناس الا القليل وفي
السنه الثانيه شي ان قد خرج فيها نهر ما هدمها اماكن كثيره وفي

منهم من العرب

261

من الهد عالم وجاني تلك السنه خير في كل شي ورخص ما راي
مثله وفي ذلك الوقت قام بن طفح وجمع عساكره في دمشق وعصي
علي السلطان القاهر وقام بعده بن جعفر المعتني في مكانه
يقال له عبدالله الرامي وكتب الي محمد بن علي متولي فلسطين بان
يحاربه بن طفح الي فلسطين في شهر اب في سنة خمس ستين من الشطه
وجا رجال لمحمد بن علي وشدوا من ابن طفح وانكسر محمد بن علي يقال له
وهرب واخذ جميع ما يملكه ومر ودخل الي مصر وملك بن طفح
ارض فلسطين وكانت سنه شده علي كل السامره واجتمعوا
رجال عرب من حسانوط وقتلوا خمس رجال من السامره ها
واربعه من اشكر واخد من النجاسيه كانوا شيوخ ضياعهم
وقتلوا في ساعه واحده وقيل انهم احرقوهم وكانت الجمعه ها
عظيمه علي السامره وبعد هذا اجعل بن طفح يده علي السامره ها
وابتدا يعاقبهم واخذ منهم مال وافقرو اكل مقدمي السامره

وانكشفوا اهل الضياع من كل ما يملكوه وامتد البلا في كل مكان
علي السامره الصغار والكبار وصار العبد علي اقبح تغضبه بالسما
للحزن والويل ورأي في عشرة ايام من تشرين كواكب تسقط من
السما ويشتعل نيران في تروؤلها مثل البرق العظيم وبقيت من نصف
الليل الي بعد طلوع الشمس تسقط واحد خلف اخر وارسل ابن طغج
الي نابلس عامل ومعه جيش كبير وضيق علي السامره جدا وعاقب
منهم جماعه وبطلت الكنيسه منع اهل الصلاه في ايامه

في طريق الرمله

العصف ولا الناموسه في الكنيسه من شدة الظلم والبلا الذي
بان في ملك ايام وبعد هذا بن السبي واخذ منه
مال كثير وتفضل الله تعالي واعانه وخلص فقام رجل سامري
واسمه كذاش لا رحمه الله تعالي ولا رضي عنه وكان يخدم بن طغج
وسلس له ويكتب له اسما السامره الذي لهم مال واخذ مالهم والخذ

رزهم

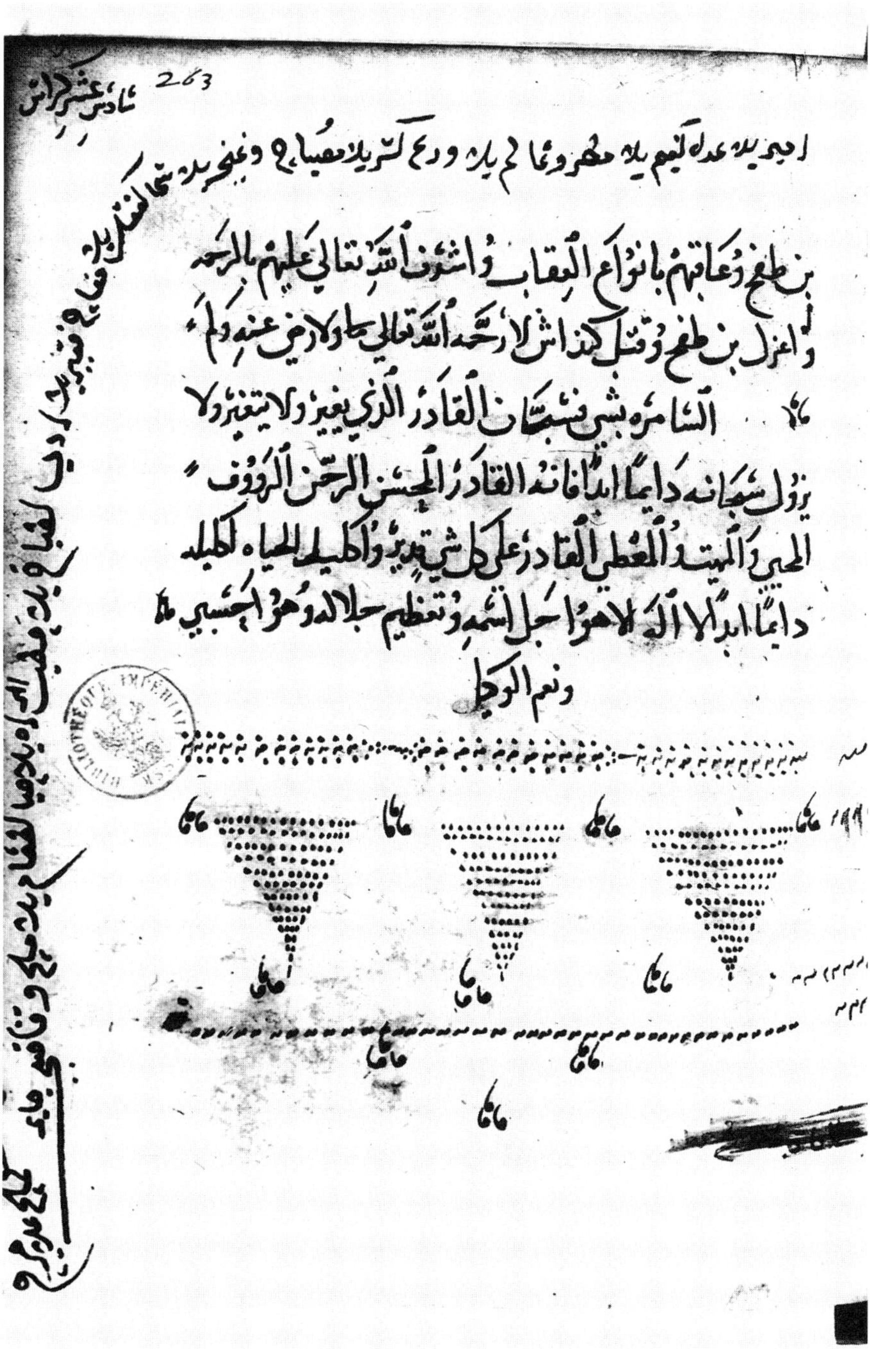
بن طمع وعاقبتهم بانواع العقاب واشرف الله تعالى عليهم بالرحمة
واعزل بن طمع وقتل كذلك اش لا رحمه الله تعالى بها ولا رضي عنه ولا
الشامر وبشي فسبحان القادر الذي يغير ولا يتغير ولا
يزول سبحانه دايما ابدا فانه القادر المحسن الرحمن الرووف
المحيي والمميت المعطي القادر على كل شي قدير واكمل الحياه لكمليه
دايما ابدا لا اله الا هو اجل اسمه وتعظيم جلاله وهو حسبي
ونعم الوكيل

264

بشر بعوده

تم هذا الكتاب المبارك

بعون الله تعالى ولطفه وحسن توفيقه

في نهار الخميس المبارك عشرين شهر رمضان

المعظم قدره سنة ثلاثين وتسع مائة على اسم كاتبه

لنفسه المملوك الاصغر الاذل الاحقر المعترف بالذنب والتقصير

في يوم القصاص المملوك مسلم بن يوسف بن ابرهيم بن محمد بن قاسم الشاكر

اليوسفي النسب الموسوي المذهب غفر الله تعالى له ثم لوالديه ثم لمن

طالع فيه ودعى لكاتبه بالمغفرة والمعونة ولجميع اهل بيت آل

اجمعين وشلوم بيتي على نفسه ومن فضل القارئ

لا يعتب على المملوك في الخط لانه متعلم ٥

والكلام صفة المتكلم والحمد لله ٥

رب العالمين ولا يضيع

اجر المحسنين

GEOGRAPHICAL APPENDIX

Names surveyed here are arranged alphabetically. Major cities and sites which are well known and widely discussed in the literature (e.g. Nablus, Jerusalem) are not surveyed in this appendix. References to bibliography and sources may be found in Tsafrir, *Tabula Imperii Romani*; Wilkinson, *Gazeteer*; Avi-Yonah, *Holy Land*; S. Marmardji, *Textes géographiques arabes sur la Palestine* (Paris, 1951). Map references are given according to the standard topographical grid of the Survey of Israel. The reference is given in six digits (i.e. in proximity of one sq. km).

Afāzim, text p. 238. Unidentified location.

'Aqdīd (?), text p. 232. Unidentified location.

'Aqraba, text p. 234. Map ref. 182/170. An ancient town in eastern Samaria, densely populated by Samaritans. It was the capital of the Toparchy of 'Aqraba in the Byzantine period. See Ben Zvi, pp. 72–73; Tsafrir, *Tabula*, pp. 56–57.

Arsūf, text p. 220. Map ref. 132/178. A city along the coast between Jaffa and Caesarea, called Apollonia in the Hellenistic and Roman periods; in the Byzantine period it was called Sozousa. The settlement, later called Arsūf, continued to exist during the early Muslim period and the Crusader period. See Tsafrir, *Tabula*, "Apollonia, Sozousa," p. 65; on the Samaritan settlement and finds see I. Roll and E. Ayalon, *Apollonia and Southern Sharon* (Tel Aviv, 1989), pp. 66–67, 274–78 (Hebrew); on Arsūf in the early Muslim period see *ibid.*, Appendices 6 and 7 by A. Elad: "Arsuf in the Early Arabic Period," pp. 289–302; "Arabic Inscriptions from Arsuf," pp. 303–308.

Ashkarū, text p. 261. Unidentified location.

'Askar, text pp. 204, 223. Map ref. 177/180. An ancient Samaritan village, nowadays an Arab village east of Nablus; identified with Socher or Sychar, where according to Christian tradition Jesus met the Ṣamaritan woman (John 4:5). The well itself, however, was shown not in 'Askar but in Balāṭa, one km. away (map ref. 177/179). See Ben Zvi, p.

66; Avi-Yonah (Hebrew), p. 123; Tsafrir, *Tabula*, p. 238; Wilkinson, *Gazeteer*, p. 172.

'Atīl, text pp. 236, 237, 238. Map ref. 157/197. A village in western Samaria, northeast of Ṭūl Karem. There is no additional information concerning this site, although the text (p. 238) implies that it was an important Samaritan settlement.

'Awartā, text p. 247. Map ref. 177/174. An ancient Samaritan village south of Nablus, recorded from the days of Baba Raba (third or fourth century) until the seventeenth century. According to Samaritan, Jewish and Muslim tradition, this was the the location of the tomb of El'azar, son of Aharon the High Priest, his son Pinḥas, and the Seventy Elders (Numbers 11:16). Now a Muslim village. See Ben Zvi, p. 60; Marmardji, pp. 151, 165.

Baṣalīya, text p. 233. This site should probably be identified with Khirbat Baṣalīya, map. ref. 194/177, about 15 km. east of Nablus and 14 km. northeast of 'Aqraba. According to the text, apparently a Muslim settlement.

Bayt Fūrīk, text p. 254. Map ref. 181/176. An ancient Samaritan village southeast of Nablus. See Ben Zvi, p. 73. Also mentioned in the *Tolidah*, Neubauer, p. 22.

Bayt Jibrīn, text pp. 227, 230. Beth Govrin/Eleuthoeropolis; map ref. 140/112. An important town during the Hellenistic, Roman and Byzantine periods in the Judaean inner plain. There is additional evidence of its continued existence during the early Muslim and Crusader periods. See Tsafrir, *Tabula*, p. 118; Marmardji, pp. 22–23; *The New Encyclopedia of Archelogical Excavations in the Holy Land*, I (Jerusalem, 1993), pp. 195–201; It was apparently a central chalk quarry in the early Muslim period, a fact attested to both by the excavations (*ibid.*, p. 201), and by al-Muqaddasī, p. 174, who also notes that it was the capital of the province. He refers to its granary and storehouse and describes it as a land of harvest and abundance, yet laments its decline since it now harbours "effeminate men".

Bayt Ṣāmā, text pp. 205, 220, 245, 246. According to al-Balādhūrī, *Futūḥ*, p. 158, Bayt Ṣāmā was a Samaritan village in the province of Nablus.

It should be noted that although the Mss. read Bayt Ṣāmā, the editor chose to correct the text to Bayt Māmā, since this is Yāqūt's version (I, 781); yet Yāqūt is, in fact, quoting al-Balādhūrī, and as the latter's reading is confirmed by our text, the copying error must be Yāqūt's.

Būrīn, text p. 246. Map ref. 173/176. Village 5 km. southwest of Nablus.

Dājūn, text pp. 240, 248. Map ref. 134/156. A town near Ramla, today Beit Dagon. Dājūn was a settlement that according to al-Muqaddasī, pp. 165–66, was inhabited in the tenth century mostly by Samaritans. See also Yāqūt, II, 515. There is also an ancient Samaritan village by this name in Samaria, *ca.* 10 km. east of Nablus, map ref. 185/177.

al-Jīb, text p. 230. An Arab village 10 km. north of Jerusalem (map ref. 167/139, the site of Biblical Gibeon); see Tsafrir, *Tabula*, pp. 126–27; Yāqūt, II, 170.

Jimsāfūṭ, text p. 261. Jinṣāfūṭ, map ref. 162/176. A large village in central Samaria, between Qalqīlīya and Nablus. The name is already recorded in documents from the time of Ramses II. See F.M. Abel, *Géographie de la Palestine*, II (Paris, 1938), p. 26. There is no mention of it being a Samaritan settlement, and the text here seems to be an early record of it being a Muslim settlement.

Kafar Tiya (?), text p. 245. Unidentified location.

Niḥāsa (?), text p. 261. Unidentified location.

Qaryat Qūzā text p. 234. Map ref. 173/171. Also called Ṣaqta, an ancient Samaritan settlement *ca.* 10 km. south of Nablus. See Ben Zvi, p. 74. Nowadays a small Arab village.

Rāmīn, text p. 237. Map ref. 164/187. An Arab village in central Samaria, 12 km. northwest of Nablus, on the main road to Ṭūl Karem.

Rās al-ʿAyn, text p. 255. See *al-Ṭawāḥīn*.

Sālim, text pp. 220, 222, 234. Map ref. 181/179, Shalem Rabtha. An ancient Samaritan village in eastern Samaria, *ca.* 8 km. east of Nablus. See Ben Zvi, p. 62; Avi-Yonah, *Holy Land*, p. 154; Tsafrir, *Tabula*, "Salem II," p. 219.

al-Sārīn, text p. 231. This place is also mentioned in Neubauer, *Tolidah*, pp. 29, 30 (trans. pp. 69, 70), where it is called Qiriath Hasarin. Ben Zvi (p. 70–72), followed by Avi-Yonah (Hebrew, p. 123), suggested that it should be identified with the village of Sīrīn (next to ʻAyn Sīrīn) near Balāṭa, southeast of Nablus, map ref. 177/178. Ben Zvi emphasizes that there is an ancient burial ground for priests on the site. In addition, it seems to have served as a religious centre where important assemblies were convened and ceremonies initiated. Nearby, in Decatus, the Samaritans had a cult centre where the Passover sacrifice was made.

al-Shiʻr, text p. 233. In Jordan. Probably the biblical "Mount Seʻīr" or "land of Seʻīr" in Edom, i.e. southern Transjordan, known in the Muslim sources as al-Sharāt. See relevant note in the text.

Sinjil, text pp. 222, 237. See note to text, p. 222.

al-Ṭawāḥīn, text p. 233. Map ref. 143/168. Also called in the text Rās al-ʻAyn (p. 255), near the sources of the Yarqon river. The Hellenistic and Roman Antipatris, this was the site of the famous battle between the armies of Khumārawayh and al-Muwaffaq (see text and notes, pp. 254, 255). See Tsafrir, *Tabula*, "Antipatris," p. 63; Yāqūt, III, 554.

ʻUskūn, text p. 259. Unidentified location. May be identified perhaps with biblical Socho, now Shweika, map ref. 153/193 in western Samaria, north of Ṭūl Karem.

Wādī ʻĀrā, text p. 237. Separates Mount Carmel and the mountains of Samaria, and is part of the *Via Maris*.

Zaytā, text pp. 220, 246, 248. Map ref. 155/199. An ancient Samaritan village in western Samaria, 8 km. north of Ṭūl Karem, inhabited by Samaritans from the fourth to the ninth centuries. See Ben Zvi, p. 88.

BIBLIOGRAPHY AND ABBREVIATIONS

This bibliography includes only those items cited in the text or notes of the present work. In alphabetizing romanized Arabic names and titles, the definite article "al-" has been ignored. The listing also includes all bibliographical abbreviations utilized in this Bibliography and elsewhere in this work.

Abel, F.M. *Géographie de la Palestine*. Paris, 1938.

ADAJ = *Annual of the Department of Antiquities of Jordan*

Adler, E.N., and M. Seligsohn. "Une nouvelle chronique samaritaine," *Revue des études juives* 44 (1902), pp. 188–222; 45 (1902), pp. 70–98, 223–54; 46 (1903), pp. 123–46. Repr. Paris, 1903.

Arav, R., L. Di Segni, and A. Kloner. "An Eighth-Century Monastery near Jerusalem," *Liber Annuus* 40 (1990), pp. 313–20.

'Arīb ibn Sa'd al-Qurṭubī. *Tabari Continuatus*, ed. M.J. de Goeje. Leiden, 1965.

Ashtor, E. "The Social Isolation of Ahl adh-Dhimma," in O. Komlos, ed., *P. Hirschler Memorial Book* (Budapest, 1949), pp. 73–94; repr. in Ashtor's *The Medieval Near East: Social and Economic History*. London, 1978.

Avi-Yonah, M. *The Holy Land from the Persian to the Arab Conquest (536 B.C.–A.D. 640): a Historical Geography*. Grand Rapids, 1977.

Bacharach, J.L. "The Career of Muḥammad b. Tughj al-Ikhshīd: a Tenth-Century Governor of Egypt," *Speculum* 50 (1975), pp. 586–612.

al-Balādhurī, Aḥmad ibn Yaḥyā. *Ansāb al-ashrāf*, III, ed. 'Abd al-'Azīz al-Dūrī. Beirut, 1978.

________. *Futūḥ al-buldān*, ed. M.J. de Goeje. Leiden, 1866.

al-Balawī, Abū Muḥammad 'Abd Allāh ibn Muḥammad al-Madīnī. *Sīrat Aḥmad ibn Ṭūlūn*. Damascus, 1939.

BASOR = *Bulletin of the American Schools for Oriental Research*

Ben Hayyim, Z. *The Literary and Oral Tradition of Hebrew and Aramaic amongst the Samaritans* (in Hebrew). 5 vols. Jerusalem, 1957–77.

Ben Zvi, I. *The Book of the Samaritans* (in Hebrew). Jerusalem, 1970.

BF = *Byzantinische Forschungen*

BGA = M.J. de Goeje, ed. *Bibliotheca geographorum arabaicorum*. 8 vols. Leiden, 1870–94.

BJRL = *Bulletin of the John Rylands Library*

Blau, J. *A Grammar of Christian Arabic Based Mainly on South-Palestinian Texts from the First Millenium*. 2 vols. Louvain, 1966.

________. *The Emergence and Linguistic Background of Judaeo-Arabic*. Oxford, 1965.

________. "The Importance of Middle Arabic Dialects for the History of Arabic," *Scripta Hierosolymitana* 9 (1961), pp. 206–28.

Boern, P.C., ed. *Rorgo Fretellus de Nazareth et sa description de la Terre sainte, histoire et edition du texte*. Amsterdam, 1980.

Bóid, I.R.M. "The Samaritan Halacha," in Crown, *Samaritans*, pp. 624–49.

Bosworth, C.E. "Christian and Jewish Religious Dignitaries in Mamlūk Egypt and Syria: Qalqashandī's Information on Their Hierarchy, Titulature, and Appointment," *IJMES* 3 (1972), pp. 59–74, 199–216.

Bowman, J. *Transcript of the Original Text of the Samaritan Chronicle Tolidah*. Leeds, 1954.

BSOAS = *Bulletin of the School of Oriental and African Studies*

CCSL = *Corpus Christianorum, Series Latina*

Chabot, J.-B., ed. and trans. *Chronique de Michel le Syrien*. 4 vols. Paris, 1899–1924.

Cohen, M. *Jewish Self-Government in Medieval Egypt*. Princeton, 1980.

Conrad, L.I. "Syriac Prespectives on Bilād al-Shām during the 'Abbāsid Period," in *Bilād al-Shām During the 'Abbāsid Period: Proccedings of the Fifth International Conference on the History of Bilād al-Sham* (Amman, 1991), pp. 1–44.

________. "A Nestorian Diploma of Investiture from the *Tadhkira* of Ibn Ḥamdūn: the Text and its Significance," in W. al-Qāḍī, ed., *Studia Arabica et Islamica: Festschrift for Iḥsān 'Abbās on his Sixtieth Birthday* (Beirut, 1981), pp. 83–104.

________. "The Quṣūr of Medieval Islam," *Al-Abḥāth* 29 (1981), pp. 7–24.

________. "Theophanes and the Arabic Historical Tradition: Some Indications of Intercultural Transmission," *BF* 15 (1990), pp. 1–44.

Creswell, K.A.C. *Early Muslim Architecture*. 2 vols. Oxford, 1932–40.

Crone, P. *Slaves on Horses: the Evolution of the Islamic Polity*. Cambridge, 1980.

Crown, A.D. "Samaritans in the Byzantine Orbit," *BJRL* 69 (1986), pp. 96–138.

________, ed. *The Samaritans*. Tübingen, 1986.

________. "The Byzantine and Moslem Period," in Crown, *Samaritans*, pp. 55–81.

________, and L. Davey, eds. *Essays in Honour of G.D. Sixdenier: New Samaritan Studies of the Société d'études samaritaines III & IV*. Sydney, 1995.

Dexinger, F. "Samaritan Eschatology," in Crown, *Samaritans*, pp. 266–92.

al-Dhahabī, Abū ʿAbd Allāh Muḥammad ibn ʿUthmān. *Duwal al-Islām*. Hyderabad, 1945.

Diem, W., and H.P. Radenberg. *A Dictionary of the Arabic Material of S.D. Goitein's A Mediterranean Society*. Wiesbaden, 1994.

Donner, F.M. *The Early Islamic Conquests*. Princeton, 1981.

DOP = *Dumbarton Oaks Papers*

Dozy, R.P.A. *Supplément aux dictionnaires arabes*. 2 vols. Paris and Leiden, 1967.

Eisenstein, H. "Die Erhebung des Mubarqaʿ in Palästina," *Orientalia* 55 (1986), pp. 454–58.

el-Hibri, T. "The Regicide of the Caliph al-Amīn and the Challenge of Representation in Medieval Islamic Historiography," *Arabica* 42 (1995), pp. 334–64.

Elad, A. "The Coastal Cities of Palestine during the Early Middle Ages," *The Jerusalem Cathedra*, 2, ed. L.I. Levine (Jerusalem, 1982), pp. 146–67.

________. "Two Identical Inscriptions from Jund Filasṭīn from the Reign of the ʿAbbāsīd Caliph, al-Muqtadir," *JESHO* 35 (1992), pp. 301–60.

Fattal, A. *Le statut legal des non-Musulmans en pays d'Islam*. Beirut, 1958.

Fossum, J. "Sects and Movements," in Crown, *The Samaritans*, pp. 293–389.

Gabrieli, F. "La successione di Hārūn al-Rashīd e la guerra fra al-Amīn e al-Ma'mūn," *Revista degli studi orientali* 11 (1926–28), pp. 341–97.

Geyer, P., and O. Cuntz, eds. *Itinerarium Burdigalense*, in *Itineraria Hierosolymitana*. *CCSL* 175. Turnhout, 1965.

Gil, M. "The Story of Baḥīra and its Jewish Versions," in H. Ben Shammai, ed., *Hebrew and Arabic Studies in Honour of Joshua Blau* (Jerusalem, 1993), pp. 193–210 (in Hebrew).

________. *A History of Palestine 634–1099*, trans. Ethel Broido. Cambridge, 1992.

Goitein, S.D. "Government Installation of Gaons and Jewish Judges," in J. Hacker, ed., *Palestinian Jewry in Early Islamic and Crusader Times in the Light of the Geniza Documents* (Jerusalem, 1980), pp. 70–81 (in Hebrew).

_________. "New Sources on the Palestinian Gaonate," in S. Lieberman, ed., *Salo Whitmeyer Baron Jubilee Volume on the Occasion of his Eightieth Birthday* (Jerusalem, 1974), pp. 503–37.

_________. *A Mediterranean Society: the Jewish Communities of the Arab World as Portrayed in the Documents of the Cairo Geniza*, II: *The Community*. Berkley, 1971.

Goldziher, I. "Lā Misāsa," *Révue africaine* 52 (1908), pp. 23–28.

Gottschalk, H.L. *Die Madara'ijjun*. Berlin, 1931.

Griffith, S. "Anthony David of Baghdad, Scribe and Monk of Mar Sabas: Arabic in the Monasteries of Palestine," *Church History* 58 (1989), pp. 7–19.

_________. "Greek into Arabic: Life and Letters in the Monasteries of Palestine in the Ninth Century: the example of the *Summa Theologiae Arabica*," *Byzantion* 56 (1986), pp. 117–38.

_________. "Stephan of Ramleh's Arabic Writing," *JEH* 36 (1985), pp. 23–45.

_________. "The Arabic Account of ʻAbd al-Masīḥ an-Nağrānī al-Ġassānī," *Le Muséon* 98 (1985), pp. 331–74.

Guérin, V. *Description géographique, historique et archéologique de la Palestine*. Paris, 1875.

Hadas, G. "Nine Tombs of the Second Temple Period at ʻEin Gedi," *ʻAtiqot* 24 (1994), English abstract, pp. 1*–9*; Hebrew, pp. 1–75.

al-Harawī, Abū l-Ḥasan ʻAlī ibn Abī Bakr. *Kitāb al-ishārāt ilā maʻrifat al-ziyārāt*, ed. J. Sourdel-Thomine. Damascus, 1953.

Hassan, Z.M. *Les Tulunides: étude de l'Egypte musulmane à la fin du IX siècle, 868–905*. Paris, 1933.

Hasson, I. "The Penetration of Arab Tribes in Eretz Israel during the First Century of the Hegira," *Cathedra* 32 (1984), pp. 54–65 (in Hebrew).

Hava, J.G. *Al-Farā'id: Arabic-English Dictionary*. Beirut, 1964.

Hawting, G.R. *The First Dynasty of Islam*. Carbondale, 1987.

Hieronymus. *Commentarium in Sophoniam*, ed. M. Adriaen. *CCSL* 76. Turnhout, 1970.

Hill, D.R. *The Termination of Hostilities in the Early Arab Conquests*. London, 1971.

Hinz, W. *Islamische Masse und Gewichte*. Leiden, 1955.

Holum, K. "Archeological Evidence for the Fall of Caesarea," *BASOR* 286 (1992), pp. 73–85.

________, and R.L. Hohfelder, eds. *King Herod's Dream: Caesarea on the Sea.* New York and London, 1988.

Hoyland, R. *Seeing Islam as Others Saw It: a Survey and Evaluation of Christian, Jewish and Zoroastrian Writings on Early Islam.* Princeton, 1997.

Humbert, J.P., and A. Desreumaux. "Huit campagnes de fouilles au Khirbet es-Samra (1981–1989)," *RB* 97 (1990), pp. 252–69.

Ibn ʿAsākir, Abū l-Qāsim ʿAlī ibn al-Ḥasan. *Taʾrīkh madīnat Dimashq*, vol. 37. Amman, 1989.

Ibn al-Athīr, ʿIzz al-Dīn Abū l-Ḥasan ʿAlī ibn al-Karam. *Al-Kāmil fī l-taʾrīkh.* 13 vols. Beirut, 1965–66.

Ibn Khaldūn, Abū Zayd ʿAbd al-Raḥman ibn Muḥammad. *Kitāb al-ʿibar wa-dīwān al-mubtadaʾ wa-l-khabar.* 8 vols. Beirut, 1958.

Ibn Manẓūr, Abū l-Faḍl Muḥammad ibn Mukarram. *Mukhtaṣar taʾrīkh madīnat Dimashq.* 29 vols. Damascus, 1988.

Ibn Saʿīd, ʿAlī ibn Mūsā Nūr al-Dīn. *Kitāb al-mughrib fī ḥulā al-Maghrib*, Book IV, ed. K.L. Tallqvist. Leiden, 1899.

Ibn Taghrībirdī, Abū l-Maḥāsin Yūsuf. *Al-Nujūm al-zāhira fī mulūk Miṣr wa-l-Qāhira.* 16 vols. Cairo, 1929–1972.

IEJ = *Israel Exploration Journal*

IJMES = *International Journal of Middle East Studies*

JEH = *Journal of Ecclesiastical History*

JESHO = *Journal of the Economic and Social History of the Orient*

MacAdam, H.I. "Settlements and Settlement Patterns in Northern and Central Transjordania, ca. 550–750," in G.R.D. King and A. Cameron, eds., *The Byzantine and Early Islamic Near East*, II: *Land Use and Settlement Patterns* (Princeton, 1994), pp. 49–94.

Kaegi, W.E. "Some Seventh-Century Sources on Caesarea," *IEJ* 28 (1978), pp. 177–81.

Karcz, I., and A. Elad. "Further Comments on the 'Sabbatical Year' Earthquake," *Tarbiz* 61 (1992), pp. 67–83.

Kazimirski, A. de Biberstein. *Dictionnaire arab-français.* 2 vols. Paris, 1860.

Kedar, B.Z. "The Frankish Period," in Crown, *Samaritans*, pp. 82–94.

Kennedy, H. *The Early ʿAbbāsid Caliphate.* London, 1981.

———. *The Prophet and the Age of the Caliphates*. London and New York, 1986.

Khalīfa ibn Khayyāṭ. *Ta'rīkh*, ed. A.Ḍ. al-'Umarī. 2 vols. Baghdad, 1967.

Kimber, R.A. "Hārūn al-Rashīd's Meccan Settlement of AH 186/AD 802," *University of St. Andrews, School of 'Abbāsid Studies, Occasional Papers* 1 (1986), pp. 55–79.

Kister, M.J. "'An Yadin (Qur'ān IX/29)," *Arabica* 11 (1964), pp. 272–78.

———. "The Social and Political Implications of Three Traditions in the *Kitāb al-Kharāj* of Yaḥyā b. Ādam," *JESHO* 3 (1960), pp. 326–34.

Knutsson, B. *Studies in the Text and Language of Three Syriac-Arabic Versions of the Book of Iudicum with Special Reference to the Middle Arabic Elements*. Leiden, 1974.

Levy-Rubin, M. "New Evidence Relating to the Process of Islamization in Palestine in the Early Muslim Period: the Case of Samaria," *JESHO* 43 (2000), 258–76.

Madelung, W. "The Sufyānī between Tradition and History," *Studia Islamica* 63 (1984), pp. 5–58.

al-Maqrīzī, Abū l-'Abbās Aḥmad ibn 'Alī. *Kitāb al-mawā'iẓ wa-l-i'tibār fī dhikr al-khiṭaṭ wa-l-āthār*. 2 vols. Bulaq, 1853.

Marmardji, S. *Textes géographiques arabes sur la Palestine*. Paris, 1951.

McDonald, J. "An Unpublished Palestinian Tradition about Muhammad," *Australian Journal of Biblical Archeology* 1 (1969), pp. 3–12.

Mingana, A. "A Charter of Protection Granted to the Nestorian Church in A.D. 1138, by Muktafi II, Caliph of Bagdad," *Bulletin of the John Rylands Library* 10 (1926), pp. 127–33.

Montgomery, J.A. *The Samaritans*. Philadelphia, 1907.

al-Muqaddasī, Abū 'Abd Allāh Muḥammad ibn Aḥmad. *Aḥsan al-taqāsīm fī ma'rifat al-aqālīm*, ed. M.J. de Goeje. *BGA*, 3. Leiden, 1906.

Nau, F. "Résumé de monographies syriaques," *Revue de l'orient chrétien* 9 (1914), pp. 113–34.

Neubauer, M.A. *Chronique samaritaine*. Paris, 1873.

The New Encyclopedia of Archaeological Excavations in the Holy Land. Jerusalem, 1993.

Noja, S. "The Samareitikon," in Crown, *Samaritans*, pp. 408–12.

Noth, A. *The Early Arabic Historical Tradition: a Source-Critical Study*. Princeton, 1994.

Nutt, J.W. *Fragments of a Samaritan Targum*. London, 1874.

Omar, F. *The Abbasid Caliphate*. Baghdad, 1969.

Palamas, G. *A Short History of the Holy City of Jerusalem* (in Greek). Jerusalem, 1862.

Papadopoulos-Kerameus, A. "Passion of the Twenty Martyrs," *Pravoslavnii Palestinski Sbornik* 57 (1907), pp. 1–41 (in Greek).

Piccirillo, M. *Chiese e mosaici di Madaba*. Jerusalem, 1989.

________. "Le chiese di Quweismeh Amman," *Liber Annuus* 34 (1984), pp. 329–40.

________. "Le iscrizioni di Um er-Rasas-Kastron Mefaa in Giordania I (1986–1987)," *ADAJ* 30 (1986), pp. 341–51.

________. "Una Chiesa nell'Wadi 'Ayoun Mousa ai piedi del Monte Nebo," *Liber Annuus* 34 (1984), pp. 307–18.

Powels, S. "The Samaritan Calendar and the Roots of Samaritan Chronology," in Crown, *Samaritans*, pp. 691–742.

al-Qāḍī, W. "Madkhal ilā dirāsat 'uhūd al-ṣulḥ al-islāmīya zaman al-futūḥ," in Muḥammad 'Adnān al-Bakhīt and Iḥsān 'Abbās, eds., *Proceedings of the Second Symposium on the History of Bilād al-Sham During the Early Islamic Period up to 40 A.H./ 640 A.D.* (Amman, 1987), II, 193–269.

al-Qazwīnī, Zakarīyā ibn Muḥammad ibn Maḥmūd. *Āthār al-bilād*. Baghdad, 1960.

RB = *Revue biblique*

Roll, I., and E. Ayalon. *Appolonia and Southern Sharon*. Tel-Aviv, 1989.

Rubin, M. "Arabization versus Islamization in the Palestinian Melkite Community during the Early Muslim Period," in A. Kofsky and G. Stroumsa, eds., *Sharing the Sacred: Religious Contacts and Conflicts in the Holy Land, First to Fifteenth Century C.E.* (Jerusalem, 1998), pp. 149–62.

Sadan, J. *Le mobilier au proche orient medieval*. Leiden, 1976.

Schick, R. *The Christian Communities of Palestine from Byzantine to Islamic Rule*. Princeton, 1995.

Sharon, M. "The Cities of the Holy Land under Islamic Rule," *Cathedra* 40 (1986), pp. 83–120 (in Hebrew).

________. *Black Banners from the East*, II: *Revolt: the Social and Military Aspects of the Abbasid Revolution*. Jerusalem, 1990.

Shehadeh, H. "The Arabic of the Samaritans," *New Samaritan Studies of the Société d'études samaritaines III & IV–Essays in Honour of G.D. Sixdenier* (Sydney, 1995), pp. 551–75.

________. "When did Arabic Replace Samaritan Aramaic?," in M. Bar-Asher *et al.*, eds., *Hebrew Language Studies Presented to Professor Zeev Ben Hayyim* (Jerusalem, 1983), pp. 515–28 (in Hebrew).

________. *The Arabic Translation of the Samaritan Pentateuch*, I: *Genesis–Exodus*. Jerusalem, 1989.

Sokoloff, M. *A Dictionary of Jewish Palestinian Aramaic in the Byzantine Period.* Ramat Gan, 1990.

Stenhouse, P. "Samaritan Arabic," in Crown, *Samaritans*, pp. 585–623.

________. "Samaritan Chronicles," in Crown, *Samaritans*, pp. 218–65.

________. *The Kitāb 'l-Ta'rīkh of Abū 'l-Fatḥ–A New Edition with Notes*. Ph.D. thesis: Sydney, 1980 (available in microfiche form from "The Mandelbaum Trust," University of Sydney, Sydney, Australia).

________, trans. *The Kitāb 'l-Ta'rīkh of Abū 'l-Fatḥ, Studies in Judaica*, I. Mandelbaum Trust, University of Sydney, 1985.

al-Suyūṭī, Jalāl al-Dīn ʿAbd al-Raḥmān ibn Abī Bakr. *Kashf al-ṣalṣala ʿan waṣf al-zalzala*, ed. ʿA.L. al-Saʿdānī. Fez, 1971.

al-Ṭabarī, Abū Jaʿfar Muḥammad ibn Jarīr. *Ta'rīkh al-rusul wa-l-mulūk*, ed. M.J. de Goeje *et al.* 15 vols. Leiden, 1879–1901. English trans. *The History of al-Ṭabarī*, ed. Ehsan Yarshater. 38 vols. Albany, 1985–proceeding.

Tal, A. "Samaritan Literature" in Crown, *Samaritans*, pp. 413–67.

Tobler, T., and A. Molinier. *Itinera Hierosolymitana et Descriptiones Terrae Sanctae*. Geneva, 1879.

Tritton, A.S. *The Caliphs and Their Non-Muslim Subjects*. London, 1930.

Tsafrir , Y., and G. Foerster. "Urbanism at Scythopolis–Beth Shean in the Fourth to Seventh Centuries," *DOP* 51 (1997), pp. 85–146.

Tsafrir, Y., and G. Foerster. "The Dating of the 'Earthquake of the Sabbatical Year' of 749 C.E. in Palestine," *BSOAS* 55 (1992), pp. 231–35.

________. "From Scythopolis to Baysān: Changing Concepts of Urbanism," in G.R.D. King and A. Cameron eds., *The Byzantine and Early Islamic Near East*, II: *Land Use and Settlement Patterns* (Princeton, 1994), pp. 95–115.

Tsafrir, Y., L. Di Segni, and J. Green. *Tabula Imperii Romani: Judaea, Palaestina and Eretz Israel in the Hellenistic, Roman and Byzantine Periods*. Jerusalem, 1994.

van Brechem, M., ed. *Matériaux pour un Corpus Inscriptionum Arabicarum*, Part 2B, vol. 2: *Jérusalem–Haram*. Cairo, 1925–27.

Vilmar, E., ed. *Abulfathi Annales Samaritani*. Gotha, 1865.

Watson, A.M. *Agricultural Innovation in the Early Islamic World*. Cambridge, 1983.

Wilkinson, J. *Jerusalem Pilgrims*. Jerusalem, 1977.

al-Yaʿqūbī, Aḥmad ibn Abī Yaʿqūb. *Ta'rīkh*, ed. M.T. Houtsma. Leiden, 1883.

Yāqūt ibn ʿAbd Allāh. *Muʿjam al-buldān*, ed. F. Wüstenfeld. 6 vols. Leipzig, 1866–1873.

GENERAL INDEX

SLAEI Studies in Late Antiquity and Early Islam

LAWRENCE I. CONRAD, EDITOR

Published Titles

1. *The Byzantine and Early Islamic Near East* (proceedings of the workshops on Late Antiquity and Early Islam):

   I. *Problems in the Literary Source Material* (Papers of the First Workshop on Late Antiquity and Early Islam), edited by Averil Cameron and Lawrence I. Conrad. 1992. xiv, 428 pp. ISBN 0-87850-080-4

   II. *Land Use and Settlement Patterns* (Papers of the Second Workshop on Late Antiquity and Early Islam), edited by G.R.D. King and Averil Cameron. 1994. xiv, 270 pp. ISBN 0-87850-106-1

   III. *States, Resources and Armies* (Papers of the Third Workshop on Late Antiquity and Early Islam), edited by Averil Cameron. 1995. xvi, 491 pp. ISBN 0-87850-107-X

2. Robert Schick, *The Christian Communities of Palestine from Byzantine to Islamic Rule: A Historical and Archaeological Study.* 1995. xviii, 601 pp. ISBN 0-87850-081-2

3. Albrecht Noth, *The Early Arabic Historical Tradition: A Source-Critical Study.* Second edition in collaboration with Lawrence I. Conrad, translated by Michael Bonner. 1994. xi, 248 pp. ISBN 0-87850-082-0

4. Martin Hinds, *Studies in Early Islamic History.* Edited by Jere L. Bacharach, Lawrence I. Conrad, and Patricia Crone, with an Introduction by G.R. Hawting. 1996. xix, 262 pp. ISBN 0-87850-109-6

5. Uri Rubin, *The Eye of the Beholder: The Life of Muḥammad as Viewed by the Early Muslims (A Textual Analysis).* 1995. ix, 289 pp. ISBN 0-87850-110-X

7. Elizabeth Savage, *A Gateway to Hell, A Gateway to Paradise: The North African Response to the Arab Conquest.* 1997. x, 206 pp. ISBN 0-87850-112-6

8. Suliman Bashear, *Arabs and Others in Early Islam.* 1997. viii, 161 pp. ISBN 0-87850-126-6

10. Milka Levy-Rubin, *The* Continuatio *of the Samaritan Chronicle of Abū l'Fatḥ al-Sāmirī al-Danafī.* 2002. xiii, 202 pp. ISBN 0-87850-136-3

11. Josef Horovitz, *The Earliest Biographies of the Prophet and Their Authors*, edited by Lawrence I. Conrad.
2002. xxxviii, 158 pp. ISBN 0-87850-118-5

13. Robert G. Hoyland, *Seeing Islam as Others Saw It: A Survey and Evaluation of Christian, Jewish and Zoroastrian Writings on Early Islam.*
1997. xviii, 870 pp. ISBN 0-87850-125-8

14. Fred M. Donner, *Narratives of Islamic Origins: The Beginnings of Islamic Historical Writing.* 1998. xv, 358 pp. ISBN 0-87850-127-4

17. Uri Rubin, *Between Bible and Qur'ān: The Children of Israel and the Islamic Self-Image.* 1999. xiii, 318 pp. ISBN 0-87850-134-7

20. *Ibn 'Asākir and Early Islamic History*, edited by James E. Lindsay.
2002. xii, 157 pp. ISBN 0-87850-120-7

21. David Cook, *Studies in Muslim Apocalyptic.*
2002. xii, 472 pp. ISBN 0-87850-142-8

Published by:
The Darwin Press, Inc.
Box 2202, Princeton, NJ 08543
Tel: (609)737-1349 **Fax:** (609)737-0929
E-mail: books@darwinpress.com **Web site:** www.darwinpress.com